Praise for *Lawyers, Liars, and the A*

Jonathan Shapiro's *Lawyers, Liars, and the Art of Storytelling* is so witty that for a while I was certain I had written it.

—**Alan Zweibel, original *Saturday Night Live* writer and Thurber Prize winner for his novel *The Other Shulman***

Storytelling—the art of connecting with, captivating, and persuading one's listeners—is the key to courtroom success. For the new generation of lawyers raised on texting, tweeting, and e-mailing, the art of old-fashioned storytelling has proven elusive, as those who can truly teach this ancient art form are fast disappearing. Thankfully, here comes Jonathan Shapiro—one of America's greatest trial lawyers and storytellers—to the rescue.

—**Steve Zipperstein, General Counsel, Blackberry***

Jonathan Shapiro is a terrific writer: incisive, informative, entertaining, and always engaging.

—**Erwin Chemerinsky, U.S. constitutional law and federal civil procedure scholar and current and founding dean of the University of California, Irvine School of Law**

Lawyers, Liars, and the Art of Storytelling is a masterful book about storytelling by the master himself. Shapiro reveals the rewards of storytelling in the real and fictional legal worlds. Most importantly, he divulges the secrets to being a successful storyteller. It is a fun and interesting read for lawyers and non-lawyers alike.

—**Laurie L. Levenson, professor of law and David W. Burcham Chair of Ethical Advocacy, Loyola Law School, California**

This is an important read for anyone who appreciates telling or hearing good stories, which should include anyone who cares a fig about the art of human communication. Thinking of this book as simply a "how to" guide for trial lawyers is as misguided as thinking of Norman McLean's classics as field manuals for anyone who plans to do some firefighting or trout fishing in Montana.

—**Ralph Alldredge, president of the California Newspaper Publishers Association and *California Magazine* Trial Lawyer of the Year**

The art of advocacy is the art of taking the truth and fashioning it into a compelling story. No one does this better than Jonathan Shapiro. Shapiro jumps from story to story so quickly that you don't realize how much you've learned until the book ends.

—**The Honorable Jeffrey Bleich, U.S. Ambassador to Australia**

If Jonathan did not exist, one might have to invent him in order to have this book written correctly.

—**from the Foreword by Robert C. Berring, Walter Perry Johnson Professor of Law, Berkeley Law School**

LAWYERS, LIARS, AND THE ART OF STORYTELLING

LAWYERS, LIARS, AND THE ART OF STORYTELLING

Using Stories to Advocate, Influence, and Persuade

JONATHAN SHAPIRO

Cataloging-in-Publication data is on file with the Library of Congress.

ISBN: 978-1-62722-926-5

Write stories for those you love. It makes you try harder.
This book is written for my fellow lawyers, writers, and storytellers.
My wife Betsy is a writer, my brother David is a lawyer, and all my closest
friends seem to be one or the other. Now my children—Abraham, Sarah,
and Ezekiel—are becoming writers and storytellers in their own right.
This book is dedicated to all of them.

Foreword the First

Humanity's legacy of stories and storytelling is the most precious we have. All wisdom is in our stories and songs. A story is how we construct our experiences. At the very simplest, it can be: "He/she was born, lived, died." Probably that is the template of our stories—a beginning, middle, and end. This structure is in our minds.

Doris Lessing[1]

Come and listen to my story about a man named Jed, a poor mountaineer barely kept his family fed.[2]

Telling stories is as natural to human beings as breathing. Thousands of years ago, storytellers provided entertainment just as they do today, but they also passed on the cultural heritage of civilization. Recorded as epic poems or stylized ballads, stories told of heroes, villains and gods. Religions and national epics are limned by stories. The development of the printing press and movable type replaced the centrality of the storyteller as recorder of events, but it never removed her from the collective consciousness. Storytelling carries on in each newly developed form of media. Books, television, movies, and now the pervasive blasts of creativity on the Internet are all elaborations on the telling of a story. Even the rarefied atmosphere of academia is currently fixated on the use of the story as a conveyor of informa-

---

1. http://www.brainyquote.com/quotes/keywords/storytelling.html#Q1CRXRMAdW1X6zx2.99
2. "The Ballad of Jed Clampett," written by Paul Henning, famously performed by Flatt and Scruggs. It merits its own entry in Wikipedia. http://en.wikipedia.org/wiki/The_Ballad_of_Jed_Clampett

tion. What is the difference, after all, between data and understanding? It is the ability to put the data into a comprehensible package, something about which a person can make sense. Political regimes understand this fact.

Many governments labor mightily to control stories, to control the narrative. Holding the power to tell the story, to indicate the forces of good and the forces of evil, to explain what really happened in Tiananmen Square, or in the Ukraine or in Viet Nam, is vital. Planning a trip to the Balkans, one discovers competing stories, historic accounts that tell stories relating totally opposite facts. The winners write the final version of the tale; it is when competing entities survive that the competing sagas remain.

Yet storytelling often is not taken seriously. Children do it. Charlatans live by it. Popular culture is littered with con men and sharp characters who manipulate and deceive. Lawyers who pride themselves on technical skill are especially suspicious of honoring the storyteller. Stories lack rigor, stories are malleable. The charm of the teller may empower a foolish story just as the lack of grace of a teller can undermine a truthful one. What else explains the American legal system's distrust of juries? Why else have the system's elaborate rules of evidence that narrow how the story can be told in court? Storytellers can transport us, make us laugh and cry, make us learn and understand. Perhaps the power of the storyteller is too much.

When I began the study of law as a first-year student, the edited judicial opinion in the casebook drove me to distraction. A fascinating story might be set up: a young man whose hand was transformed into a hideous hairy appendage sues his doctor who had guaranteed a fully functional hand. Here was drama, a compelling story, absurd but enthralling, it pulled me in. But the story veered off into abstraction in the opinion. The reader learned about the use of the expectation measure in contract damages, but what happened to the boy with the hairy hand? If pressed, a professor would deflect the question. The end of the story does not matter. Oliver Wendell Holmes Jr. long ago opined that while a woman might care who the plaintiff was or if she was wearing a hat, the law cared nothing for such human details. The law is cold and hard-edged. Focus on the question of contract damages. The first year of law school is designed to bleach away the stories.

Jonathan Shapiro gives us the stories back. He demonstrates the power of storytelling and its inevitable importance. More important, he offers advice on how to do it well. Running at the subject from a variety of directions, he moves storytelling to center stage. If Jonathan did not exist, one might have to invent him in order to have this book written correctly. He is buried in stories. A journalist before coming to law school, Jonathan never stopped telling stories. Nor did he renounce the power of telling a good story. Years as an Assistant United States Attorney, a lawyer in private practice, a journalist, and a screen writer have immersed him in the power of the narrative. This unique background produces a book that ranges from the three pillars of Aristotle to remembrances of Professor David Daube to the theories of Professor Erving Goffman to David E. Kelly and Harvey Weinstein, with many stops in between. The author shows the reader how to tell stories by telling stories. Fortunately, he has some great stories to tell.

There are great truths in this book. Jonathan Shapiro has shared his knowledge and his life with us to make his point. Two final thoughts: First, if the last few pages do not inspire you, you have no soul. In the end we tell our own stories. Second, after reading this you will want to share a beverage with Jonathan Shapiro and hear more tales. I guarantee it.

Robert C. Berring
Walter Perry Johnson Professor of Law
Berkeley Law School

Foreword the Second

The great Swiss modernist painter Paul Klee once explained the process of artistic self-discovery as "taking a line for a walk." Creative endeavors depend as much on the eraser as the pen—how different is the comic's post-mortem of his fifty-minute stand up set from Veronese's decision (deliberate perhaps) to leave intact his corrections and restatements on the paper itself. The great polymaths—Da Vinci, Michelangelo, and Jefferson—reveal in their scribbling the relentless process of innovation as much by what was left on the cutting room floor.

Unforgiving self-editing is critical, to be sure, but you also have to have a vision, a point of view, a point to be made, and an answer to the eternal question on the lips of any reader, judge, juror, or filmgoer: "Why should I care?" Too often I find myself asking this question—sometimes out loud, and usually during an oral argument—when faced with a farrago of rhetoric, or a meandering ramble decoupled from the facts, the law, or the record itself. I'm listening—often times I worry that the lawyer isn't. And when that happens, the audience pulls a reverse Timothy Leary, and turns off and tunes out.

I like understatement as a rhetorical device. My favorite example, told by an Amsterdam Jew who narrowly escaped death at Sobibor, summed up his ordeal as follows: "*Wir hobben gehobbt ein schwitz.*" It leads the listener to a conclusion by letting him paint him own picture, without having to knock him over the head. Tricky, to be sure, but potent when executed deftly.

Technical mastery of the law is also a good start. Knowing the facts is essential. But a good brief, like a good detective story, requires a compelling narrative, a roadmap, and the effortless synching of the wind-up and the pitch. Raymond Chandler explained it this way: "The grim logician has as much atmosphere as a drawing board. The scientific sleuth has a nice new shiny laboratory, but I'm sorry I can't remember the face."[1]

Drama and pathos is part of the law, and part of the tool kit of effective advocacy. Judges care about the impact of their decisions on the lives of ordinary folks—you don't have to be a legal realist to understand that. The story matters, and if used sparingly, the occasional reminder of the larger stakes in any given dispute might cause the audience, or the jury, to sit up and pay attention.

Among my favorite examples is the one told by Philip Elman, the great Supreme Court advocate and former assistant to the Solicitor General during the *Brown v. Board of Education* era. Elman described one oral argument before the Court in the restrictive covenant cases. An elderly attorney made what Elman charitably described "an argument that as a professional piece of advocacy was not particularly distinguished." He argued the 13th Amendment, which wasn't the issue before the Court. He tried to distinguish cases that were indistinguishable. "He didn't cut through all the underbrush; he got caught in it." "It was," as Elman remembered it, a "dull argument until he came to the very end."

He concluded his argument by saying—maybe my memory is not accurate, but this is the way I remember it—he said, "Now I've finished my legal argument, but I want to say this before I sit down. In this Court, this house of the law, the Negro today stands outside, and he knocks on the door, over and over again, he knocks on the door and cries out, 'Let me in, let me in, for I too have helped build this house.'"

All of a sudden there was drama in the courtroom, a sense of what the case was really all about rather than the technical legal arguments. The Negro had helped build this house, and he wanted to be let in the

---

1. Raymond Chandler, *The Simple Art of Murder*, New York (1950), Houghton Mifflin, Introduction: *The Simple Art of Murder: An Essay* at 2; reprinted by Vintage Crime/Black Lizard Books, Kindle edition, at Location 75.

door. Well, I've never forgotten this man whose name I don't remember, who in a few sentences made the most moving plea in the Court I've ever heard.[2]

Storytelling, at its core, is about persuasion, and Jonathan Shapiro's breezy narrative of the architecture of persuasion is a pretty close-to-perfect demonstration of that art. You'll get too caught up in the first-person narrative of the frustrations and pleasures of the creative process to realize that you have actually been taught something, both by its exemplary exposition and its content.

It's a book worth reading, and not just by lawyers or screenwriters, or lawyer/screenwriters. Story-telling is an essential part of the innovative process. It takes more than a vision to achieve the technically-next-to-impossible. Someone has to translate that vision into a compelling narrative, to persuade the skeptic that it can be done. We can marvel at the Pantheon, perhaps the greatest technological leap forward until Neil Armstrong set foot on the moon. It remains the largest unreinforced concrete dome in the world. It survived looters, fires, and the fall of the Roman Empire. But it would not have been built without the leadership and persuasion of Hadrian, who dared the skeptic not to subscribe to this outrageous undertaking. What might have happened if his pitch had failed?

Chief Judge Alex Kozinski
U.S. Court of Appeals for the Ninth Circuit

---

2. Philip Elman & Norman Silber, *The Solicitor General's Office, Justice Frankfurter, and Civil Rights Litigation, 1946-1960: An Oral History*, 100 Harv.L. Rev. 817, 819 (1987).

Contents

There are, then, these three means of effecting persuasion. The man who is to be in command of them must, it is clear, be able (1) to reason logically, (2) to understand human character and goodness in their various forms, and (3) to understand the emotions—that is, to name them and describe them, know their causes and the way in which they are excited.[1]

Denny Crane.[2]

---

1. Aristotle, *Rhetoric*, trans. W. Rhys Roberts (Mineola: Dover Publications, 2004), 7–8.
2. *The Practice*, season 8, ABC, 2004; *Boston Legal*, seasons 1–5, ABC, 2004–2008.

Introduction

The stories in this book are all true. But that did not convince television executives that they actually happened.

"Life is not a dramatic narrative," Alan Dershowitz once wrote.[1] Surely, I'm not the first person to think he was a funny one to have said so. The man built his career on dramatic narrative.

But he wasn't wrong. Truth is stranger than fiction. What is true is not always believable. But Alan Dershowitz, of all people, should know the job of a good storyteller is to *make* it believable.

* * * * *

Many of the stories in this book involve cases I investigated, tried or otherwise handled as a federal prosecutor. I later wrote and produced television scripts based on a number of them. Considered together, they offer a personal but practical guide to storytelling.

If the book sometimes reads like an excuse to tell stories rather than as a manual on how to tell them, then I have done my job. Stories are meant to be instructive *and* entertaining. Stories that are instructive but not entertaining are called lectures.

---

1. Alan Dershowitz, "Life Is Not a Dramatic Narrative," in *Law's Stories: Narrative and Rhetoric in the Law*, ed. Peter Brooks and Paul Gewirtz (New Haven: Yale University Press, 1996), 99–105; quoted in Jeanne M. Kaiser, "When the Truth and the Story Collide: What Legal Writers Can Learn From the Experience of Non-Fiction Writers About the Limits of Legal Storytelling," *Journal of the Legal Writing Institute* 16 (2010): 163.

Herodotus claimed that he wrote history so that great events and the lives of great men would not be forgotten. Many of the storytellers in this book are no longer with us. But their stories remain.

Finally, I note that other books have been written about storytelling. Many are more scholarly than this one. Indeed, some are downright unreadable.

If dry is what you want, you have other choices.

PART ONE

The Storyteller's Story

ONE

The Presentation

In August 2013, I was invited to present a panel to the 40th annual conference of the Association of Business Trial Lawyers (ABTL). The topic of the conference was "The Art of Storytelling."

American business trial lawyers are a tough crowd. There might be more intimidating professionals—snipers, bar bouncers—but they didn't want to hear from me.

That the ABTL did—and that it was devoting its expensive time to the topic—reflects a growing trend among business, education, and political leaders to view storytelling as the best way to advertise, teach, and campaign.[1]

I should have thanked the ABTL then politely declined their invitation. Instead, I told them I would be delighted to come.

* * * * *

The deadline for a television pilot I had sold to the FX network was fast approaching. After months of conversations with studio executives, I had written hundreds of pages of story ideas, character outlines, and series themes. But not one word of the actual script. It wasn't laziness. I

---

1. See Janis Forman, *Storytelling Business: The Authentic and Fluent Organization* (Stanford: Stanford University Press, 2013); Pete Cenedella, "Political Storytelling with Brand Obama and Brand Romney," *Huffington Post*, October 26, 2012; Laura White, "The Power of Storytelling—How Telling Stories Created a Great School," *Forbes*, October 15, 2012; Pamela Rutledge, "The Psychological Power of Storytelling," *Psychology Today*, January 16, 2011; Pamela Hsu, "The Secrets of Storytelling: Why We Love a Good Yarn," *Scientific American*, August/September 2008.

hadn't written the script because I had no idea what the script or series were supposed to be about.

Instead of trying to figure it out, I grabbed the ABTL invitation as an excuse to procrastinate, diving into my speech preparation like a fat man on a food binge.

I reread scripts I had written for television law shows and transcripts of my old trials. I downloaded ex-Pixar editor Emma Coats's "Rules of Storytelling." I suffered through Robert McKee's *Story*, considered the great guide to screenwriting, and then comforted myself with the novels of Raymond Chandler, George V. Higgins, and Jane Gardem.

I developed opinions about why some stories work while others do not and about the ways in which lawyer storytelling is unique.

As the author of one story and the simultaneous critic of another, the storytelling lawyer is like a man who spends months building a race car in his garage. When he's done, his competition is going to take a hammer to it.

The winner isn't the one with the prettiest car. It's the one whose car is still moving when the race is over. It is a cruel business, being a lawyer storyteller.

As a television writer, I hated critics and their reviews of my shows. But those critics weren't standing next to me the whole time, attacking every line I wrote while offering up their own version of the story. The worst critic in the world is the lawyer on the other side of your case.

* * * * *

The more I thought about it, the more I realized that storytelling applies to everything a lawyer does. We tell stories to get jobs and clients. We tell them to get promoted, in our dealings with bosses and opposing counsel, when we explain things to witnesses. We use storytelling techniques when we write a statement of facts for a motion or brief, create a chronology, draft interrogatories, or take depositions.

Sometimes we even get to tell stories to a judge or jury. Only lawyers on television go to trial on a regular basis. Most lawyers—most litigators—

will see their doctor more often than they will see a jury. Thanks to high costs, uncertain results, and cuts in court budgets, the number of trials has been going down for years.

But throughout their career, all lawyers will have to present compelling narratives in and out of court. The types and forms of these stories are infinite. But the fundamental purpose of lawyer storytelling never changes. The practice of law is the business of persuasion.

Storytelling is the most effective means of persuasion. No other skill so elegantly or completely combines a lawyer's ability to think, organize, write, and speak. This is why, everything else being equal, a credible lawyer capable of telling a well-reasoned story that moves the listener will always beat the lawyer who cannot.

* * * * *

The remarkable thing is how few lawyers seem to realize they are supposed to be storytellers at all.

If you doubt it, ask a lawyer what they do for a living.

They will say they do transactional work or business law, criminal defense or prosecution. They might tell you where they work and name the firm or an office or business.

Or they will describe their clients ("I work with high-tech start-ups") or cases ("I do immigration cases"). Nobody ever says that they serve justice for a living, or spend their working days protecting the rights of others, or get up every morning to ensure America remains a nation of laws. There is a reason they don't say this: they would sound insane if they did.

What lawyers actually do—all of them—is gather information and then share it with others in the most effective way possible. They do this to persuade others to do or not do something or to make a certain decision.

Of all professionals, lawyers should be the very best storytellers. After all, we begin with enormous advantages. Other storytellers must face the blank page and must choose their subject. Some must create their characters out of whole cloth and imagine their motives and desires. They must plot their actions then steer things toward a resolution.

Lawyers have great material handed to them every single day. That most don't realize it is their fault. "If one is in search of stories of fraud, deceit, cruelty, broken promises, blasted homes, there is no better place to learn them than a law office."[2]

Character, motive, conflict, and resolution are the key elements of all stories. They are also at the heart of every legal dispute and case controversy.

Cognizant of the power of words, in all their complex meanings, we are trained not only to edit our narratives, but to pick apart our opponent's counter-narrative, to find its weaknesses, to expose what is wrong with that story.

Storytelling—what it is, why it matters, how to do it—is not, therefore, a metaphor for legal advocacy. It is legal advocacy itself.

Storytelling should be a comfortable fit for lawyers. That it isn't is an indictment of how lawyers are trained, not an indication of how they should practice.

The more I worked on my speech, the more I realized that recognizing the centrality of storytelling to the legal profession is not enough. Lawyers should also study the elements and structure of stories, how they work and why. And they should learn the principles that have guided great storytellers for thousands of years.

* * * * *

Rhetoric is the study of how to persuade. It consists of a set of logical and procedural rules for how to argue propositions, present ideas, extol virtues. These rules are just as useful when applied to storytelling that aims to persuade.

---

2. Edward Herndon, *Herndon's Life of Lincoln* (New York: De Capo Press, 1983), 268.

Aristotle identified several forms of rhetoric, but our focus will be on two:

"Judicial, or forensic rhetoric, as it is sometimes called, is rhetoric that deals with the past: the rhetoric is not so much of praise and blame but of conviction and exoneration. It seeks to establish what happened, why it happened, and whether the actors involved were at fault . . . It is concerned with justice and injustice... the question of legality and illegality."[3]

It would be overstating it to say that rhetoric has become a hot topic. But it is enjoying a modest bump in interest. Recent books such as Sam Leith's *Words Like LoadPistols: Rhetoric from Aristotle to Obama*[4] and James Crosswhite's *Deep Rhetoric: Philosophy, Reason, Violence, Justice, Wisdom*[5] are excellent histories of rhetoric. They are also persuasive manifestos on rhetoric's relevance to the modern age.

Rhetoric has many applications for a number of professions, especially law, but for our purposes, we will only consider the rules and principles contained in Aristotle's "rhetorical triangle." Because, taken together, they provide the best model for writing and presenting persuasive stories.

* * * * *

The speech to the ABTL made me think about a lawyer I used to work with. He had an unhealthy love of pension planning but he was downright crazy for wills and estates.

This was the intersection of sex, death and money. This was drama and comedy. From before birth to after death, this is where the Darwinian struggle to pass on genes and property clashes with the limits of mortality and morality.

---

3. Sam Leith, *Words Like Loaded Pistols: Rhetoric from Aristotle to Obama* (New York: Basic Books, 2012), 219.
4. Ibid.
5. James Crosswhite, *Deep Rhetoric: Philosophy, Reason, Violence, Justice, Wisdom* (Chicago: University of Chicago Press, 2013).

This man's clients had illegitimate children their spouses didn't know about, weird fetishes, secrets they hoped to carry on into perpetuity, and complicated acts of vengeance they hoped to pull off from the grave.

Not that any of them thought they were going to die. "My job is to tell them 'thou art mortal,'" the lawyer explained.

The shelves of his office library were filled with biographies of great men and women. The lawyer would ask the client what they all had in common. The client almost never came up with the right answer.

They're all dead, the lawyer would say, slamming his palm on the desk. And they all died without a will.

That last part wasn't true. Napoleon, I was certain, had written several wills.

The lawyer shrugged. He wasn't under oath in his own office. The point of the story wasn't the truth. The point of the story was to get his clients to write a will.

* * * * *

Most lawyers don't acknowledge the importance of storytelling to what they do. As a result, they don't tell their clients' stories, their own stories, or the stories of their profession, as well as they could.

The odd thing is that we knew the power of storytelling long before we ever became lawyers.

There is a sculpture of a child in the gardens of the Inner Temple, one of London's bench and bar associations. The boy holds a storybook inscribed with Charles Lamb's quote: "Lawyers, I suppose, were children once."

We forget the names of teachers and friends, chemistry formulas, the dates of battles. If we ever knew algebra before, we don't know it now. Just try to help your kid with homework.

But we remember stories.

Not perfectly but well enough to retell them to our children.

We can do it because we never lost the point. No one forgets how the turtle beat the hare or why the Little Engine that Could, could.

Stories stay.

They are imprinted on our memory, stored in neat, ready-to-use packages, to be shared whenever they can do some good.

Other than sex, no other form of human interaction offers a more effective or efficient means of communication. Stories can educate, elevate, comfort, and afflict those who are too comfortable. They can create community. They can also drive people apart, justify unspeakable crimes, and destroy the most basic concepts of civil society.

You want proof? Brian Boyd's *On the Origin of Stories: Evolution, Cognition and Fiction* (2009) draws on Darwinian theory to argue that storytelling isn't just important, it is scientifically important.

There is also this, from the *New York Times*: "Brain scans are revealing what happens in our heads when we read a detailed description, an evocative metaphor or an emotional exchange between characters."[6] The research shows that stories "stimulate the brain and even how we act in life." When people read a sentence about grasping or kicking something, their brain scans show activity in the same part of the motor cortex that coordinates physical movement.[7]

Moreover, the brain "does not make much of a distinction between reading about an experience and encountering it in real life; in each case, the same neurological regions are stimulated."[8]

Many of us already knew that stories have the power to move us and make us think. We didn't need scientific proof.

* * * * *

During my training in trial advocacy at the US Department of Justice, we were told trials are stories, competitions in narrative. The winning side is the one that tells the best story.

---

6. Anne Paul Murphy, "Your Brain on Fiction," *New York Times*, March 17, 2012.
7. Ibid.
8. Ibid.

Everyone says that, but they don't mean it.

If they did, lawyers would be taught that the words "case" and "story" are interchangeable.

They would learn to develop stories from the raw material of their practice—fact-patterns, law, client and witness statements, and so on— trying, whenever possible, to follow common story genres and patterns.

They would learn to write like storytellers, plotting their arguments with pace in mind, developing characters, identifying their wants, understanding their conflicts, and reasoning to a credible resolution that moves, convinces, and persuades the listener.

They would realize that some of the most important stories lawyers tell are the stories they tell about themselves.

Most of all, they would bring the same passion and planning to their storytelling as they do to every other part of the practice.

* * * * *

I have spent a lot of time working with lawyers and writers. Most were good people. Some were not. Quite a few were addicted to one substance or another. At least three were insane.

Work with lawyers and writers long enough and nothing will surprise you except, maybe, this one thing:

Many of them do not love their work. This isn't just sad. It's limiting.

No storyteller can be great if they don't love telling stories. Whether you are a writer or a lawyer, you must *want* to connect with the audience and take joy in it when you do.

Passion matters. I have heard it from lawyers arguing a retirement fund case but never felt a twinge of it from lawyers prosecuting a murder trial. Passion is not the product of a particular set of facts or laws. It comes from the heart of the lawyer trying the case and his or her commitment to it, to the people involved, to the process, to a personal sense of professionalism and pride in the work.

The opposite of love is not hate—Elie Wiesel said in a wildly different context—it is indifference. The indifferent writer or lawyer is bad at his job. I am as indifferent to him as he is to his own work.

* * * * *

The more I prepared for my ABTL speech, the more ambitious I became. The topic was too big for one man.

So I recruited Michael Badalucco to be my co-panelist. Woody Allen's former prop man, he went from being a member of the crew to going before the cameras. A beloved character actor, a favorite of the Coen Brothers, Badalucco won an Emmy Award for playing lawyer Jimmy Berluti on the ABC drama *The Practice.*

During long lunches, sitting in the sun on the terrace of his Manhattan Beach home, eating delicious Sicilian food cooked by his wife, Brenda, Michael and I deconstructed stories of famous trials and debated the meaning of cases on the news and episodes of law shows.

The absurdity was not lost on me.

I was contemplating the issue of storytelling—for free, by the way—rather than writing the story I had already been paid for. It was unseemly, sad even. Those who can't write, write or—better yet—*talk* about writing.

* * * * *

In time I became the most annoying of all self-creations. I became an expert. Loopy with information, I developed a theory as to how lawyers—and everybody else—should tell stories.

It wasn't so much a new theory as a distillation of lessons I learned from the two best storytellers I ever knew.

* * * * *

For the last 27 years, I have been writing and performing law stories of one kind or another, as a journalist, a practicing attorney, and as a television writer.

Yet the person who taught me the most about lawyer storytelling never tried a case, never represented a client, and never watched—or owned, to my knowledge—a television set.

Professor David Daube looked like the prophets he studied: tall, stooped, his domed forehead ringed with corn-silk white hair. He wore a wool suit, frayed shirt, and ancient school tie.

One of the 20th century's greatest biblical scholars, he was able to trace his own lineage back to the medieval rabbis of Lyon. His massive body of work—on the rabbinical Jesus, the meaning and content of Jesus's teachings, on the Hellenistic influences on both Jewish and Christian law—changed how much of the world's religious and legal scholars would forever do their work.

What made him unique—what made him great—was that he recognized that "faith stories" were really law stories. In Daube's view, the Bible—Old and New Testaments—were neither divine nor understandable through faith. They were legal narratives, the products of their time, place, and context. They referred to prosaic legal conflicts governed by identifiable laws and precepts. They were told and retold in order to establish societal norms and practices.

To read Daube is to be suffused with story. His goal was not to prove or disprove an article of faith. It was to find the legal origin of the stories contained in the Bible in order to uncover their intended meaning and purpose.

"Stories were fundamental to David; absolutely fundamental," Calum Carmichael told me over the phone from his office in Ithaca, New York.

Daube's former pupil and friend (you could not be one without becoming the other), Carmichael is a professor of comparative literature at Cornell University. He is also Daube's literary executor, the editor and publisher of Daube's enormous body of work.

"Daube recognized that he could not do philosophy. Abstractions were unnatural to him. Truthfulness to life is what counted," Carmichael said. "For him, storytelling was so much better for expressing ideas and thoughts. The idea determined the story he would tell. And it was always apt."

Daube's storehouse of stories seemed infinite. He was an expert on biblical laws, Greek texts, Talmudic exegesis, the laws of ancient Rome, classical literature, politics, and law.

He was also married several times and never lost his lust for life or anything else. There was never a more engaging or interesting man. A poet as well as a scholar, his wide-ranging, insatiable intellectual curiosity led him to create new stories out of the oldest and most diverse of materials.

Daube introduced me to rhetoric. He also convinced me that it contains everything a storyteller needs to craft great stories.

Working on my ABTL speech was like going back to graduate school, where I managed to get not one but *two* useless master's degrees in history.

They cannot be traded in for one PhD, by the way. I asked.

* * * * *

My own storehouse of stories came from practicing law. For almost ten years, I was a federal prosecutor. Starting in the District of Columbia Superior Court, I handled everything from prostitution, assaults, drugs, and burglary, through illegal protests in the House Chamber during the State of the Union Address, inadvertent gun possession in the White House (a lot of tourists forget they are packing), and attempted murder.

But for a short stint helping to prepare Attorney General Janet Reno to testify at the congressional hearings into the siege of the Branch Davidian compound in Waco, Texas, most of my career was spent in Los Angeles, handling bank robberies, police brutality civil rights cases, massive white-collar frauds, battles in the drug war, and espionage.

During my 14 years writing television, I never stopped practicing law, at least part-time, handling political asylum cases for the Public Counsel Law Center or working as counsel at a law firm.

Anyone can enjoy two careers. All it takes is desire, opportunity, and the willingness to be mediocre. Born with the first, handed the second,

I have learned to accept the third. A short attention span and low television ratings can only take you so far. Still, I have thoroughly enjoyed working as a lawyer and writer, even if I have never been a lights-out success at either.

There is no better way to understand the centrality of storytelling to the law than to practice it. There is also no better way to get story material.

* * * * *

The ABTL speech was an opportunity to acknowledge a debt to Professor Daube as well as to David E. Kelley.

The creator of iconic law shows ranging from *L.A. Law*, *Ally McBeal*, *Picket Fences*, *The Practice*, and *Boston Legal*, Kelley gave me my first job in Hollywood. He employed me full-time for five years as a writer and producer. Even after I left to create my own show, we wrote several scripts together. He taught me everything I know about storytelling on television. Not everything *he* knew—that he kept to himself—but enough to keep me working.

* * * * *

Professors and members of the legal profession could learn a lot from contemplating Kelley's work. His shows are examples of how storytelling both affects and reflects the work lawyers do and the expectations of those they serve. Law reviews fill law libraries and databases. Their readership is small, but it is believed to be influential.

In contrast, tens of millions of people—literally that number—watch law-themed television shows. Sometimes these numbers represent the American viewing population on a single night.

Television law shows dwarf all other formats for explaining—or confusing—the public over what the law is or should be. Along with generating billions of dollars of revenue, these shows have the potential to significantly alter the legal landscape.

Of course, lawyers on a television series are not real; nor are the stories. But the stories reflect and influence the storytelling of real lawyers. And real lawyers could learn to tell their own stories better by studying them.

* * * * *

Finally, on October 4, 2013, I presented my results to the ABTL. It was a multimedia hour-long piece of PowerPoint performance art; not exactly an extravaganza, but close. There were video clips from television shows I had written and Badalucco acted in. I showed charts defining story elements and the principles of storytelling. I offered pointers on how to craft facts and law into compelling narratives in a myriad of contexts.

Badalucco performed a closing argument from an episode of *The Practice*. He then conducted a kind of actor's workshop on how to prepare and deliver stories in the most cogent, moving way possible.

With hubris bordering on insanity, I concluded with "Shapiro's Five Rules for Storytelling," thoughts on how to write and rewrite stories, no matter the context, client, or case.

These rules do not purport to be all the rules. Nobody blames Congress for not passing all the laws they could—quite the opposite, as a matter of fact.

That said, however, Shapiro's Five Rules for Storytelling happen to be terrific: easy to remember, handy to use, versatile, and relevant for almost every type of storytelling a lawyer might engage in. They are also cheaper than attending a McKee script seminar.

1. Have a point
2. Use the rhetorical triangle
3. Write the script

4. Edit the script
5. Rehearse the performance

Take these rules, I told the ABTL, or leave them. Better yet, write your own. The important thing is to go about the important job of storytelling in a mindful, organized, thoughtful way.

Badalucco and I were a big hit.

And I missed my pilot script deadline by a year and a half. This book is the result.

TWO

The Miscast Lawyer

Once upon a time, Harvey Weinstein and I were sitting in a Town Car being driven through Manhattan.[1] Weinstein is the greatest living movie impresario of our time. Ask him. He's not shy. He will tell you himself.

"Sorry I'm late," he said when we first shook hands, over breakfast at the Peninsula Hotel in Beverly Hills. He just flew in from the Super Bowl, he said, where he spent the whole time talking to former President W. Bush about Weinstein's latest film, *The King's Speech.*

Weinstein and another famous producer had an idea for a television series. I was hired to help sell the show to a network and then write the pilot script.

The details were fuzzy. Apparently, it was to be a one-hour drama based on a real person. He was a charismatic former law enforcement officer and bon vivant. I had not met him—or anyone like him—but I got the drift of what the show could be. It would be dark but funny, twisted but not too twisted. The hero would be handsome but not pretty, tough but not cruel, resourceful but no off-putting genius. He would be a modern-day knight errant, serving rich and famous patrons, *in* their world, you understand, but not *of* it, true to his working-class roots, street-savvy, but Protean in his ability to move in and out of the many tribes that make up modern-day America.

"But not Ray Donovan"—the Showtime hit series was already on the air at this point. "And our hero can't be a lawyer," Weinstein said.

---

1. March 2011.

19

"Got it," I said. What I should have done instead is thanked him for the offer and politely declined. I was miscast to write this story and should have said so. I didn't.

* * * * *

Now we were in New York trying to sell the show to a cable network. The early afternoon weather was cool and rainy. Dark skies and grey streets, yellow taxis and red brake lights smearing colors through the water-streaked car windows.

Several other Weinstein Company employees were with us. One had taken me to lunch at Nobu. She had been Weinstein's assistant. Now she was the head of his nascent television production company. Weinstein had been going to join us for lunch but didn't. Thanks to her previous position, she knew his to-go order.

A cell phone rang in the car. Madonna was on the line. She and Weinstein talked about the music for the final credits of a movie she had directed and he was producing: W.E.

Sitting in the white-hot center of show business should have been more fun. But something was wrong. I can't remember what exactly I ate at Nobu. I had a lot of it, and quickly too, because we were running late. Now it disagreed with me. Violently.

My stomach churned and growled. Clammy sweat sprung from my forehead. It trickled down my sides, sticking to my shirt, and pasting my hair down on my head. I stared out of the fogged-up window.

Traffic was gridlock. Not even the greatest movie producer of our age can alter time or traffic. Despite our driver's suicidal efforts, we were going to be late.

Nerves began to fray. The overheated interior of the car became suffocating. I tried to open my window. It was locked.

Suddenly, involuntarily, an internal valve in the area of my lower abdomen went into a titanic spasm. Something else, something bad and noticeable, erupted farther along my digestive tract. I wondered if

Madonna heard. "Jesus," Weinstein muttered, covering the cell phone and speaking to his assistants, "What the fuck did you let him eat?"

As the car caromed down the street, I hoped for a crash, anything to stop the disaster ahead. Unfortunately, we got to the meeting safely. But we did not live happily ever after.

The End.

* * * * *

By "the end," I mean of my career writing for Weinstein. It is a fine place to begin studying the mechanics of storytelling.

Aristotle taught that everything must have a *telos*, a purpose. But a story must not simply have a purpose. That purpose must be clear to the audience.

My purpose in telling the Weinstein story is to define what a story is, identify a few important story elements, and discuss some principles that apply to all stories. My goal is also to show that while all of us can be miscast as storytellers from time to time, there is always something we can do to make things better.

* * * * *

While writers and lawyers employ different terms when they discuss story elements, they can and should be used interchangeably.

Not because the terms and concepts are exactly alike. Save your carping; I know they are not *exactly* alike. The purpose of this book is to get lawyers more comfortable with storytelling. Whether they realize it or not, they already know a lot about the elements that make up stories, as well as the basic structure of stories themselves.

Setting/Jurisdiction
Every episode of the Weinstein series was to begin and end in a particular New York City restaurant, one that really exists. Famous for catering

to the famous and infamous, the place would become a character unto itself.

The setting of a story gives the audience a point of reference, like a giant "You Are Here" arrow on a map. The more familiar the setting, the more likely it is that the audience will bring their own knowledge and understanding of the world where the story takes place and the rules that apply there. Even if the audience has never been to the famous New York restaurant, chances are they have seen or heard stories about places like that.

The lawyer's term for setting is jurisdiction. In this, lawyers don't enjoy the writer's freedom. A case of patent infringement or murder has a limited number of potential settings. If you do get to choose, the questions to consider are: Who do you want to tell your story to? Where are you likely to get to tell the story the way you want to tell it, with as little interference and editing as possible?

* * * * *

In the early 1990s, when I was at the US Department of Justice, the odd folks across the hall made up the Child Exploitation & Obscenity Unit. Even though "child" was in their name, they tended to bring cases involving adults where no children were involved. And they always seemed to charge them in places like Utah, where the community standard of what constituted obscene material was different than New York or California. *These* were storytellers who understood the value of setting.

* * * * *

There is another aspect of setting evident in the Weinstein story. It is based on a true story. Strike that. It *is* a true story. Or as true as I remember it; though, in all fairness, I was unwell at the time and there was no court reporter present.

Claiming a story is true sets it in the real world, where the rules of physics and human nature apply. It also gives the story credibility, so long as we find the storyteller credible. Stories lawyers tell are always based on the truth. If they are not, the lawyer will soon no longer be a lawyer.

Characters/Parties and Potential Witnesses

It is inevitable that stories and cases *about* people *involve* people. It is a good thing, too. People are always the most interesting part of any story or case, particularly to other people.

People in a story are called characters. People in the real world of law can be characters and even character witnesses, but they are usually called something else—parties, clients, witnesses, etc. Again, for our purposes, we shall call them all characters. The job of the storyteller is to recognize, understand and use the characters to further the story. Because someone is a potential character does not mean they should be in the story. Not everyone who could be brought into the story should be.

Here are a few simple rules when dealing with characters: No character in a law case or story should be presented unless he or she is interesting. By definition, no one can be interesting in a case or story unless he or she is relevant. If the characters or witnesses are necessary to the story but seem uninteresting, the role of the writer and lawyer is to make them interesting.

* * * * *

In *Storytelling for Lawyers*, Philip N. Meyer analogizes lawyers to film directors.[2] But I think an equally valid analogy is with executive producers such as Weinstein. He neither writes the script nor directs the action nor plays any role. Most of the components of the story he presents exist independent of him. They were there before he arrived and could have been developed by someone else.

---

2. Philip N. Meyer, *Storytelling for Lawyers* (New York: Oxford University Press, 2014).

Yet he has become the most important, influential force in modern filmmaking. He has won numerous Academy Awards and earned hundreds of millions of dollars. What does he do, exactly? How does he do it? What is the secret to success? It isn't complicated. The man can spot a good story.

That's it. That is his genius—to know the difference between what could be a sure-fire hit or a dismal, though well-intentioned, flop—and to invest his money, time, and energy accordingly.

It is the same talent that makes plaintiff's lawyers rich, prosecutors undefeated, defense lawyers famous, the general counsel essential, and private equity lawyers worth every penny they get.

Enormous risk is involved in this kind of work. Pick the wrong story or case and the producer or lawyer can lose everything. Few Fortune 500 CEOs have Weinstein's talent for grabbing a good story and running with it. Few can boast a more successful, influential, or recognizable brand. The closest I can think of are some of the nation's best contingent fee attorneys.

As a character in a story, Weinstein is hard to beat. Gamblers and savants are always interesting.

Wants/Motives

Every character in a story, regardless of who they are, has one thing in common: they want something.

It is important that writers, and lawyers, know what they want. Because what they want reveals who they are, explains their potential biases, goes to their credibility, and suggests whether they are truth-tellers or liars.

Weinstein wanted a television hit. I did, too. It is generally believed that a hit television show is the surest way to win honor, power, riches, fame, and the love of women, not to mention men and children. Watched by millions of people, a hit generates hundreds of millions of dollars in revenue, can be celebrated as a cultural phenomenon, and always makes the writer who created it happy for the rest of his life. Or so my agents inform me.

That I, as the narrator in the Weinstein story, prayed for a car crash suggests I wasn't going to have a hit. For whatever reason—bad sushi, the pressure of the moment—I lost perspective. I became a hysteric.

What a character wants, how they try to get it, what they do when they face obstacles, all work to reveal who and what the character is. In stories, what people want is also referred to as "the stakes." All stories need stakes. The audience has to understand and relate to what is at stake. If the stakes don't matter, the story won't matter.

Conflict/Causes of Action

Characters do not all want the same thing. It would be a boring story if they did. It would certainly not be a law story.

The clash of wants creates conflict. It is what causes the action. Conflict is at the heart of law and storytelling. Without conflict, there would be no business for either profession.

While every case and story involves a conflict, there are several differences in how these narratives can be told. In fictional stories, for example, the conflict can be wholly internal, as it is in the Weinstein story. In a law story the conflict must be manifested in some external way. The storytelling lawyer must express it clearly.

My boss at the U.S. Attorney's Office, the late, great Robert Louis Stevenson Brosio, believed there was no such thing as too much clarity when it comes to explaining conflicts. Don't assume the judge or jury know anything. Spell out the conflict between your story and the other side's as often and as clearly as possible.

A lifelong student of storytelling, Brosio was named by a family friend, James M. Cain, author of *Double Indemnity* and *The Postman Always Rings Twice*. Cain was a regular at the restaurant where Brosio's father was the maitre'd.

* * * * *

There are other story elements and principles. Plot, for example, refers to the events that make up a story. The speed in which the storyteller moves from one event to the other is called pace. Lawyers don't really have a term that corresponds with either pace or plot. But they should.

* * * * *

Let us leave definitions aside and consider what else we can learn from the Weinstein story. The first question is an obvious one: what, exactly, was the point? It is a bad sign if you have to ask. It should be obvious. The Weinstein story is about failure. Film producer Lindsay Doran (*Sense and Sensibility*, among others) told me that there is as much to learn about storytelling from a bad movie as there is from a good one. Why a story succeeds can be a mystery, lightning in a bottle, as hard to explain as it is to duplicate. Why a story fails is more obvious. There are many reasons why the movie *Titanic* was a hit. There was only one reason why the ship Titanic sunk.

But the Weinstein story isn't just a story about failure. It is also an example of a failed story—a story that fails to do what a story ought to do. Understanding why it fails is an important step toward understanding how to create stories that don't fail.

* * * * *

Almost every story element in the Weinstein case has problems. For example, the fact that the story is set in the real world and is based on real characters does not make it worth telling. Many things are true but are not worth talking about.

It is good that the voice of the narrator is identifiable but it is possibly too identifiable. The whiny, neurotic, self-obsessed writer is an off-putting cliché. Just because a cliché may be true doesn't make it better.

Furthermore, invoking the ineffable name of Weinstein is obvious bootstrapping, success by association, a kind of hearsay, an attempt to establish bona fides as a storyteller through my work with a far, far more successful and established figure.

There is nothing inherently wrong with this kind of name-dropping. Indeed, as we shall see, Aristotle approved of it as a means of establishing credibility. But a little bit goes a long way. Too much of it is a credibility killer.

The story's tone also smacks of disingenuousness. Ostensibly about choking and messing up a pitch meeting, the story might also be read as the worst kind of humble brag, the sly boast hidden amid self-deprecation. Instead of enhancing my credibility, it may undercut it.

It isn't all bad. The story does have logic to it. You don't have to be a writer to understand the motives driving the narrator or the pressure he feels to make sure it all works out. It also has a nice pace; things move along.

But the story promises something that it does not deliver. The audience is prepared for a resolution it can anticipate, possibly, but does not receive. Because story elements are connected, inextricably intertwined, if you like, when one fails or a basic principle is ignored, chances are good that the story, whether it's about failure or not, will fail to achieve its purpose.

* * * * *

It turned out that my immediate fears were unfounded. Weinstein did all the talking in the meeting with the New York executives, and it was a joy to listen to him. His knowledge and love of movies is unmatched. He didn't seem to understand the show we were selling any better than I did. But then, he didn't have to; he wasn't going to have to write it.

Despite Weinstein's best efforts, the series did not sell in New York. The network executives explained that their audience did not seem to spark to shows about cops. Their two previous attempts to do cop shows had failed and they were not interested in trying again. As my father, a furniture salesman, once said, you cannot sell a credenza to a man who wants a wall unit.

* * * * *

A week or so later, back in Los Angeles, I was sitting in the offices of another network with Weinstein and two of his executives. Again, Weinstein did all the talking, and this time, he was even better—passionate, engaged, intelligent. Mostly, he talked about his love of television and his excitement about getting to work on this (whatever this was).

"And we're very excited to be working with Jeff," he said, flicking his hand in my direction, "a great writer."

I was proud. I blamed myself for not being named Jeff. I resolved to remain Jeff until the show went into syndication.

Again, the nature of the show was not clear. Again the network passed. This, perhaps, should have been a sign.

* * * * *

But Harvey Weinstein did not become great by quitting. Once again into the breach and this time, Weinstein was his most brilliant, a consummate salesman. He even got my name right. FX bought the show.

What transpired over the next year is a blur. Delays in closing the deal took up most of the time, along with meandering conversations between the various parties. During this time, I wrote countless memos and miscellanea outlining what the show could be.

The only thing that everyone seemed to agree on was that they didn't like any of it. I recall weeping in frustration, but only once, and only in front of one executive.

The network hadn't bought a wall unit or a credenza. They bought the idea of maybe being interested in some piece of furniture, the features and functions of which they could never really describe. I failed to make it for them.

The script never came together, the show never gelled, the pilot was never shot, my dream of Hollywood immortality died. However, nothing in show business ever truly dies. The idea itself went into "turn-around," all rights to the story reverting back to my partners.

* * * * *

I never spoke to Weinstein again after the show was sold, a shame because I liked and respected him enormously, and appreciated his efforts. It wasn't his fault that his success did not rub off on me.

For reasons both in and out of my control, I could not write a good story. None of the elements worked. There was no point to any of it. I am not the first writer or lawyer to have taken on a case I could not win. But it occurred to me that I should learn something from it.

The desire to be a good storyteller is not enough. Not in writing and certainly not in the law.

* * * * *

Knowing why a story fails is important. But it is not the same as knowing what makes a story work.

For many years, I was a book critic. There are worse crimes. But most of them can be defended: the perpetrator was desperate, under the influence, forced into it. I had no excuses. I volunteered for the free books, meager or no pay, the chance to see my name in print. That I never wrote a book didn't mean I couldn't render verdicts on them.

The problem with life is not that it is too short. The problem is that it is too long. What goes around comes around.

When the first show I created aired, it was subjected to hundreds of reviews. They appeared in newspapers, magazines, radio programs, television shows, and countless Internet sources. There were raves. Many were positive. But some were not and a few seemed libelous.[3] Yet no one should be a tougher critic of his own work than the storyteller himself.

Thinking you have a great story to tell does not make it true. Believing in the story with all your heart is also not enough.

---

3. The most hostile review was written by a critic who never revealed she had lobbied to produce the show herself; nor did she reveal I had once, inadvertently, called her fat. I don't blame her for being fat or biased; I just think she might have been more forthcoming.

* * * * *

One day a Mary Kay cosmetics saleswoman who looked like Sandra Bullock was driving down the street in her pink Cadillac. She saw a large man beating a small woman. Without hesitating, the saleswoman blew her car horn, pulled to the curb, jumped out, and began screaming for the man to stop, shaming him into running away. The saleswoman noticed the woman was wearing a US postal uniform. There was a satchel of mail on the ground, letters strewn everywhere. But what she remembered most, what she could never forget, was what the man looked like.

"I make my living off the faces of others," she said on the stand. "I'll never forget his face."

Who could? He had a wet, weeping Phantom of the Opera wound that ran from the side of his forehead down to his chin. He also wore his hair high, very high, Sideshow Bob high. He lived on the letter carrier's route. He often complained that she took too long delivering his mail.

The defense lawyer went to trial with the following story: misidentification. The victim and Mary Kay cosmetics woman—he argued—had pointed out the wrong man. The real culprit was another person, never identified, who must have been the same size and weight as the defendant, wearing the same hairstyle, and bearing the same hideous scar. The defense lawyer told this story with great passion. I think he really believed it.

The jury was out for ten minutes. They spent nine of the minutes arguing over who got to be the foreperson.

All of us think we can dance, kiss, and tell stories well. Many of us overestimate our abilities. But that does not mean we should stop trying.

Chances are good that you are a more talented storyteller than you realize. If you have not succeeded in the past, it could be that you just haven't found the right place to tell your stories. Or found the right way to tell them.

* * * * *

It was a dark and stormy night. If you had been there around midnight, standing in the cold, on the corner of the empty street, as the thunder caromed off the buildings, you would have seen, in the lightning flash, the ghostly image of a Catholic church.

The old priest who lived in the rectory of this church had been awakened by a noise. A light sleeper, bothered by a hip problem, he rarely slept through the night. For a moment, he wasn't even sure what woke him. Was it the thunder? He didn't know. He still doesn't. All he knows for sure is that when he tried to turn on the lights in his bedroom, they wouldn't go on. The electricity had gone out.

He heard something fall inside the church. He put a bathrobe over his sweatpants and T-shirt, grabbed a flashlight, and hobbled out of his room to see what was going on.

Going from the rectory through a side door into the church, the darkness lit only by the flashlight beam, the priest saw a shadowy, dark figure standing near the rail of the altar. It was a man holding what looked like a knife.

For a moment, both men stood in silence, shocked by the other's presence. Other people might have run away but the priest stood his ground. Partly, he wanted to find out who the man was, how he got in, why he was there. Partly, he wanted to help the man. No one, the priest thought, breaks into a church unless they have to.

Suddenly, the man barreled into the priest, using the metal object in his hand as a kind of battering ram. Involuntarily, the priest put his arms around him in a hug, as much to stop him as to catch himself from falling.

They ended up in a pile, the two men struggling in the middle of the church as the thunder crashed and exploded outside. The man was strong, smaller than the priest, younger, desperate. He twisted, turned, used the metal object in his hand to try to pry the priest off of him, grunting and cursing with effort.

But the priest would not let go. Something made him hold on. Fear, perhaps, though he thinks it was something else, something bigger.

What neither man knew—what they could not have known—was that a policeman, driving in his car, had seen a light from within the church. The priest's flashlight had pierced the darkness, glimmering through the church's window. The police officer stopped his car and ran toward the church to see what was going on.

* * * * *

Too dramatic but still better than the prosecutor's actual opening statement: "Ladies and gentlemen of the jury, good morning, my name is _____, and this is a case about the crimes of unlawful entry into a house of worship and the attempted theft of more than $500 of religious artifacts."

It was factual. It was based on the law. It was horrible.

Outside of court, this was a smart lawyer and a charming, funny man. The only way to keep him from being a great storyteller was putting him in front of a jury. There, he freeze-dried stiff, bland, and tasteless. A victim of his training, afraid of the other side objecting to what he said, scared of the judge's disapproval, he played it so safe that he never managed to advocate for anything, let alone do it creatively.

Eventually, he left court work and spent years handling mental health issues for the US Attorney's Office, becoming an expert in the field. His intelligence, humanity, and compassion earned the respect of judges, law enforcement, doctors, prosecutors, defense lawyers, patients, and their families.

Much of his success was the result of his ability to distill the cases into story terms, outlining the narrative and events that brought each person into the criminal justice system. He was a born storyteller. He just had to find the right stage. It wasn't in the courtroom. It was in the judge's chambers, in smaller venues, among professionals, advocating, in a quiet, reasoned, humane way, for what he believed should be done.

It wasn't lawyer storytelling for trial work. But the basic elements and principles of good storytelling still applied.

* * * * *

He was not at all the most miscast storyteller I ever saw in DC Superior Court. That was another young prosecutor. Cross-examining the defendant in a case, she went down her list of questions, asking them in order, failing to notice what the defendant was saying, even when he was lying.

There was no need. She had already written out her closing argument before the case began and wasn't going to change it because one of the characters went off script. That was bad.

Worse was her tendency to recount the testimony—or her version of what it should have been—in ethnically offensive accents appropriate to the witness. If, for example, the witness who saw the drug transaction was of Asian descent, the prosecutor would remind the jury what he said—or should have said—in a voice not heard since the Charlie Chan movie series was popular. Her summary of an African American's testimony was an *Amos 'n' Andy* horror show. When she was finally confronted about this, she was shocked, having no idea that she was doing it. She was such a bad listener that she hadn't even been listening to herself.

* * * * *

Listening is the most unappreciated requirement of becoming a good storyteller. But it is never taught in law schools. Perhaps because is antithetical to the temperament and habits of most lawyers.

Listening is how we gather information. It is how we make sense of the world. What we hear is the source of our story material, the foundation of all storytelling.

Yet just listening is not enough. We also have to be open to what people are telling us and write our stories based on what we hear, not what we think we hear or want to hear. Bad listeners are always miscast as storytellers.

* * * * *

I heard that one of the series regulars on the original *Law and Order* series began to believe he actually *was* a prosecutor in the Manhattan District Attorney's Office. If a script called for him to appear at an arraignment hearing, he would send a note to the producers on prop office stationary from the DA's office, asking that they find a junior attorney to handle it.

"I'm too senior for arraignments," he said.

Writers hate this. *We* created the character, *we* write what they say; only card-carrying members of the Writers Guild of America are allowed.

A gaffer wouldn't dare do props. If he did, he'd get grief from both unions. If anybody yelled "action" or "cut" the Directors Guild would file a grievance. The reason writers don't act isn't just because they have no talent and aren't particularly easy on the eyes. It's also because it's not our job. Just like writing is not the actor's job.

Lawyers can get just as defensive about clients telling them how to do their business.

But not listening to the opinions of others is always a mistake.

* * * * *

In a script for *The Practice*, Charles Dutton had to give a three-minute speech; an eternity in television.[4] He nailed it, first try, and got a rare ovation from the crew.

"Thank you, sir," he said to me, adding quietly, "I wanted to change a few things but I didn't want to bother you."

He won an Emmy Award for the role.

During that same episode, Steve Harris, one of the series regulars, cornered me, unhappy with his lines.

"Where's my music?" he yelled. "You don't have my music in my lines!"

Once, when a series regular told me that he didn't feel comfortable delivering a particular line, I asked if he felt comfortable cashing the

---

4. "Killing Time," *The Practice*, ABC, September 30, 2001.

check. Another time I made an actor cry by demanding he say the words of the script *exactly* as written.

It was a mistake. Like most mistakes, it was based on ego and insecurity, the desire to control everything, and the fear of what might happen if I let other people get involved in my storytelling.

The actors embody the characters, understand them—*become* them—in three dimensions. The more I listened to actors, the more I realized they were right about what they had to say. They were also bringing a level of understanding to the character that even the writer who created them did not have.

It is remarkable how many lawyers make the same mistake. Too many tell the story they want to tell the way they want to tell it. They fight with strong-willed clients who disagree with them. These lawyers believe they have been hired to do a job, to develop a vision, a story. Once they have created that story, the lawyer wants to protect it.

They are right to do so but only up to a point. Maintaining the vision comes at too high a price if you can't hear good advice. Lawyers, like writers, have to understand that storytelling is a team effort—it is collaboration, not a dictatorship. When we don't listen to the characters in our story or case, the story, the case, and the law suffer.

Of all people, my mother had to teach me this.

* * * * *

She was a bank teller for over 30 years and was never wrong. At the end of the day, when she balanced out her cash drawer, it came out even, to the penny—she hadn't made a mistake by giving out or taking in the wrong amount of money.

It is nerve-racking to have such a mother.

She was held up four times as a bank teller, the last two times by the same group of heavily armed robbers. Repeat customers, if you will. There were quite a few eyewitnesses in the bank both times that this group hit. All but one of the witnesses swore the robbers were African Americans.

My mother was the lone dissenter.

"They were not black," she said firmly. It was the only way she said anything. "They were white men and they were wearing wigs and make-up."

They tried to talk her out of it. They didn't know her well.

"They did not have Negroid facial features," she insisted, making me cringe a little. In the 1950s, she had taken anthropology at LA City College and gotten an A. She did not claim to be an expert, but she knew what she saw.

And she would not be moved.

Black men were arrested as suspects in the robbery. My mother was shown photos, taken to line-ups, brought to show-ups. She did not budge. It wasn't them.

Little pleaser that I was, it troubled me that she wasn't helping the authorities. What if she were wrong? She was, after all, a lifelong liberal, conservative in all things except politics. Her mother had voted for Henry Wallace over FDR, a fact we whispered since it was akin to confessing she had been a Stalinist.

Mom walked precincts for Helen Gahagan Douglas when she lost to "That Son-of-a-Bitch Nixon." This was the only swearing my mother did. She voted for Eugene McCarthy over Robert F. Kennedy in the California Primary because RFK was not liberal enough. On civil rights, she was left of Paul Robeson.

She did not like the FBI, did not trust it, still held a grudge over the Rosenbergs, detested J. Edgar Hoover almost as much as Nixon himself, and didn't even like Efrem Zimbalist Jr., star of the television series *The FBI*—and he was a regular customer at the bank.

I feared she was wrong about the robbers out of some sympathetic bias toward black people or out of hostility toward the FBI agents.

* * * * *

Weeks went by. Finally, the robbers were arrested. The FBI found make-up and wigs in the trunk. The robbers were all white men.

"But did the FBI listen?" my mother asked. She is the queen of the rhetorical question.

* * * * *

How does one become a good listener?

If I knew that, I could save the world a lot of unhappiness.

Still, there is a great deal to learn from producers like Weinstein, not to mention marketing experts, studio executives, and network promotional departments.

In order to make their living, they have to be practical and pragmatic. It is called show business, not show fun. To quote rock promoter Bill Graham, when they say it's not about the money, what they mean is . . . it's about the money.

Not only are producers such as Weinstein and studio executives good listeners, they pay millions of dollars to have people talk to them. Would anyone talk to them if they weren't getting paid?

* * * * *

Television and movie studios focus-group test every movie and television show they produce, often many times. They do it to find out what people want, what they like, and what they would enjoy watching, so that they can give it to them as often as possible. It's no different than soap makers or political candidates.

For television shows, focus group tests are conducted for every pilot in at least three different markets—the East Coast, West Coast and Las Vegas—on the theory that these three areas represent the whole of America. Think about that.

* * * * *

The company conducting the focus group test for my first series fanned out at Universal City Walk, a vast outdoor mall, looking for volunteers.

Those that agreed got something like $50 and a packed lunch in return for filling out a questionnaire, watching a TV pilot, and then talking about it.

The questionnaire, perhaps 25 to 30 questions, asked about their income levels, family and educational background, and television viewing habits. There were also more specific questions about their attitudes toward lawyers and law shows, the justice system, and their experience with it.

Next, they sat in a room watching the pilot. Each held a small electronic box with a dial on it. They were told to turn the dial to the right when they liked something, to the left if they did not, and to push the tune-out button if something displeased them so much that they would turn the channel—turning off the television entirely is never an option. The producers watched them watching the show through a two-way mirror.

A decade or so earlier, I sat in the same type of room in a similar focus group testing facility, not for a show, but as a member of the large team of lawyers involved in the federal prosecution of the LAPD officers who beat Rodney King. The federal government was paying then, an almost unprecedented expense, reserved for the most important cases. Now, I was doing the same thing for a WB show, and the stakes somehow, absurdly, embarrassingly, felt higher.

* * * * *

After screening the pilot, a young, heavily tattooed woman in a halter top and flip-flops said that she would have enjoyed the show more if the characters were more interesting.

"More interesting how?" the focus group consultant asked.

"I dunno," she said, and thought about it. "Could they fly?"

Not in an airplane but on their own, like Superman or something.

I still think she was kidding.

The executive sitting next to me stroked his chin. "You know what . . . it's not such a bad idea."

My pilot aired without flying lawyers. It bombed.

NBC put on a show called *Heroes* the next season. It involved regular folks, not a lawyer among them, but some of them could fly.

It was a hit.

* * * * *

Writers hate dial testing. A compelling story has unexpected twists and turns. It is not a steady climb upward; there are peaks and valleys. Variety makes the journey interesting. In a dial test, however, peaks and valleys do not make executives happy. It suggests the show is upsetting, confusing, too intellectual, will not appeal to a large audience. Nobody wants a "thinker," the network's term for something bad.

"They are not happy," an executive hissed to me as the lines from the dials dipped on the screen. "Why aren't they happy?"

At that moment in the pilot, the young lawyer was being interviewed for a job and not doing well. The audience wasn't supposed to be happy; they were supposed to be worried about whether the character was going to get the job.

"It's a thinker," he said. "We're going to have to smooth that out."

I started nervously chewing a pen. Someone poured me a glass of wine.

Fortunately, the lines went up and stayed there. But then there was a sharp dip. It was a trial scene, when our inexperienced hero made a mistake cross-examining a witness.

"They feel bad for him," I said. "That's good, right? They care about whether or not he's winning the case."

The executive shook his head sadly. "No, that's not the problem," he said. "The problem is the whole cross-examination thing is a 'thinker.'"

The theory is that you can't make the audience work hard. Give it to them simply. Cut out the complexity; otherwise, they don't like it. If they don't understand something, they won't keep watching.

It's an ugly fact. Lawyers ought to keep it in mind.

The lines went up as steady as a conservative stock; overall, a good but not great return on the studio's investment. Only three people hit the tune-out button. One man fell asleep.

It was nerve-racking, like watching jury deliberations on a second-by-second basis. At some point, I bit through the pen I was chewing, ink going down my throat and chin. Someone refilled my wine glass then later refilled it a few more times.

Seinfeld, among the most popular television shows of all time, was sold into syndication for a bit more than a billion dollars. It had a notoriously terrible dial test score. Larry David, one of the show's creators, had the results framed. It hung for years over the guest bathroom toilet.

* * * * *

After the dial testing, as the producers sat behind the two-way mirror, a tall, cadaverous-looking man led the focus group through a discussion of what they had just seen.

They liked the show a lot.

But they didn't love it.

They enjoyed it and would watch it again.

But they wouldn't change their social plans to stay home to do it. They might or might not record it to watch later.

The moderator moved onto their attitudes about lawyers.

All of them had been called to jury duty at some point or had legal cases of their own. Their experiences and understanding of the system varied.

But they all had a surprising and gratifying view of the legal profession. They believed lawyers were people who could help other people and often did. What they hated were arrogant lawyers who only cared about money.

It was remarkable what they missed. For example, they hadn't realized the show was about lawyers until five minutes into it, even though the characters said so.

Once they realized they were lawyers, a few never managed to grasp who the defense lawyer was and who the prosecutor was. Not everyone walking around an outside mall in Los Angeles is necessarily a brain surgeon.

Their likes and dislikes were also strange.

One woman tuned out the show because she didn't like the name of the defendant. It seemed like a silly name to her.

Another would watch the show because she liked the music; her understanding of the show itself was otherwise vague.

The woman who wished they could fly also wished there had been more mystery, like a *CSI* show. This sounded good to me. Except that Jerry Bruckheimer was the producer of the entire *CSI* franchise *and* my show. The one thing we could not do was steal from one of the senior partner's other shows.

I asked if there was any wine left. No, they said, I had finished it. In fact, not only had I finished the wine for my pilot's focus group, I had also finished the wine for the next two pilot focus groups scheduled that night.

My contributions to show business are small, perhaps, but significant. Warner Brothers no longer provides alcohol at focus group tests.

* * * * *

I have written, created, produced, or run shows considered "procedurals" (workplace drama) or "dramedies" (comedy with dramatic elements). My only half-hour comedy aired on NBC in 2011.

"I love it!" my boss at the studio said after seeing the pilot. "I just wish it were funnier."

So did I. So did America. We were canceled after two episodes.

One of the characters, played by the Tony Award-winning actor Ben Shenkman, was named Jonathan. He wore my glasses, my suits, and my ties; he spoke and acted just like me.

According to the test results, the focus groups hated him the most.

THREE

Becoming a Storyteller

Her name is Sandrine Chapon. She is an academic at the University of Grenoble, France. We have never met. But I love her.

* * * * *

One night while *canal* flipping, Chapon happened on an episode I wrote of the ABC television series *Boston Legal* involving Louisiana's decision to execute a mentally disabled man accused of raping a child.

It was an unusual, even unprecedented episode.

Since the Supreme Court bans cameras, we wanted to show the American public a version of what actually happens there.

Comparing the show's production calendar and broadcast schedule with the Court docket, we based the episode on a pending case, *Kennedy v. Louisiana*, with the hope that it would air the week before the actual argument was held.[1]

The question before the Court—and television version of the Court—was whether capital punishment for a crime in which no one died amounted to cruel and unusual punishment in violation of the 8th Amendment of the Constitution.

It was the easiest script I ever wrote because the appellate briefs provided the facts and law.

Writing the justices' dialogue was easy, too.

---

1. Due to a network preemption, it ended up airing six days after the actual argument. See Tony Mauro, "David E. Kelley's 'Boston Legal' Takes on the Roberts Court," *Legal Times*, May 5, 2008.

The Supreme Court isn't just the highest in the land—it is also the longest-running law show in history, with a rotating cast of regulars. You love them, you hate them, but most of all, you know them; how they think, how they talk, what they want.

You don't have to guess what they would ask or how they would ask it. Putting words in their mouths was like lawyer fantasy camp.

Walking into casting sessions, however, was surreal. Who knew there were so many actresses in Hollywood who looked like Ruth Bader Ginsburg? The man we cast as Chief Justice John Roberts was so perfectly bland in appearance, so sneakily smart that he should make a career out of playing the role.

The only hard part was finding a credible Clarence Thomas. I don't think we succeeded.

The script's structure was also obvious. Supreme Court practice has its "got-to-have" scenes, including the inevitable mock argument, with all its own stresses. The arguments had already been written by the parties. The challenge was to boil them down in an accessible and entertaining way.

The Court's interior was built on the production stage. Some license was taken. Denny Crane's only interest in the case was a betting one. He wagered $10,000 that they could get the otherwise silent Justice Thomas to say something during the argument. He won the bet.

Stanford Law School professor Jeffrey Fisher, who argued the real child rape case on April 16, has seen and was impressed by the episode. . . "It was striking how closely the episode hewed to the real facts in *Kennedy*, down to the most minute detail, and (certain rants aside) to the real legal arguments the parties are advancing," Fisher said in an article about the episode. "The producers obviously had studied our briefing quite closely."[2]

We had indeed. As Tony Mauro noted in the *Legal Times* article cited here, our research indicated that James Spader's attorney character, Alan Shore, would never in a million years have said some of the things he said, such as when he attacks the "overtly and shamelessly pro-business"

---

2. Ibid.

Court, and takes a sharp detour from the rape case to slam Justice Antonin Scalia for his seemingly likely support for ExxonMobil in the case—also argued recently—involving punitive damages awarded after the *Exxon Valdez* oil spill. "Nineteen years after the *Valdez* oil spill and the plaintiffs are still waiting to be fully compensated," Shore says.

When the Scalia character interjects sharply, "You are getting so far off point," Shore shoots back: "My point is, who are you people? You've transformed this court from being a governmental branch devoted to civil rights and liberties into a protector of discrimination, a guardian of government, a slave to moneyed interests and big business and today, hallelujah, you seek to kill a mentally disabled man."[3]

[Shore eventually] concludes, "If mercy truly lives within these walls, within your hearts as justices, as people, you cannot cause this man to be injected with chemicals for the purpose of killing him."[4]

Fisher told Mauro:

"I thought the episode did an admirable job of exploring one of the paradoxes of Supreme Court practice—namely, that lawyers represent clients who usually have personal goals, but the Court is much more interested in resolving legal issues than doing individualized justice . . . Most Supreme Court advocates have been in the position, one way or another, of having to explain to a client that even though a certain result in a lower court is wrong and does an injustice, the Court will not care about that. . . There are good reasons for that reality, of course, but I do think it strikes some in the public as odd."[5]

Mauro noted that the "remarkable level of detail and accuracy in its portrayal of the Court—including references to little-known sculptures and customs at the Court—has given the episode a life of its own.'"[6]

Mauro also quoted *Slate*'s Supreme Court correspondent Dahlia Lithwick, who wrote: "'I can't recall another time I've seen anything as close

---

3. Ibid.
4. Ibid.
5. Ibid.
6. Ibid.

to the real justices represented on prime-time television, or a moment in which someone in the popular culture. . . really took on the Roberts Court as a collection of political actors.'"[7]

*   *   *   *   *

The real life Court's ruling would not come down for several months. When it did, it affirmed our show's holding, striking down the Louisiana law as unconstitutional. And we managed to get it all done in less than one hour. Not that it counted.

Still, until the Court allows cameras to broadcast their arguments, the episode will be as close as most people will ever get to seeing what the Justices do and how they do it.

*   *   *   *   *

When my FOX show *Justice* aired, I made up hats with the show's name on it for the crew.

When *Justice* was canceled, I had a box of unused hats.

I sent one to Supreme Court Justice Anthony Kennedy with a note saying that he was one of the few people I could think of who could legitimately wear a *Justice* hat. He sent back a very nice thank-you note, promising that he would wear it during his walks around the Court.

The rest of the hats I gave to the Jewish Council Thrift Shop.

Several months later, just as I was getting over the cancellation, a homeless man outside the local Starbucks asked me for change. He was wearing one of the Justice hats. I bought it from him and threw it out in the Dumpster in the parking lot.

I never want to see those hats again.

---

7. Ibid.

A few years after the *Boston Legal* episode, we took a family trip to Washington, DC. The highlight was a tour of the Supreme Court, arranged by a friend and former Court Clerk. One of the justice's secretaries was kind enough to take us into the main chamber, conference rooms, offices, and basketball court where Justice Byron White enjoyed charging over clerks.

Walking down a stairwell toward the end of the tour, I turned to say something to the woman, tripped, and went tumbling head over heels down the entire length of the staircase.

As I lay flat on my back, searing pain running up my leg, the woman stared down at me.

"You can't sue. The Court has immunity."

Back in the hotel, I could not get my shoe off without two of the kids pulling. You can make fun of the Court all you want. But the Court gets the last word.

* * * * *

Chapon turned the *Boston Legal* episode and others I wrote into a research article for one of France's academic journals,[8] providing a comparative study of how complicated legal issues are presented in the United States.

"TV series are not yet regarded in France as a serious source of information," she explained to me via e-mail. "It is considered as a subculture whose only purpose is to entertain desperate housewives. The whole point of my dissertation is to prove the contrary."

From "a didactic point of view," she concluded, the episode "conveyed the highest amount of information about the law and legal culture in the shortest amount of time to the largest number of people."

Furthermore, the specialized "discourse is highly accurate, being written by a lawyer, so it is a highly reliable source in order to increase

---

8. Sandrine Chapon, "La peine capitale aux États-Unis à la croisée de la fiction à substrat professionnel et de la source primaire: une étude comparative," *ASp* 60 (2011): 21–39.

the legal vocabulary of French law students" who are trying to understand basic American principles, as well as "language teachers who have no legal training."

Storytelling, Chapon concluded, it a great way to teach law and to understand it. It is a shame American students are not taught how to do it.

* * * * *

Everyone who graduates law school almost immediately realizes how poorly law school prepared them for the actual practice of law.

Law students are taught how and when law developed, by whom, what the law is generally, and where they can find answers about it if they don't know. In general, they are not taught how to convey information in a cogent, persuasive way to the client who needs the help; to opposing counsel, who has a different client and point of view; or to the decision-maker who has to make the final call.

Despite the fact that all law school graduates who practice law will have to write statements of facts for briefs, memos, and client letters, law schools don't teach them how to marshal facts and law into coherent stories.

Instead, lawyers are taught to communicate with other lawyers or judges rather than simply learning how to communicate with people.

Storytelling is a creative process. But creativity is not just discouraged in law school—it is banned. Only "legal" writing can be taught, and it must be coupled with "research." The emphasis is on the proper forms of citations rather than on the mechanics of how to tell a good story. Talking is strictly controlled. Students speak when called upon to do so in the context of being graded.

Professor Daube thought law schools don't teach storytelling because of intellectual snobbery. Academics see the subject as unworthy of their time and effort. No one has received tenure for it. Law reviews don't publish stories. Thus, storytelling has no place in the curriculum.

* * * * *

Even in the rare cases where law schools do teach storytelling, they treat it as a novelty, an elective, less important than, say, property law or civil procedure.

Others fall back into academic tropes, turning what should be of practical use into unhelpful theory. They twist storytelling into a pedantic exercise; agitprop only other academics could love.

Richard A. Posner calls it "legal narratology,"[9] the tendency of some law professor to produce incomprehensible textual analysis and their own didactic stories.

In *Law's Stories: Narrative and Rhetoric in the Law*, Professor Peter Brooks posed a reasonable question: "Why doesn't the law pay more attention to narratives, to narrative analysis and even narrative theory? They would seem to be almost as relevant as economic or social theory to understanding how cases come to the law and are settled by the law."[10]

Dershowitz, as noted, rejected the notion that narrative has a place in legal cases. It is misleading, he says. Stories have logic, but cases are not logical; people often don't behave rationally. Presenting cases like stories edits out the possibility that our eyes deceive us, that what appears to be true is really just a lie.[11]

He makes a point. The rule in the US Attorney's Office in Los Angeles was to never let a writer, actor, or director stay on a jury. They tend to want happy endings with plenty of twists and turns. As prosecutors, we wanted simple, easy to follow stories with unhappy endings. Justice is not sweet. At best it is bittersweet. Guilty verdicts are often warranted but almost never the cause of happiness.

To present a case as a story brings to it certain expectations. It suggests a logical resolution should be reached. But that is what makes storytelling so important. Dershowitz confuses dramatic narrative itself

---

9. Richard Posner, "Narrative and Narratology in Classroom and Courtroom," *Philosophy and Literature* 21 (October 1997): 2; quoted in Peter Brooks and Paul Gewirtz, *Law's Stories: Narrative and Rhetoric in the Law* (New Haven: Yale University Press, 1996), 99–105.

10. Quoted in Peter Brooks and Paul Gewirtz, *Law's Stories: Narrative and Rhetoric in the Law* (New Haven: Yale University Press, 1996), 99–105.

11. Ibid.

with badly crafted narratives. Stories that fail to adhere to the rhetorical triangle aren't usually worth listening to in or out of court, not just because they fail to reflect the actual experiences of the audience, but because they lack credibility.

"The life of the law is not logic: it has been experience," Holmes said. The same is true of persuasive storytelling.

The illogical experiences of life are what make stories real. Failing to account for the illogical is bad storytelling.

* * * * *

As for the illogic of Alan Dershowitz criticizing lawyer storytelling, has anyone benefited more from storytelling, or been more responsible for blurring the lines between legal fact and fiction? The man wrote the book *Chutzpah* for a reason.

Ron Silver portrayed Dershowitz in the movie *Reversal of Fortune*, the story of how Dershowitz got his client Claus von Bulow acquitted of murder through what can only be called extremely creative legal narrative.

We cast Silver to basically play Dershowitz again in an episode I cowrote of *The Practice*. Silver played attorney John Mockler, a tart-tongued, combative, media-savvy defense attorney with a love of confrontation.

A friend of mine visited the set during shooting. I was giving him a tour. Silver stormed up and said he wanted to change the name of the character.

Why?

"John Mockler is a stupid name," Silver declared. "I mean, yeah, I get it," Silver said sarcastically, rolling his eyes. "Mockler, like he's mocking the law, oh, like the writer is being so clever."

When he finished his rant, I introduced Silver to my friend—John Mockler—one of the moving forces behind the Supreme Court decision that struck down inequality in public school financing.

Silver muttered something and slinked away. Several years later, Silver died, presumably not of embarrassment.

* * * * *

Maybe law schools have a problem with storytelling because of misplaced ethical concerns. Storytelling carries a whiff of charlatanism. To create is to make-up, to imagine; to call someone a storyteller can be a gentle way of calling him or her a liar.

The issue is one of nomenclature rather than reality. No proponent of storytelling by lawyers advocates perjury. It is unethical, improper, and wrong to tell stories for the purpose of deceiving someone else.

Show business takes a more liberal view.

* * * * *

Law schools should add storytelling to the curriculum if, for no other reason, because nothing else seems to be working.

Law student enrollment continues to fall. New graduates are saddled with enormous debts and many are having a hard time finding a job to repay their loans.

Anything that has the potential to make law school more relevant (and enjoyable) cannot be bad. And anything that makes lawyers better communicators deserves at least some consideration.

Granted, storytelling is a less objective subject than others. It is not a science. It is a personal practice, filled with artistic choices and subjective decisions; it is a creative process, not a mechanical one. Spot ten writers a white whale and a one-legged sea captain and you will get ten different stories.

Lawyers, in contrast, like bright-line rules. Storytelling, for the most part, doesn't have any. Norman Mailer described writing as a scary art for a reason.

But that doesn't mean it isn't serious. If you doubt it, get to know some writers. You won't find a more thoughtful, neurotic, obsessed group of professionals anywhere.

Furthermore, there is a well-established, long-standing, highly serious, classical method available to law schools to teach the art of storytelling.

* * * * *

Why *isn't* rhetoric taught as a first-year class? Instead of civil procedure or contracts, why not a course that teaches the best way to organize and advocate every conceivable type of information and to tell every single type of law story?

Those are rhetorical questions.

* * * * *

Had Professor Daube been the dean of the law school—the idea made him laugh—he would have added two subjects to the curriculum: poetry and rhetoric.

Poetry is a practical skill. To study poetry involves understanding the meaning of language and its capacity for representation. It is to learn how to convey information that invokes emotion. It involves parsing each word down to its basic part, interpreting the writer's intention through syntax, word choice, and sentence structure. It is to become a craftsman of language.

Nothing could be more useful for lawyers, whether they are deciphering the terms and conditions of a contract, the meaning of the administrative order, or the purpose of a constitutional provision.

Rhetoric is of equal value. Daube wrote and lectured on its history, its development in Greece and Rome, its different schools, its basic tenets, and its influence on Talmudic exegesis, classical learning, the Renaissance, and the Enlightenment.

Daube was old, *old* school. But he did not harbor the illusion that the classical language of rhetoric was coming back. Nor did he think his students needed or cared much about what Aristotle had to say.

But he believed telling a persuasive story was at the heart of what lawyers do. And he felt strongly that the classical past offered relevant information on how to do it.

* * * * *

Aristotle's rhetorical triangle, its elements and uses, remains the lawyer's best tool for building persuasive and effective stories. Stories told by lawyers in the context of their work are most effective when they utilize all three parts of the rhetorical triangle.[12]

Such stories establish the lawyer's expertise as someone worth listening to. They utilize the facts and events in a reasoned way to support the lawyer's arguments. And they move the audience to feel connected to the lawyer's point of view.

Aristotle classified arguments into three separate categories:

- Ethos referred to a speech about credibility.
- Logos referred to speech using logic and reason.
- Pathos was an argument that relied on emotion.

Aristotle did not specifically describe these arguments in terms of storytelling. But they clearly apply to any and all storytelling that aims to persuade.

Nor did Aristotle teach these arguments in terms of a triangle. Rhetoricians and high school debate coaches did that. Pythagoras was the triangle man, not Aristotle. In truth, Aristotle might not have approved of the whole triangle concept. He treated each element as a separate argument unto itself, not necessarily as part of a whole.

Still, a triangle is a pleasing shape and has long been a handy pedagogical device, easy to portray, easier to imagine.

---

12. See Paramjit L. Mahli, "The Power of Storytelling in Your Legal Practice," *ABA Practice Management Section*, April 2008.

NBA Hall of Fame Coach Phil Jackson made a fetish of another type of triangle.[13] But Coach Jackson never suggested that each leg was of equal importance. What made him a great coach—and a Zen master of the obvious—was to see that Michael Jordan was the most important leg of the triangle.

Of course, visuals can be misleading. Invariably in books on the subject, the three sides of the rhetorical triangle are depicted with equal lengths. Advocacy and storytelling don't always have such pleasing symmetry. In the real world, the length of each leg of the rhetorical triangle depends on the circumstances of the case, the facts, the law, the people involved, and any number of other factors.

It is the lawyer's job to tell the right story, to build the appropriate triangle for his or her client, to make subjective judgments based on the variables as to whether to spend more or less time on establishing ethos, displaying logos, or eliciting pathos.

Every triangle has three sides. But each triangle has its own unique shape and appearance. And while each leg of the triangle deserves its own consideration, it must never come at the expense of the whole.

Ethos without logos is a losing strategy. The age's overreliance on pathos is almost always fatal. The triangle cannot stand if one of its legs is missing or too weak. The triangle is the strongest where two or three of the legs overlap.

Only the lawyer telling her story can know which leg is her strongest—ethos, logos or pathos—but she must never fail to have all three present in her story.

To be clear, merely invoking Aristotle's triangle won't suddenly make you a great storyteller. As we will see, storytelling takes thought, preparation, practice, talent and experience.

But all storytellers would benefit from understanding how the triangle works and how to build stories with the legs of the triangle in mind.

---

13. The triangle offense uses the three sides of the triangle, with the center at the low post, the forward at the wing, and the guard at the corner. Simple enough until you try to use it in your kid's youth league.

Coach Jackson's triangle worked for the Chicago Bulls and the Los Angeles Lakers, too; not as smoothly, perhaps, but enough to win four championships.

The year after Professor Daube died, one of the legs of the Lakers' triangle, Shaquille O'Neal, began referring to himself as "The Big Aristotle."

Daube admired any practical application of classical learning to modern contexts.

He would have *loved* The Big Aristotle.

PART TWO

Building the Story

FOUR

Ethos

"Of the modes of persuasion furnished by the spoken word there are three kinds. The first kind depends on the personal character of the speaker."[1]

Your mother doesn't need to prove that she is trustworthy. You know her, you're familiar with her work—you know she's trustworthy.

Everyone else has to earn ethos.

Ethos is about getting the listener's attention, grabbing the audience, convincing them that you are a credible storyteller.

In writing and law, ethos must be earned through externals, associations with others, actions or behaviors that can be read and interpreted as meaning this narrator deserves our attention.

* * * * *

Federal prosecutors are instructed to introduce themselves to the judge and jury this way: "My name is [your name here], and I am here representing the UNITED STATES OF AMERICA." That is a statement that carries ethos. I always felt bad for the defense lawyer who had to follow that.

The late Mort Boron, a beloved Los Angeles defense lawyer, used to joke that so many of his clients were convicted that they named the federal prison at Boron for him.

---

1. Aristotle, *Rhetoric*, trans. W. Rhys Roberts (Mineola: Dover Publications, 2004), 7.

A thin scarecrow of a man with a wild thatch of white hair, an eye-patch, and the gravelly voice of a pirate, Boron once introduced himself and his client this way: "Mort Boron and his friend," he growled, "up against it."

Everyone loves an underdog.

* * * * *

The current website of the era's most famous storytelling teacher begins with a strong declaration of ethos:

"Robert McKee, A Fulbright Scholar, is the most sought after screenwriting lecturer around the globe. He has dedicated the last 30 years to educating and mentoring screenwriters, novelists, playwrights, poets, documentary makers, producers, and directors internationally."[2]

Notice Fulbright Scholar is the first thing mentioned. If that isn't enough ethos, the website notes that among the more than 100,000 people who have taken his seminars are 60 Academy Award and 170 Emmy Award winners, as well as winners of other honors and hundreds of nominees.

Relying too much on ethos is often seen as a sign of insecurity.

* * * * *

During the 2014 State of the Union address, CNN caught Associate Justice Ginsburg entering the chamber wearing a raincoat and scarf.

Moments later, they showed her listening to the president, along with the other members of the Court, in the appropriate, credibility-building costume: her robe. In a robe, Ginsburg was as commanding as the biblical Ruth. Out of her robe, she was my mother-in-law.

* * * * *

Costumes can make the blandest characters seem like part of the story. Off the bench, judges are nondescript. Meet them at a bar and they dis-

---

2. "About McKee," http://mckeestory.com/about/.

appear into the woodwork. It's impossible to remember their names, let alone believe what they do for a living.

Put them in a simple black dress, however, and they take on an air of mystery, of danger. They become captivating; you can't take your eyes off of them.

But more than just clothes give the judge ethos. The big entrance also helps.

The Honorable, the Chief Justice and the Associate Justices of the Supreme Court of the United States. Oyez! Oyez! Oyez! All persons having business before the Honorable, the Supreme Court of the United States, are admonished to draw near and give their attention, for the Court is now sitting. God save the United States and this Honorable Court.

Shakespeare understood the value of a big entrance. He tells us Julius Caesar or Henry IV is coming; everybody get ready, they are almost here. Then he has the other characters talk about the big men before they arrive. Then he provides stage directions so that the actors know to stand up and bow and generally look impressed when the king finally arrives.

It's a neat trick, the big entrance, one favored by divas and dictators. The showy entrance means attention must be paid. All rise and face the judge. Judges don't actually need the gavel, by the way. Thor without the hammer looks like a singer in an ABBA tribute band. Nothing says decisive like a mallet.

Judges don't really need to sit on an elevated stage, either. But go to any court, from the US Supreme Court down to small claims, and notice who gets the best lighting. A raised bench and overhead bulbs make anyone a star.

None of this is meant as a criticism of judges. Many judges are fine people. Several could, if pressed, establish ethos without the stagecraft and props, through the force of their personality, the wisdom of their rulings. What is interesting is how few try.

It was not so long ago, in the context of history, when American judges eschewed the robe, the gavel, and the elevated bench, opting for something less majestic, more egalitarian; more democratic. A suit and tie, a desk, and the American flag behind them. Ethos was what they earned through who they were, not through what they wore.

* * * * *

Have you ever wondered what your bar dues pay for?

When you pay bar dues you are buying ethos.

For the most part, that is all you are getting, too. Ethos is the whole reason why there is a legal profession. The purpose of the profession is to instill confidence in the consumer and convince regulating bodies that the profession's members are credible and are allowed to practice for money.

Bar associations are ethos makers. By ensuring only "the right people" get in, licensing only those who pass certain requirements, appearing to maintain standards of ethics and competence, the bar provides lawyers an invaluable, blanket ethos.

* * * * *

Joe Dunn, the director of the California State Bar, once pitched me an idea for a television show. It was based on the misconduct of attorneys. "You simply cannot imagine how bad some of these lawyers are," he said.

Unfortunately, I can. I prosecuted several of them. And every state bar association in the country publishes disbarment reports in their newspapers and journals.

As a young lawyer, I read them the way old people read the obituaries: to make sure they are still alive. The feeling they invoke is not schadenfreude—there was no pleasure in the suffering of the fallen lawyers—but the Germans probably do have a perfect word for it. It is the comfort you get when you realize that as bad as you may be at your job, others are much worse.

But the disbarment pages are not there to comfort lawyers. They are there to comfort the public, to assure them that standards are being upheld, that *their* lawyer can be trusted and the profession itself is credible.

In fact, disbarment reports don't comfort anyone and don't work as cautionary tales to deter bad behavior. They are good examples of terrible storytelling.

* * * * *

The stories are too familiar and sad. The misconduct is almost always the symptom, rather than the cause, of the lawyer's downfall. It isn't moral turpitude or an inability to understand the Parole Evidence Rule that destroys legal careers. It is usually drug and alcohol abuse, mental problems, emotional struggle.

To read about these lawyers feels like an invasion of privacy, a violation of confidential privileges, a peek into files best maintained by doctors, lawyers, and clergy. For some reason, convention demands that these sad stories be written in bureaucratic prose that aims at objectivity. But the result is banality that verges on the cruel.

What are we supposed to feel for and about lawyers who have been kicked out of our ranks? That they deserved it? That we are better, as a profession, now that they are gone? That we are better, as individuals, because we are still here?

If the answer is that we are to feel nothing, then these should not be presented as stories to begin with. Stories are intended to persuade through reason and emotion. Notice of disbarment should go to the lawyer's clients, opposing counsel in his cases, and the courts. It should be reported in a purely factual way, with the lawyer's name and change of status published by itself without further comment.

In its current form, like all bad storytelling, the disbarment reports manage to accomplish the exact opposite of what was intended in the first place.

Most of the misconduct—stealing from client accounts, falsifying evidence or obstructing justice—is far beyond the pale of professional conduct. The public's confidence in the profession is not enhanced when a criminal loses his or her license to practice law.

If anything, the public is right to wonder how the criminal got a license to begin with, why it took so long for him or her to lose it, and how many innocent clients suffered because the profession lets in the wrong people.

The additional fact that a criminal conviction does not *automatically* lead to disbarment—that it only follows after yet another legal proceeding—only serves to reinforce the public's worst suspicions about lawyers and the profession.

Perhaps worst of all, rather than deterring unethical or criminal lawyers, the stories of disbarments only offer comfort to the least capable among us.

The rules of professional responsibility tell a story of high aspirations and competence. But the disbarment page teaches a different lesson: Nobody ever gets disbarred for being grossly incompetent.

If you don't believe it, read the suspensions section under the disbarment reports. It is amazing how bad you can be and *not* get disbarred.

* * * * *

I pitched Dunn's idea to Jason Carbone, executive producer of reality television shows such as *The Real World*, *Road Rules*, and *The Bachelor*. He wasn't interested.

"Nobody to root for," he said.

Bad lawyers might be an element of a show. Everybody can get behind hating a bad lawyer, he said, but they want to cheer for a good one. Lawyers can still be heroes.

I found that comforting. The profession's blanket ethos has not been lost entirely. Yet.

* * * * *

How else does one build ethos into a story?

One way to do it is through a kind of hearsay—ethos by association.

The Weinstein story illustrates this. I must know something about storytelling. Why else would Weinstein have hired me? But ethos is never dispositive. The fact that I had written good scripts before did not mean I was going to write a good one this time.

Establishing ethos is not risk free. Name-drop too much and you alienate Harvey Weinstein. You may never eat lunch in this town again, at least not in the same restaurant where he is eating. Though, I am pretty sure he still thinks my name is Jeff.

* * * * *

Expert witnesses are another form of ethos by extension. This is why writers and lawyers are eager to introduce an expert into their story. The field of expertise almost doesn't matter. What makes an expert an expert is ethos. If they didn't have it or couldn't establish it, they would not be experts.

To add an expert to your story is a classic means of building ethos.

* * * * *

How does one cast an expert?

In the Pulitzer Prize-winning book *Anti-Intellectualism in America*—mentioning an award is always a good credibility/ethos builder—Richard Hofstadter argued that Americans love intellect when it's put to practical use. What they hate are intellectuals.

Hofstadter's book sought to explain why Americans loved Dwight D. Eisenhower more than Adlai Ewing Stevenson II.

Ike, the brilliant technocrat, was the hero as CEO, a warrior who never fired a shot or personally faced an enemy. He commanded vast armies as the head of a military board of directors comprised of world leaders and their generals. Stevenson, in contrast, was an "egg-head," an ivy-towered intellectual, the kind of know-it-all who does pure research or philosophy or liberal arts. Americans don't like that. Bill Gates is famous and respected because he gave us Windows and became a multibillionaire. The fact that he is giving much of his fortune away has added to his popularity, perhaps, but did not create it.

American admiration for intellect is in direct proportion to how much that intellect helps improve the lives of other Americans, makes money, or wins wars. This is no country for philosophers or saints. Cast your expert accordingly.

* * * * *

Scientific experts are especially popular, but casting such experts is a complicated matter. Richard Feynman or Neil deGrasse Tyson aside, the best people in their field are not necessarily the best people to explain it.

Furthermore, Americans have funny notions about science. Congressman Rush Holt, for many years the one and only scientist in the House of Representatives, noted that people think anecdotally and personally, not statistically and objectively.[3]

Holt announced that he was leaving Congress at the end of his fifth term, even though he had a lock on re-election. Still a relatively young man, Holt swore he still believed in the *idea* of Congress. But you got the sense he was tired of dealing with all those Congressmen who think the same way most people do: anecdotally and personally.

Recent surveys have shown that a remarkable number of Americans don't know the earth revolves around the sun. And they don't believe many of science's basic tenets—witness the debate on evolution versus creation myths.

Holt noted that until we reach a "Golden Age," when the average voter begins to think scientifically, dealing with issues like climate change is going to be nearly impossible.

* * * * *

---

3. Congressman Rush Holt, interview, *Jansing & Co.*, MSNBC, February 28, 2014.

"Shapiro's Postulate on Law and Science" recognizes that in any legal matter involving science of any kind, two things are true:

1. Everyone involved in the case—the lawyer, the client, the judge, the jurors, the opposing counsel—has strongly held, highly personal, subjective attitudes about science itself, and

2. Most of them have no idea what they are talking about.

* * * * *

Sociologist Erving Goffman wrote about the many ways doctors presented themselves in order to establish ethos. Goffman argued that expertise is a kind of story in itself, told through clothing, speech patterns, office furnishings, body language, and use of jargon.

Goffman also observed that much expert ethos-building is disturbingly similar to the ways in which con artists operate. It stands to reason. The con is based on convincing a victim that something fraudulent is instead the real thing. Looking and sounding like the real thing is a necessity. Precisely because it is hard to understand, science is a fertile ground for the expert as well as the flimflam man.

Take any legitimate subject, one endorsed by society as important, essential, even. Add complexity and a fluid, changing set of beliefs, no matter how appropriate. Couple it with its own specialized, complicated language. Toss in a shaming element—the idea that smart people understand science and anyone who does not is stupid—and you have the perfect conditions for selling people almost anything.

Lawyers who tell science stories, therefore, have two choices: buck reality or benefit from it. Try to enlighten and educate or take advantage of the confusion. Our duty of loyalty to the client makes the answer clear. Obfuscation on behalf of a client is no vice. And trying to enlighten anyone other than the client is no virtue.

* * * * *

The public's fascination with experts is reflected on television. From *Quincy, M.E.* through the *CSI* franchise, the expert of the crime scene has become the hero. Perhaps this is why enrollment in criminal justice programs for crime scene techs has gone up almost as much as law school enrollment has gone down.

For those of us in television, the challenge is finding a new area for someone to be an expert in. Results have been mixed.

In *Lie to Me*, Tim Roth's character, Dr. Cal Lightman, was an expert on body language. This expertise gave him the ability to know when someone was lying.

The premise proved hard to sustain ("Know wat?" Roth's character would say in his East London accent. "This bloke's lyin' to me, he is!").

The show ran for two seasons longer than any of the shows I created.

More successful was *The Closer*, in which Kyra Sedgwick played the deputy chief of the LAPD whose expertise was getting suspects to confess. That show ran seven seasons longer than any of my shows.

Sometimes the expert is not so much trained to be an expert as simply born with the gift.

The expertise in *The Ghost Whisperer* was obvious. So was the fact that she could solve crimes by speaking with the dead victim. The show ran for 107 episodes (CBS, 2005–2011). In *Medium*, Patricia Arquette played the title character, a paid consultant for the district attorney's office of Phoenix, Arizona, who solves crimes through her ability to peer into the otherwise unknowable past and future. It ran on NBC for five seasons, then ran two more years on CBS.

Those interested in selling a television series need only find an unexplored field of expertise.

* * * * *

Ethos is often established through appearance. If that sounds shallow, if that offends you, if you feel that appearances are irrelevant, that what is inside is more important than what is outside, then you should skip the rest of this chapter.

* * * * *

Lawyers don't have the luxury of assigned uniforms, manufactured respect, or most of the tools of stagecraft that build ethos. Lawyers have to write, produce, direct, perform, and generally create ethos as a part of their story.

It is a shame law schools don't generally read Goffman's *The Presentation of Self in Everyday Life*. It would help. Goffman was the father of "dramaturgy," the notion that all social interaction is a kind of presentation, a form of storytelling. Applying a theater metaphor, Goffman argued that each of us assumes many roles during our lives—the son or daughter, the parent, the judge, the judged, and so on.

The roles are based on an infinite number of variables and contexts. Like trained actors, we play out the scenes of our work and personal lives, motivated by our desires, often in conflict or in conjunction with the other actors—the people we interact with.

How much of this is a choice depends on fate and circumstance. Often we are cast in roles we did not seek. We are forced to act out scenes we have no interest in being in. Many of us often don't even realize they are in a scene at all.

Those that do know, Goffman suggested, enjoy a kind of tactical advantage. They can opt out of certain scenes, alter their dialogue, modify the setting, cast additional actors to be involved, and participate more directly in the storytelling process. They can present themselves consciously to achieve their desired ends.

* * * * *

To be a lawyer is to present oneself in the role in any number of contexts. Goffman believed presentation included all the activity that a professional does in the presence of those he serves.[4] It also includes all the places and things the professional uses during the course of his activity to build ethos.[5]

For lawyers, these include fixed standing sets, everything from the courtroom to the office. But it also includes the law firm logo and stationery, the quality of the office furniture, the law school diplomas and awards on the wall, the costumes we wear, and the props on our desks.

The first step to making a good presentation is realizing that everything you do is part of that presentation. To build ethos, one must present themselves in a professional way.

* * * * *

Goffman's influence on the late 1960s and 1970s self-actualization movement, among other things, was profound. One can almost hear the late Dennis Hopper right now: "Look at your scene, man…this is a bad scene."

Aristotle may be fresher in most people's minds than Goffman, but the sociologist remains worthwhile. Every aspect of the practice of law involves the very type of performance he was writing about. Putting aside psychological implications or benefits, dramaturgy has as much to offer lawyers now as it did when Goffman was writing.

The strange part is that so few lawyers seem to be aware of the role they have cast themselves in. Or how much control they could exercise over how that role is played.

* * * * *

What would Goffman make of the legal profession's tendency to wear casual clothes? That it reflects a general loosening of cultural standards? Or a desire to be more accessible to the client, who also, regardless of the profession, tends to dress like a slob?

---

4. Ibid.
5. Ibid.

Thanks to Steve Jobs and the Silicon Valley, jeans and a sweater has become the standard for a certain type of billionaire—the innovator, the plutocrat as artist.

There are exceptions. Warren Buffett, Bill Gates—and their lawyers—still wear conservative clothing. But the trend is toward no suit, no dress. As to whether that also means no service—or less service—is an open question.

Good lawyers know that appearances tell their own stories. They can add to the lawyers' ethos or detract from it.

* * * * *

Dylan McDermott was the handsome star of *The Practice*. During the presidential debate between Al Gore and George W. Bush, I asked him what he thought.

"Gore had bad lighting," McDermott said sagely. "And his suit didn't fit."

As far as McDermott was concerned, the race was over.

* * * * *

When it came to ethos, Edward Bennett Williams and Johnnie Cochran had different styles, but they sought to achieve the same effect.

At trial, Williams wore less expensive suits and a cheaper watch than he usually wore because he wanted to establish his credibility as a regular guy. Cochran took a slightly different approach.

My only case against Cochran occurred before the O.J. Simpson trial. He was, when I met him, still considered a treasure, a civil rights leader, one of the finest trial lawyers in Los Angeles, and one of the most respected.

I was thrilled to meet him, and even happier when his client took my generous plea offer. No prosecutor wanted to go to trial against Johnnie Cochran.

A year or so later, still years before the Simpson case, I saw him again. He was at Spago's for the Academy Awards dinner, holding court.

There was no reason that Cochran should have remembered me. Ours had been a nothing case. I was nobody. Yet he rushed over, hugged me, and insisted on introducing me to his table-mates as "one of the finest prosecutors he ever faced."

It was as flattering as it was untrue. It was manipulative. I loved it.

And, god help me, I loved his clothes.

During our first meeting, Cochran wore a purple double-breasted bespoke suit with a matching tie and pocket square and a white-on-white tailor-made shirt.

The suit he wore that night at Spago's was the flashy version . . . in burnt orange. When he hugged me, I noticed the padding, shoulders, and sides and wondered if they were meant to give the suit shape or to give Cochran size.

Williams' clothing told one story. Cochran's clothes told a different story.

But their behavior was the same. Williams always said to be nice to the most junior lawyers on the other side; one day, they will be the senior partners. Cochran was wrong about me being good or important. But he had the same idea as Williams.

* * * * *

Dressing poorly does little to convey competence. But dressing too well or too stylishly may well convey information that hurts rather than helps your client. Lawyers should dress if they were going to meet the president or the Pope. Clean, tasteful, not too low-cut, heels, but not too high. Nice.

* * * * *

Nothing establishes ethos like the appearance of success. McKee's book, Story, is to be found on the shelves of many a Hollywood executive trying to pass as creative.

No one can say how many have actually read it. It is not an easy book to get through. Dry and technical, it is a manual of concepts rather than a set of compelling narratives.

There are three ways to look at McKee: One view is that McKee's system must be credible because so many people have benefited from it. McKee would agree with this view.

The second view is that any system of storytelling that's reasonable and based on the actual experience of someone who has tried it and been happy with the results, is better than no system at all. I would agree with this view.

The third—most cynical—view is that McKee's real success is not teaching people how to write stories, but in persuading people that he has taught them to write stories.

Read McKee and decide for yourself.

* * * * *

McKee was portrayed in the Charlie Kaufman movie *Adaptation*. He was played by the actor Brian Cox. Kaufman wrote the movie, and also gave his own name to the movie's central character, who goes to a McKee seminar because he is unable to overcome writer's block.

McKee stands before the students, sharing his thoughts on the meaning of story, when Kaufman, played by Nicolas Cage, gets up the courage to ask a question about the movie he is unable to write. Cox/McKee barks back, peppering him with questions about the story, the characters, and the world in which the story is set. In response, Cage/Kaufman stammers that not much happens in his story.

Cox/McKee's response is worthy of a federal judge or senior partner: if nothing happens in your story, he asks, "Why the fuck are you wasting my two precious hours with your movie?"

To which Cage responds, as any beaten-down writer or lawyer would, by quietly thanking Cox/McKee for the abuse and sitting back down.

McKee *brags* about this portrayal on his website.

Nothing imparts ethos more than being played in the movies.

* * * * *

One way to appreciate the power and importance of ethos is to study examples of its abuse.

A police officer's uniform, badge, and gun are strong ethos-builders. The law enforcement officer or agent, as a character, is by definition law-abiding, brave, and honest.

Prosecutors live and die off the ethos of law enforcement officers. They cannot win a case without it. For a prosecutor to accuse a police officer is to undermine essential, established ethos. It is to tell a kind of counter-productive, self-damaging counter-narrative—to violate the fundamental expectations upon which the prosecutor's entire body of work rests.

This is why prosecutors hate prosecuting officers. They are hard cases to win. But they are even harder cases to bring, unless one is committed to doing it exclusively. The practice in the US Attorney's Office when I was there was to leave it to the DOJ Civil Rights Division or handle it as the last case you did in the office.

After prosecuting a cop, the prosecutor is seen by law enforcement officers as tainted, unfit for other work—not to be trusted.

* * * * *

The first police officers I prosecuted were out of a David Lynch movie.

Adelanto, California, is a wind-swept desert city near Victorville and Apple Valley, in the big nowhere between Los Angeles and Las Vegas. It boasted an Indian casino, the High Desert Mavericks minor league baseball team, and a closed US Air Force base. Many of the streets were unpaved. The public schools were so bad that parents eventually sued to take them over. The newest and nicest building in town, next to City Hall, was the police department, a bright, shiny building.

At the time, a number of the Adelanto police force had tried but failed to get hired in other departments.

The two officers in question were veterans, well regarded on the force. There were rumors about them being too aggressive, a little rough, but nothing substantial enough to get them fired.

Who knows why they ultimately snapped? All that's clear is that they did, twice beating confessions out of innocent men. One man was arrested during a drug operation, accused of resisting arrest and spitting on the officers. He was forced to lick up his own blood after they beat him.

The other man was accused of a crime that defies belief—raping and beating his girlfriend's baby. The attack happened. There were hospital records. Yet the crime was not committed by him.

The state charged but failed to convict the officers. There was no truth to the allegations against them, the cops argued. But if there was, it wasn't their fault.

After the state dropped the charges against them, the two cops sued the City of Adelanto for wrongful termination and received sizeable settlements.

* * * * *

The police are the rarest of defendants. They begin their case with a presumption of innocence and a presumption of heroism. If they occasionally snap and lash out, so do soldiers in times of war. Juries don't like to hold it against them.

There was reluctance to take the case federally. There always is. The man in charge of civil rights cases in the office was happy to pass the buck to someone else.

It is hard to overcome ethos, to convince jurors that the police could or would act like thugs. Plus, the two officers were no longer on the force. Jurors might think the two men had been punished enough, that the Feds were kicking the ex-cops while they were down.

Furthermore, the accusation of the rape and beating of a baby was so horrible that it carried its own perverse, lingering doubt about the actual innocence of the suspect. It shouldn't have, but it did.

The other suspect, wrongly accused of a drug crime, was named Henry Easley. He was not exactly the most sympathetic victim. A small, sunburnt raisin of a man, a self-proclaimed desert rat, Easley lived alone in a small, battered trailer sitting unevenly on concrete blocks on a dirt patch off an unpaved road outside Adelanto city limits.

He had been at the wrong place at the wrong time. This was not uncommon. He had been for much of his life. The night he was arrested, he happened to be walking past a house being raided by the two officers. Naturally curious and also drunk, he decided to find out what was going on, barging into the search and demanding to know who was in charge.

Easley was not unknown to the two cops. *Town drunk* is an unkind term but accurate. On this night, Easley swore he had not been belligerent. But it was not outside the realm of possibility. Nor had he spit on the officers, he said, no matter what they claimed, though on several occasions, he accidentally spat on me during one of his many rants.

Easley admitted arguing with the officers back at the police station. He did not remember cussing them out. But he denied telling them he had AIDS (he didn't) in order to scare them. What is clear—because it was partly caught on a closed circuit video camera—is that both officers beat Easley up and then forced him to kneel down and lick his own blood off the floor.

* * * * *

Getting Easley from the high desert to the grand jury in Los Angeles was an adventure. He refused to leave his trailer. He couldn't find his shoes. He got sick in the car.

Later, he left phone messages on my answering machine, his words slurred, apologizing for being too terrified to testify, then calling back to apologize again and promise he would be better when he sobered up.

Fearing the police were out to kill him, he begged to be put into witness protection, to have 24-hour-a-day security, and to be given a pistol so he could protect himself.

One morning, after the case had been indicted, the FBI agent on the case called. "Turn on your television."

Easley had managed to book himself on a daytime talk show to discuss the beating. For a frightened guy, he seemed eager to tell his story to as many people as possible. The defense was going to have multiple prior statements for cross-examination.

* * * * *

It was a bad ethos mismatch—the two clean-cut-looking former officers who had received wrongful termination settlements versus the gibbering, high-strung Easley and a man accused of such a horrible crime that it was hard not to suspect him of *something*.

We went to interview the other man, the one wrongly accused of raping a baby. His luck hadn't gotten any better.

A year or so after he was beaten, he was almost killed when a tractor trailer plowed into the side of his pickup truck. He was in a coma for weeks. The crash left him with significant brain damage.

His memory of the arrest was sketchy, his ability to speak limited, and his demeanor heartbreakingly child-like. If the defense intended to make their case off of this guy, they were going to have a hard time of it.

* * * * *

The FBI investigated and discovered that one of the new Adelanto Police Department's witness interview rooms had been wired for sound. The system was automatically activated by the human voice. The two cops didn't know it.

Going through the department's stacks of tapes from the time of the arrest, the FBI found a partial recording of the beating of the suspect accused of the rape. On it, the officers can be heard entering the room, obviously not for the first time.

"We're baaaaack," one of them says with a laugh, a line from the movie *Poltergeist*.

The suspect begins to cry. The other officer asks if he's ready to confess to what he did. The suspect wails that he didn't do anything.

The officers call him a liar. In possibly the worst good cop/bad cop effort ever, one cop speaks calmly to the suspect, suggesting that maybe the baby made the suspect angry, that was understandable; maybe the suspect lost his temper. Before the suspect has time to respond, the other officer screams at him to quit crying and confess to what he did.

There is silence, then what sounds like a scuffle. It is quickly followed by a blood-curdling scream, less human than terrified animal. One of the officers laughs. The other officer shouts again for the suspect to confess. The suspect begs them to quit torturing him.

"Torture?" one of the officers says. "Who the fuck are you to say anything about torture?!"

* * * * *

Years later, I tried to use the accidental taping as a plot twist in an episode. Studio executives made me take-out.

"Too convenient," the one in charge said. "It lacks credibility."

I brought him the public case file and played him a copy of the tape. He didn't care. Just because it happened and I could prove it didn't mean he or anybody else was going to believe it was true.

* * * * *

Easley did not bear up well under the pressure. As the case went on, he became more unpredictable. He drank, which made him more paranoid, which made him drink more.

He *had* been the victim of police abuse. But the more you got to know him, the more time you spent listening to him, the more he spat on you, the more you could understand how and why someone might want to hit him.

Not all victims are lovable. Easley was a victim only his mother could love.

We debated not calling him as a witness, but ruled it out. The jury would wonder where he was or why we were trying to hide him. Plus, if we didn't call him, the defense would and treat him as hostile (which he surely was) and slam his motives. The jury would hate him, and us, for bringing the case.

My phone rang one weekend during trial preparation. It was the FBI. Easley was dead.

* * * * *

His body had been found at the bottom of a desert wash a mile or so from his trailer. The coroner immediately conducted an autopsy. Those present recall smelling alcohol the moment he made the first incision into Easley's abdomen. His blood alcohol level turned out to be somewhere over 2.0. The wash contained Easley's overturned ATV, purchased with the proceeds of his settlement money from another civil case. There was also a plastic gallon container of Stater Bros. Markets store brand vodka.

The two officers were never suspects. They had solid, provable alibis. We no longer had any living or competent victims to testify against the officers, which was the best thing that could have happened for our case.

The defendants had no choice but to enter guilty pleas.

Without the ability to attack our credibility by portraying Easley or the other victim as unbelievable or worse, the two Adelanto cops had no defense at all.

Nowhere was the power of police ethos clearer than at sentencing. The judge actually apologized to the two defendants for having to sentence them at all, so much did he love the police. He gave them two years in prison.

One of the officers told the press that if he had known he was going to prison for what he did, he would not have beaten Easley. He would have killed Easley instead.

Apparently, he resented being charged federally. It seemed unfair. He didn't believe he should have to face state *and* federal charges.

The defendants in the federal Rodney King prosecution registered the same complaint in that case.

Ethos, they seemed to think, meant forever.

FIVE

Logos

"In the beginning was the Logic, and the Logic was with God, and logic was God."[1]

Logos is the bread and butter of good storytelling. It is what convinces the listener that not only are you credible and worth listening to, but you are right about what you are saying. You are making sense.

Of all the legs of the triangle, logos comes the closest to being non-subjective.

Ethos can be bought. Pathos is the stuff of dreams; it can be manipulated. But logos cannot be faked.

* * * * *

A confession: Many if not most books on the art of storytelling, including this one, are gross simplifications of Aristotle's approach, bastardizations of complex logical theories of deduction and induction, an abomination of what has been the life's work of a small but impressive group of scholars, living and dead.

It doesn't excuse anything to admit it but it does give you a choice.

You don't like it?

---

1. John 1:1, as translated by Gordon Clark (1902–1985), American philosopher and theologian. The original Greek word can mean both "word" as well as "logic." Clark objected to the more conventional choice: "Any translation of John 1:1 that obscures this emphasis on mind or reason is a bad translation." Daniel Calder, "Gordon Clark vs. John Calvin on John 1:1," *St. Petersburg Christianity Examiner*, January 19, 2014. Clark's use of the word *logic*, or *logos*, in the place of "the Word," he acknowledged, had shocked the devout. "But the shock only measures the devout person's distance from the language and thought of the Greek New Testament." Ibid. Like Daube, Clark believed in reading the Bible as it was written, not as it was mistranslated.

Read the *ipissima verba* yourself.

Nobody is stopping you.

* * * * *

Shapiro's Formula for Constructing Logos:

First, begin with the elements of the story that are commonly understood and agreed to;

Second, look to the agreed-upon past—to history and precedent—to see what helps you, what hurts you, and what reasonable assumptions you can draw from it;

Third, listen to the other side's story, accept it as valid, and use common sense and reason—without emotion—to find its flaws.

A second confession: It sounds easier than it is.

* * * * *

One night in the early 1950s, Daube's colleague, Lord Sommerville, "a quick mind and lawyer," returned from London to Oxford, excited. He had just spoken to Winston Churchill.[2]

Eager to take advantage of the moment, Sommerville decided to ask the former Prime Minister an impertinent but memorable question:

How would Churchill defend himself on Judgment Day for his role in dropping the atom bombs on Japan?

"I shall say to the Almighty," Churchill said, "why did you unleash that secret [of the atom] at a time when passions were running high?"

Daube loved Churchill's logos, not to mention his courage:

"It is not simply a defense; he immediately counter-attacks. 'Why did you . . . ' The argument he instinctively hits on is of an historical character: God's timing was wrong."[3]

---

2. David Daube, *The Jottings of David Daube*, ed. Calum Carmichael (New York: YBK Publishers, 2008), 2.
3. Ibid.

If you are not smart, if you cannot reason well, building logos into your story is going to be harder, but not impossible. Dumber lawyers than you have done it for years. Street smarts count, too. Unlike philosophy, physics or economic theory, common sense is at the heart of logos in the legal profession. [4]

* * * * *

In 2013, television camera crews and news vans staked out the Los Angeles County Courthouse. They were there in "Trial of the Century" numbers not seen since the Phil Spector or O.J. Simpson cases.

And nobody had even been murdered.

It was a civil trial about the ownership of a decedent's property, about as dry as the law gets.

But, really, they were there for a love story.

Boy meets girl.

Boy loses girl.

Boy gets girl back.

Except this case was a variation on the theme:

Boy meets girl.

Boy loses girl.

Because girl died.

In the movie *Love Story*, handsome but wooden Ryan O'Neal played the boy, Ali MacGraw the doomed girl. It was a huge blockbuster back in the day. Now it's a kitsch classic. Then it was the great date movie, big enough that it spawned a sequel, *Oliver's Story*, in which O'Neal's character played a high-powered lawyer.

Marx said history repeats itself, first as tragedy, then as comedy.

The sequel bombed.

---

4. Sam Leith, *Words Like Loaded Pistols* (Basic Books: New York, 2012), 64.

O'Neal went on to make other movies with Stanley Kubrick, with Norman Mailer, and with his own daughter, Tatum. His personal life was tumultuous even by show business standards. There were multiple divorces, battles with substance abuse, complicated relationships with children, and dust-ups with paparazzi.

He married Farrah Fawcett-Majors, a *Sports Illustrated* model turned actress and 1970s superstar, big enough that Andy Warhol did her pop art portrait.

Fawcett-Majors and O'Neal divorced. O'Neal gave her back the Warhol for safekeeping, not to keep forever, he claimed. When she died of cancer, O'Neal went into her home and took the Warhol back.

Love means never having to say you're sorry.

The University of Texas didn't agree.

Fawcett-Majors had willed a great deal of her fortune and estate, including the Warhol, to the University. Texas claimed O'Neal took what he was not entitled to keep. They wanted it back. This wasn't a love story. It was a story about O'Neal's greed.

The media's interest was intense, even though one of the stars was dead and the other looked only vaguely like the star he once was. If any of the jurors were familiar with Fawcett-Majors or O'Neal, it was most likely through their short-lived reality shows. Celebrity does not last forever but it can be maintained with very little effort.

The stakes were high. The Warhol was worth tens of millions of dollars. And O'Neal's reputation, such as it was, hung in the balance. Did he act in good faith, or was he a burglar, robbing from the dead?

The attorney for the university presented a strong case built on documents and the statements of witnesses. He wasn't going to let this turn into a soap opera.

O'Neal took the stand and gave a powerful performance. That is not meant as an insult. He isn't that good an actor. A comedy troupe used to run ads for a Ryan O'Neal Film Festival of all of his greatest moments on screen: "Airing at 5:00 p.m., 5:01, 5:02 . . ."

But the real star of the show was not O'Neal. Nor was it the lawyer for Texas.

It was the unlikely figure of Marty Singer, O'Neal's attorney, a large, ungainly man, sporting chunky black-framed glasses, blackish hair, and a suit—if not of many colors then at least of much fabric.[5]

Singer knows the law. He probably even knows some property law. Like his opponent, he didn't make this a love story either. He agreed it was all about greed.

But his client wasn't the greedy one. The University of Texas was. They were not satisfied with getting the bulk of Fawcett-Majors's estate, oh, no—they wanted *both* Warhols, too.

Did I forget to mention there were *two* Warhol portraits of Fawcett-Majors? Or that the University of Texas already had the other one?

Solomon tried to split one baby to figure out who the mother was. The jury in the O'Neal trial got twins. It wasn't hard for them to decide to give one to Texas and one to the grieving ex-husband. It was common sense.

O'Neal got to keep the painting. He may even have been entitled to it.

* * * * *

History and experience are important elements of logos.

Three days after 9/11, I asked David E. Kelley for permission to do a script about how the terrorist attacks would alter the legal system.

I had some credibility on the issue. Having done work for the Terrorism Unit of the Department of Justice during the early 1990s, I knew about the Foreign Intelligence Surveillance Act, the legality of searches without warrants, the hazy rules that govern when uncharged individuals can be held as material witnesses.

I began with the commonly agreed-to elements. The entire country was afraid and angry because an enormous crime had been committed.

---

5. He is movie director Bryan Singer's attorney in lawsuits stemming from allegations involving sexual assaults against young men who attended parties. The Singers are not related.

They wanted justice. Law enforcement would respond. But because of the scope of the crime and the fear it generated, it would be under enormous stress to do something quickly.

There have been other times in the country's history when it was attacked, when enormous and understandable stress was put on the law and the government to do something about it. During the Civil War, the law of habeas corpus was suspended and the government imposed military justice. In World War I, undesirables were deported. During World War II, Japanese and German Americans were interned. During the Vietnam war, the FBI spied on leftist groups. It was reasonable to assume that past was prologue, that what had happened before might happen again.

Since our characters would be defending a terror suspect, I imagined what the government's case and attitude would be against them, accepted their view as true, then used common sense to imagine what flaws I could find.

* * * * *

The script became the earliest network television episode to address how the war on terror would affect civil rights.

Directed by David Semel, its title was "Inter Arma Silent Leges." I learned the phrase from Professor Daube: "In war, law is silent."

The plot revolved around a series regular, Rebecca Washington, played by Lisa Gay Hamilton.

She is hired by a woman whose Arab American husband is detained on unknown charges; when Washington, as his lawyer, tries to see him, the federal prosecutors invoke then-existing laws governing classified information, which prevented lawyers without security clearances from seeing the evidence against their client—or even the client or herself.

At one point, the Assistant US Attorney explains to the defense lawyer what is going to be needed if she wants to defend an accused terrorist:

"I'll need your address, social security number, names of family members, how you know Mr. Habib . . . I need to warn you, anything you say can and will be used against you and your client . . . This case involves national security. You want to defend Habib, you need clearance. To get it, you need to go through us, answer our questions, if you lie to us, it's perjury. Plus, *everything* we tell you is privileged. If you divulge *any* of it to anyone, you'll be prosecuted."[6]

The defense lawyer asks what happens if she refuses, objecting that it's a violation of *her* rights.

"Then Mr. Habib gets no lawyer," the prosecutor says.

When the defense lawyer gets the clearance, her client has already been moved to an undisclosed location. When she finally tracks him down, he refuses to speak with her. Eager to prove his patriotism, he would rather stay in prison, quietly, respectfully, than rock the boat by asserting his constitutional rights.[7]

In producing the episode, the only challenge was finding an Arab American or other nationality to play the role of Mr. Habib. None of the actors we saw seemed right for it. Later, I heard some casting agents were reluctant to have their clients play a suspected terrorist, even if he was innocent.

* * * * *

Toward the end of the episode, the defense lawyer wonders if her client was tortured into agreeing to cooperate with the authorities. Whether he actually *was* tortured was left an open question.

As of this writing, it remains open.

Despite the continued pleas of US Senator Dianne Feinstein (D-CA) and others, the CIA's own memo on that issue has yet to be de-classified.

* * * * *

---

6. "Inter Arma Silent Leges," *The Practice*, ABC, December 9, 2001.

7. A Japanese American teacher at my junior high school had been interned as a boy in Manzanar, the windswept camp in the Eastern Sierras. He told me that the saddest thing about it was how some of his fellow internees thought accepting their fate quietly was the patriotic thing to do.

Was the script liberal agitprop?

Not from me.

I am a pro-prosecution, pro-enhanced technique type of American. The question, from a storytelling point of view, was how to dramatize the issues in a way that was credible, logical, and compelling.

* * * * *

For the lawyer storyteller, the past is more than prologue. It is the basis for logos, its essential building block.

Judge Learned Hand wrote that the common law "stands as a monument slowly raised, like a coral reef, from the minute accretions of past individuals, of whom each built upon the relics which his predecessor left, and in his turn left a foundation upon which his successors might work."[8]

The law, like much storytelling *about* the law, lends itself to serialized storytelling because notions of precedent and stare decisis all but demand it. The common law and jurisprudence is an aggregation of connected stories, a long narrative consisting of countless smaller stories, tied together by previous holdings.

* * * * *

Whenever I argued appellate cases in federal court, it always felt like a literary debate. The justices or their colleagues wrote the relevant holdings. I was there to say they did a great story (when I wanted them to affirm) or a terrible one (when I wanted them to reverse).

Law, not history, is one damn thing after another. There are no stand-alone stories. Every story is part of a larger, ongoing narrative.

* * * * *

---

8. "Book Review," *Harvard Law Review* 35 (1922): 479.

Human beings can be lazy thinkers, easily distracted, overly emotional. It is a sad, ironic fact that even a good story built with logos can fail to persuade stupid people. The foes of logos are legion.

* * * * *

Ivan C. Namihas was a gynecologist in Orange County, California. According to his fellow doctors, Namihas was a very skillful surgeon. He had privileges at two hospitals in the area and a thriving practice.

He was also a sadist. Over 120 women filed complaints with the California Medical Board alleging that he sexually assaulted, abused, or otherwise mistreated them. Some of them claimed that he performed excruciating medical procedures on them without anesthesia. After Namihas laid out money for an expensive laser device for his practice, he began to tell women they had cancer or precancerous conditions that required immediate removal. He would then burn off parts of their skin without numbing the area. He also convinced two men to submit to the torture, telling them that if they didn't, they would die of cancer.

Namihas was born near one of the tributaries to the Amazon River and looked like something that might have climbed out of it. With pockmarked, scaly skin, beady, dead black eyes, and a leering smile, he was a bad casting agent's candidate for the serial killer role.

Even though Namihas racked up the highest number of complaints against him, more than any doctor in the history of California, nobody did anything about it for years. Finally, the California Medical Board got shamed into action thanks to one persistent investigator and press stories. Before they could strip him of his license, however, Namihas folded without a fight and retired from the profession.

It could have ended there, but the victims wouldn't let it die. I was home one night watching an ABC news program, *20/20*, and their report on the case. The angry victims expressed outrage that Namihas had been allowed to voluntarily give up his license rather than be stripped of it. They were also disgusted that the Orange County district attorney refused to charge Namihas with rape or sexual battery.

I wanted to make a federal case out of it. But there was no federal rape statute to charge him with. There still isn't.

My theory was not clever but it seemed clear enough. If a doctor sexually abuses a woman in his office during a medical exam and then sends a bill for medical services, it is mail fraud.

Defense lawyers called this overreaching. It was the best storytelling we could do in light of the legal limitations. It was better than doing nothing.

Getting all the elements together to tell the story was tough. There were statute of limitations and evidence problems. Once Namihas retired, his office records were moved and could not be fully reconstructed. The California Medical Board hadn't bothered to keep them.

Trying to get medical records through third-party sources—the hospitals where Namihas had privileges, the insurance companies that paid his bills—was slow and frustrating.

Several doctors who could have helped refused. They justified it on the grounds that they were protecting the sanctity of the peer review process and doctor-patient privilege. In fact, they didn't want to be seen as snitching out a colleague, even if he was a monster.

Namihas seemed to target poorer members of the Latino community who were also non-English speakers. Fear prevented a number of them from speaking to us.

Eventually, we were able to identify a handful of victims within the statute of limitations who might be willing to go forward with a case. One woman described how Namihas told her she had cervical cancer. Devastated, she and her husband went back together to see Namihas in his office. Not only did the doctor confirm the diagnosis, he also told the woman's husband that he needed to have biopsies of his penis because the wife's cervical cancer might have spread to him. Namihas later confirmed what he said in a letter: "There was no error in my diagnosis. I expect to be paid."[9]

You couldn't make this guy up. I tried. Studio executives did not buy it.

"He's not a credible villain," one said to me.

* * * * *

Getting women—and two men—to testify in a public trial about the most intimate aspects of their health history meant persuading them that we were credible, the case was logical, and with their help, we could punish Namihas for what he did and achieve some type of justice.

We cast a good person to tell this story.

Susan Watson, US postal inspector, was smart, tough, and no-nonsense, a Texan with close to 20 years of law enforcement experience, a woman who said what she meant, and admitted what she didn't know or couldn't guarantee.

She disliked bullshit and bureaucracy but flat-out hated lawyers—me especially—although she accepted they were a necessary part of the process.

She was forthright with the victims, laying out a version of the case, but also downplaying the joy they might feel when it was all over. She managed client expectations. She said we might lose.

* * * * *

We seized the laser. Curious over how it worked, I turned it on and aimed it at a yellow legal pad. It burned a hole through the pad, the carpet, all the way down to the floor slab.

---

9. Reporter's transcript, vol. 9, at 1753–1754, *United States v. Namihas.*

We drew a great judge. She understood mail fraud and evidence law. She knew that certain relevant but uncharged prior bad acts can and should be admitted to prove the defendant's motive, intent, modus operandi, and plan. She would surely let us introduce the fact that Namihas raped some of the patients he later billed. Plus, she took an Old Testament approach to sentencing—swift, harsh, and just.

Then without explanation she took herself off the case.

The new judge was the late Linda H. McLaughlin.

This was not a good plot twist. When I found out, I got off the phone with the court clerk, closed my office door, and face-planted on the desk full force, my enormous nose bent all the way back to the cheek, tears and snot making puddles on the desk.

One should never speak ill of the dead. Judge McLaughlin was not stupid, just very literal. She worked hard and was capable of narrow but intense reasoning. If unflinching commitment to the letter rather than the spirit of the law is the standard, she was the most magnificent jurist I ever saw. Nothing could alter her point of view once she fixed her grim stare on it. Her strengths were consistency and persistence. Her hold on what she believed to be correct was as tenacious as the jaws of a Gila monster in its death grip.

* * * * *

"You're overreaching," the defense lawyer said.

Was it overreaching when they used tax charges to get Al Capone?

"My guy isn't Al Capone."

Of course he said that. You have to be careful writing dialogue for law shows. It is easy to slip into cliché because cliché is often how lawyers actually talk. Like sportscasters and athletes, lawyers compete in an arena where the same thing happens according to the same rules involving the same people, day in and day out.

It is hard to come up with new material.

* * * * *

The defense moved to exclude all evidence of sexual abuse or sadism. It was too prejudicial. Of course it was prejudicial—we were trying to convict his client, and our job was to introduce prejudicial evidence, as much as possible—but it wasn't unfairly prejudicial.

Judge McLaughlin disagreed and pruned our case down to the barest root. Evidence of sexual abuse or sadism was irrelevant. The only question, in her mind, was whether the doctor carried out a scheme to defraud patients out of money, and whether he used the mails to carry it out.

We were left with a small class of victims. All of them had been lied to about having cancer or precancer. All had been burned with the laser. All of them were billed for unnecessary and tortuous treatments. It was only a portion of the overall story. But at least it was a narrative with a beginning, middle, and end. It was a narrow area but big enough to build a solid triangle.

* * * * *

Life will kill you, Warren Zevon said.

Everything is precancerous, potentially, but doctors are only supposed to treat cancer or tissue on the road to cancer.

We just needed to cast an expert who would say so.

I went to a medical library, walked to the aisle devoted to gynecological oncology, and went through the main treatises. Most were written by or cited the works of Dr. Philip DiSaia, one of the world's great doctors, a renowned expert on questions involving the cancer and precancerous conditions in our case.

He was also local, an esteemed member of the UC Irvine Medical School, right down Interstate 5 from Judge McLaughlin's courtroom. He was not a hired gun. On the contrary, he never testified as an expert before and had no interest in doing so now.

Persuading him to testify required yet another form of storytelling. The credibility of our office did not impress him at all. Furthermore, he brought a clear-eyed understanding of the emotions involved in treating life-threatening conditions. He devoted his life trying to save and comfort women facing cancer and was deeply sensitive to the victims' claims. But he also knew that patients in the throes of a terrifying situation do not always hear or understand everything their doctor tells them.

Dr. DiSaia was all about logos. He was a scientist who would only offer an opinion on provable facts, documents, or what he could observe himself. He would only testify if he could prove to himself that our case had merit.

Lawyers make a mistake when they try to do too much with each character in the story. Dr. DiSaia's dispassionate, unemotional testimony was foundational. It set the stage and earned the pathos that was delivered by the victims.

* * * * *

Judge McLaughlin wasn't all bad. The trial should have taken a month. She got it done in less than a week and a half. It helped us. The best stories are well paced. They move smoothly from one character to another, along an easy-to-follow, flowing narrative. Having the train run on time is better for the prosecutor and plaintiff. The defense calls it railroading someone. We prefer to think of it as good storytelling.

The defense team put on their expert witness. He was unappealing and combative with a South African accent and a sneer. For the most part, he agreed with our expert about everything except Namihas's guilt. By law, he was not supposed to offer his opinion on the ultimate question in the case. Judge McLaughlin, strict on so many things, took a surprisingly permissive view of defense expert opinion.

Then Namihas testified. A viperous man with a weird tic—his tongue darted from one side of his mouth to the other—it was if he were *trying* to look evil.

I could not imagine any scenario in which we would lose. But I hadn't started writing for television at that point. I didn't appreciate the importance of audience targeting.

* * * * *

It isn't quite accurate to say the best story wins at trial. Prosecutors always have to tell the more compelling story. The burden of proof and jury unanimity demands it. In terms of the audience, they have to produce a flat-out hit, one that appeals to every segment of the population, a ratings bonanza.

The defense is more like a cable show—their story can be a hit with even the lowest possible ratings, so long as they attract a small but passionate audience.

The Namihas team targeted one specific demographic: women, age 49 or older, who don't trust the government, who have a bizarre, quasi-religious love of doctors but distrust science and scientists.

Such people exist.

We had one on the jury.

* * * * *

Judge McLaughlin's courtroom was housed in a converted double-wide trailer. The Ronald Reagan Federal Courthouse was in the process of being built next door. Through the thin door that led to the jury room, we could hear the jurors yelling at one another.

Four days later, they were still at it. Jury notes came in asking the court how they were to handle a deadlock, what to do with a hold out, how to force someone to participate in deliberations. They filed into court for further instructions looking beaten down, frustrated. Several jurors cast angry glances at one juror in particular.

Judge McLaughlin scolded them, refused to answer their questions, and ordered them back to finish their job. They tried hard but couldn't. The judge finally declared a mistrial.

Later we learned that the problem wasn't any one part of our storytelling. The hold-out juror did not believe *any* part of our story.

Having failed to disclose her own medical history, or her unshakeable belief that doctors were heaven-sent ministers of goodness, she would not even entertain the notion that Namihas—or any doctor—would or could ever lie to a patient.

Doctors don't care about money, she argued. Doctors are healers, not hurters; end of story.

* * * * *

Because our postal inspector had built up such credibility with the victims, because Dr. DiSaia had been so credible, and because there had been satisfaction in telling their story, the victims agreed to try again.

There was a second trial. We tried the case the same way. The only difference was that we got luckier with the jury. They convicted Namihas in no time flat.

* * * * *

As I said, Judge McLaughlin got some things right. Moments after Namihas was found guilty, she remanded him into custody to await sentencing.

The US marshal was a giant, bald-headed, African American man. When he stepped Namihas back to cuff him, Namihas began to cry. It was the first emotion he showed throughout the entire process.

The marshal leaned down, his back to the gallery, and whispered toward Namihas's ear, loud enough so I could hear.

"Look at you, crying like a bitch," he said.

It was not a logical thing to say. Not everything in law or life is logical.

Gerald T. Nowak, a colleague at Kirkland & Ellis, once catalogued errors in logos. The list included making false comparisons, suggesting a set of false choices, reaching for illogical conclusions, committing the sin of tautology.[10] Nowak's point was that even the smartest lawyers can occasionally make such mistakes.

On April 15, 2013, the Supreme Court witnessed an interesting struggle with logos.[11] The case involved patents. Not always a rich area for riveting storytelling, except that these patents involved a portion of human DNA that contains a mutation linked to breast cancer.[12]

The question before the Court was whether DNA material could be patented by those responsible for taking it out of the human body and sequencing it.

The issue turned on whether DNA sequencing was a product of nature (not patentable) or the product of human ingenuity (patentable).

The attorney for the group challenging the patent, Christopher Hansen, knew his audience and understood how the justices tended to hear these stories. None of the justices are scientists. They struggled with the issue.

Like any confused audience, the justices grasped for analogies—in essence, other stories—to make sense of things. Hansen was happy to provide them.

"This Court has said repeatedly that just extracting a natural product is insufficient. For example, this Court has used the example of gold. You can't patent gold because it's a natural product," Hansen said. You could patent earrings made from gold but not the gold itself.

---

10. Gerald T. Nowak, "Classical Methods for the Modern Lawyer: The Interplay between Ethics, Morality and Efficacy in the Transactional Context," *Practising Law Institute: Drafting and Negotiating Corporate Agreements 2011*, CLE, February 10, 2011.

11. Official transcript of the oral argument in the Supreme Court of the United States at 37, *Association for Molecular Pathology v. Myriad Genetics*, 569 U.S. 12 (2013) (No. 12-398).

12. *Association for Molecular Pathology v. Myriad Genetics*, 569 U.S. 12 (2013).

Justice Alito wondered if the whole thing wasn't more like a plant in the Amazon. If the natural substances in it were found to help treat breast cancer, could the leaves be patented?

Depends on what you did to the leaves, Hansen said. Transform the leaves by concentrating the molecules and you give them a function as a drug they did not have in their natural state.

Gregory A. Castanias, attorney for the company seeking the patent, was confronted with Justice Sotomayor's story.

"I can bake a chocolate chip cookie using natural ingredients—salt, flour, eggs, butter—and I create my chocolate chip cookie," she said. She was not right about flour being a natural ingredient, of course, but nobody was going to correct her, so she went on about the cookies:

"If I combust those in some new way, I can get a patent on that. But I can't imagine getting a patent simply on the basic items of salt, flour and eggs, simply because I've created a new use or a new product from these ingredients."

"Analogies prove nothing," Sigmund Freud once wrote, "but they can make one feel more at home."[13]

Castanias politely replied that what his clients did was nothing like baking cookies.

"But that's the problem with using the really simplistic analogies, with all due respect, Your Honor, about, you know, like coal ... like leaves, and that sort of thing." It missed the important ingenuity that his clients brought to the task.[14]

Having made the point, however, Castanias couldn't help himself. He had already won in the lower court with his own simple analogy. Even though he had just told the Court, less than a minute before, that simple analogies missed the point, he used one.

"I'll use my own simplistic analogy which we offered in our brief and

---

13. Sigmund Freud, *New Introductory Lectures on Psycho-Analysis* (London: Vintage Classics, 2001), 64.

14. Oral argument at 36, *Association for Molecular Pathology v. Myriad Genetics*, 569 U.S. 12 (2013) (No. 12-398).

which we offered to the lower court," he said. It worked once. Why not try it again?

"A baseball bat doesn't exist until it's isolated from a tree. But that's still the product of human invention to decide where to begin the bat and where to end the bat."[15]

DNA wasn't like gold, he was suggesting. It was like a baseball bat.

Justice Alito could not let go of the bat: "To get back to the baseball bat example, which at least I—I can understand better than perhaps some of this biochemistry, I suppose that, in you know, I don't know how many millions of years trees have been around, but in all of that time possibly someplace a branch has fallen off a tree and it's fallen into the ocean and it's been manipulated by the waves, and then something's been washed up on the shore, and what do you know, it's a baseball bat ..."

At which point, according to the transcript, there was laughter, because, let's face it, no one had any idea what Justice Alito was talking about.

The lawyer tried to get back on track, arguing that the DNA was composed of molecules, and molecules have been patentable for a long time in the form of drugs.

"Well, I don't understand how this is at all like that, because there you're obviously combining things and getting something new," the chief justice said, still swinging the bat. "Here you're just snipping, and you don't have anything new, you have something that is a part of something that has existed previous to your intervention."[16]

It got so bad Justice Sotomayor asked the lawyer for the other side to come up with a plausible story for patenting the DNA.

"How could they write it to do what he thinks would be patentable?" she asked. "I know you are helping your adversary by answering the question."[17]

---

15. Ibid., 37.
16. Ibid., 60–61.
17. Ibid., 62.

Hansen couldn't do it, either.

Castanias is wonderful attorney, but he lost the case. Perhaps no one could have won it based on the facts and the law. But a better storyteller might have followed his own instincts and stayed away from the analogies. Better to have spent the time describing all the hard work and effort that went into his client's success, a story that connected with the justices on an intellectual but also a human level.

If a lawyer as smart as Castanias can't always tell the best story, it has to be hard.

SIX

Pathos

Humans love a story, especially if it's shocking, weird or emotionally arresting . . . As a consequence, a jury story can psychologically trump a dry statistic, even when the statistic is rather more informative.[1]

Pathos is the crack cocaine of storytelling. It is easy to make, feels good to use, and is addictive.

Bad storytelling is bad for many reasons, but unearned pathos is the most common and pernicious one.

Overreliance on pathos is the curse of our age. It fuels our political debates, clouds our policy discussions. It makes heroes of talk radio rage-mongers. It replaces rational thought with irrational feeling.

One could write volumes on each segment of the rhetorical triangle, but the most timely and relevant would address the uses and abuses of pathos.

Ethos requires credibility. Logos demands reason. Neither is harder to earn than real pathos. It requires subjective abilities, an understanding of human nature, a sense of proportion.

Like dynamite, pathos is unstable. It can move mountains or blow up in your face. Pathos must be handled with care.

* * * * *

---

1. Stephen Law, *Believing Bullshit: How Not to Get Sucked into an Intellectual Black Hole* (Amherst: Prometheus Books, 2011), 187.

Nancy Grace, the Madame Defarge of cable news, is the queen of pathos, a woman who has made her life's work pursuing her own version of bloody-minded justice.

Just because someone is a master storyteller does not mean we have to like him or her. Respect the skill; learn from it, even if you loathe the storyteller.

If it seems a bit late in the day to attack Grace, rest assured, I have been on the case a long time. I cast the actress Katherine LaNasa to play a toned-down, slimmer, but equally obnoxious version of Grace as a recurring character on the FOX television series *Justice*.

The late Dominick Dunne watched the show and mentioned it in his *Vanity Fair* column. We became friends. He thought LaNasa did a good but not a great job as Grace. Not passionate enough, Dunne said.

* * * * *

Selling outrage is how Grace made her living. The former prosecutor-turned-commentator-turned-author-turned-celebrity-turned-*Dancing with the Stars* contestant is an important example of modern lawyer storytelling. Her success reflects the qualities that increasingly seem to be required. If they did not, she would never have attracted or kept the audience that she has.

I once appeared on her show. This is when she was still at Court TV. The crime was a vehicular manslaughter case. A driver had plowed into an Amish family's buggy, killing several of the occupants.

Grace's outrage was calculated. It went on and off with the red light on the camera. On air, she seemed to expand, her big eyes going wide as she vented.

During commercial breaks, when the light went off, she seemed to shrink back into a smaller, more Southern, warmer persona. She asked about my work, where I lived, how I liked California. She was not listening to the answers, just trying to mimic human behavior.

But the moment the floor director told her we were coming back on the air, she expanded again like a blowfish, spiky and trembling with rage over the defendant's obvious guilt.

Grace proves that two legs of the triangle can take you far in a number of fields.

Her experience as a lawyer—and crime victim—gives her credibility. Her outrage provides pathos. What is missing is logic. She dispenses with the presumption of innocence, assumes facts not in evidence, often at the expense of the defendant, and rants rather than reasons. She understands her stage and audience. It isn't a judge or a client. It is everybody else.

Is she artificial?

All storytelling is artificial. All human societies engage in it, but it is not a spontaneous act. It is calculated. It is planned. It is a performance.

But that doesn't make it any less impressive.

Great storytellers feel the roles they play. Whether the emotions they conjure up are sincere is irrelevant. They are convincing.

"Politicians, ugly buildings and whores all get respectable if they last long enough," John Huston's character says in *Chinatown*. Grace is still not respectable. But her longevity is a testament to her ability to fake emotion.

But what she does is not lawyer storytelling. It is entertainment.

* * * * *

One cannot rely too much on pathos. But one can't ignore it, either. In fact, writers and lawyers do themselves and their clients an injustice when they fail to explore the emotional potential of their stories.

* * * * *

In 2014, Kerry Kennedy was charged with driving under the influence of a drug; a generic form of Ambien. The story from the Westchester District Attorney's Office was straightforward. A police officer pulled her over, suspecting she was DUI. The blood test confirmed it.

Gerald B. Lefcourt, head of the defense team, played for pathos, casting his client as the hero, "American political royalty."[2] He put Kennedy on the stand and asked her to describe her background. She said she was one of 11 children raised by a single mother after her father died when she was eight years old.

Lefcourt asked how her father, Robert F. Kennedy, died. It was irrelevant and unnecessary but safe. No lawyer would be gutsy or dumb enough to object.

"He was killed when he was running for president," Kennedy replied.

Oh. *That* Robert F. Kennedy.

* * * * *

But Lefcourt did not ignore logos. Unable to deny that the drug was in Kennedy's system, Lefcourt could only explain that Kennedy was not responsible for putting it there.

Yes, she had ingested it, but only because she mistook it for a similar-looking drug. It was an accidental doping. The defense introduced the bottles and the pills. CVS packaged the generic pills in similar containers. Kennedy just took the wrong one. It could have happened to anybody.

A "there but for the grace of God" story isn't so easy to pull off when you're a Kennedy. They are not like the rest of us.

Her use of a sleep aid, for example: Kennedy testified that her work on issues relating to social justice required that she travel the world, which means ever-changing time zones. Not the most relatable problem on earth. But the perfect detail to reveal character: this was a good person, devoted to helping others. And she was losing sleep over it.

---

2. Joseph Berger, "Kerry Kennedy Hits Back as Prosecutors Question Story Line at Trial," *New York Times*, February 26, 2014.

Lefcourt's real point—that his client was not a drug abuser—addressed a darker aspect of the Kennedy legacy.

Lefcourt didn't ask how Robert F. Kennedy died because he didn't know. Lefcourt knew, and the jury knew, and Lefcourt *knew* that the jury knew.

Lefcourt had to also assume at least one of the jurors also knew about other aspects of the Kennedy family's legacy, including its history of fatal crashes where alcohol was a factor. That past was just as irrelevant to the case as was how Robert F. Kennedy died. But like all good storytellers, Lefcourt knew what part of the past to leave in and what part to leave out.

* * * * *

Lefcourt also knew that if his client was the hero, he needed to have a villain.

The candidate was not obvious. The public despises DUI. Thanks to the efforts of victims' groups such as Mothers Against Drunk Driving and law enforcement, sentences for drunk and drug driving have become Draconian. The public approves of this.

Lefcourt made a risky but clever choice. He turned Westchester County's zero tolerance policy toward DUI into the problem, not the solution. He accused prosecutors—not the police—of pursuing every single case, regardless of extenuating facts. They were not protecting the public. They were wasting the public's resources in a mindless effort that put form and precedent over reason and consistency over compassion.

The trial took four days.

The jury was out for less than an hour before they acquitted Kennedy.

* * * * *

A more gracious winner might have thanked the jury and quietly retreated. Instead, Kennedy continued to rip the DA, telling the same story she and her lawyers told the jury. But now she told it to Matt Lauer on *The Today Show*—so much for the Kennedy legacy of winning with grace.

For public figures, the storytelling does not end with the trial. Win, lose, or draw, they must continue to control the narrative even after the case is over. Not forever, perhaps, but long enough to control the news cycles until the story itself dies.

As to whether justice was served, I am sure Kennedy and others will be more careful with their medications. No public service announcement could ever have gotten the attention this case did. Deterrence, after all, is a worthwhile purpose of prosecution. It was probably too much to expect that any defendant would have been saintly enough to acknowledge the good done, or the lives saved, by the prosecution. Not even a Kennedy is that good.

But Kennedy's claim that the case was a waste of resources was wrong. She *did* have the drugs in her system. The case was credible and reasonable. Had it not been brought, charges of special treatment would have been leveled against the DA, and rightly so.

The DA simply did not do a good enough job telling *that* story. Having established two legs of the triangle, the DA lost because he failed to account for the third.

For all its uses and abuses, pathos remains an essential part of the triangle. It is as much a mistake to use it too much as it is to ignore it completely.

* * * * *

Though we have considered pathos in the trial context, it is just as relevant and important in other situations.

In the DC Superior Courtroom where I served most of the time, the court clerk was an older woman. One day, she kept moving a particular sentencing back to the end of the calendar, as if a delay might change things.

The courtroom was nearly empty when she sighed and finally called the case. The defendant stood, a big, strong, handsome man in his 20s. Legs and wrists manacled, he short-stepped it to the podium, mouth clamped shut, the muscles of his jaws flexing, his face set in rage.

His lawyer shambled to join him, a tubby man in a wrinkled suit, disheveled after a long day. He lazily waved a legal pad at his client, less of a greeting than a reminder to keep his distance, like a man fanning away a fly. The pad had the lawyer's handwritten argument for leniency. I saw him scribbling it while we waited for the case to be called; it was written in large, looping letters, in the style of a child. It didn't fill half the page.

I cannot remember a word of it. The trial itself had been a slow guilty plea. If there had been a defense, his lawyer never raised it. The sentencing was just as pro forma.

I submitted on the papers and didn't say anything. I didn't have to once the office filed life without possibility of parole papers.

Blame the office. Blame Congress. Blame politics. Don't blame me.

Sadly, if my children ever ask, that's what I will have to say Dad did in the War on Drugs.

* * * * *

The judge asked the defendant if he had anything to say before he was given the sentence required by law. The defendant grunted like a boxer taking a body shot. The clerk looked down at her papers, adjusted the heavy frames of her black glasses, and shook her head slightly, sadly.

No, the defendant choked out, he had nothing to say. The sentence was imposed, the deed was done and the marshals led him away. The judge sprinted off the bench. I slunk out of the courtroom, avoiding the clerk's stare.

I followed an older woman into the elevator. We were alone. She had been the only spectator in the courtroom, though neither the defendant nor she acknowledged one another. She was his mother.

We rode down in silence. I did something I had never done before. I told her I was sorry. I didn't say for what.

"Well," she said quietly, her voice soft as a sigh. "At least now, I'll always know where he is."

I wished she had said it in court.

* * * * *

A television character like Nancy Grace need not be subtle in seeking to generate pathos. A real lawyer, however, cannot be so direct. To do so would undermine the lawyer's credibility and destroy the sense that he is a reasonable, logical person. The goal is to elicit emotion, not mimic it for effect.

This is best achieved after the other legs of the triangle have been established through the most understated, least obviously emotional appeal possible.

There was still a time, in the nineteenth century, when breast-beating and tears made up for bad facts and law. Those days are gone.

* * * * *

When Timothy McVeigh was on trial for the Oklahoma City bombing, federal prosecutors had a tragic amount of evidence available to draw from.

There were witnesses who tied him to the truck that carried the bomb, his own writing and statements, his flight from the scene. There were also the lives of the dead and injured, hundreds of them, a heartbreaking mountain of pathos.

But in his opening statement, the prosecutor focused on a small pair of earplugs. After leaving the truck with the bomb inside before it exploded by the child-care center, McVeigh stuck the earplugs into his ears to protect himself from the sound of the blast.

The prosecutor's burden of proof was to prove McVeigh committed premeditated murder. The earplugs showed the extent of his planning, his deliberation, and his commitment to detail.

But it also showed character, the nature of the man, someone concerned with his own hearing and avoiding his own discomfort when the bomb went off and killed 168 people, many of them children. The smallest and most minor of factual details, it conveyed everything you needed to know and feel about Timothy McVeigh.

* * * * *

The power of earned pathos is profound. Not even the greatest storyteller can overcome it.

* * * * *

When the double-murderer Robert Alton Harris was about to be executed in San Quentin, I was assigned by my newspaper to do profiles of the two appellate lawyers in the case.

Central casting could not have come up with better characters. Defense lawyer Charles Sevilla was tall, lanky, and bearded. The prosecutor, Louis Hanoian, deputy state attorney general, was short, squat, and as solid as a brick house, with about as much personality.

It was Lincoln versus Douglas, updated, and set in San Diego.

Sevilla was a great wit, considered the best trial lawyer and comedian of the San Diego bar. He also wrote a terrific series of books about a fictional defense lawyer and the absurd judges he appears before.

If Hanoian had a sense of humor, he wasn't showing it to me. Deadly serious, by the book, and professional, as one would hope, his job was to beat back any effort to delay Harris's execution. This was no time for levity.

So what, I asked, was the deal with the plastic skeleton hanging on his office door. He stared at me across his desk.

"Maybe it's a joke," he said. He wasn't smiling.

Harris earned his spot on death row by robbing and then killing two teenage boys. Sevilla told me the story of Harris's life: the abusive parents, the possibility of fetal alcohol syndrome.

Hanoian talked about procedures and told only one story about Harris. It was about the hamburgers.

After Harris shot the boys to death, he reached into the fast-food bag next to their bodies and ate the lunch the boys had just purchased. Heartless, inhuman, and unforgettable, it was the detail that elicited the most emotion. It sealed Harris's fate.

* * * * *

My editor put our newspaper into the media lottery to get one of the witness chairs to the execution. As I was the one who suggested he do it, I was given the prize ticket when we won.

The warden sent out do's and don'ts with the invitation: where to park, what to wear. No running in the prison yard was mentioned.

The Supreme Court issued a stay, the date was moved, and I didn't have to watch Harris die. I was relieved.

* * * * *

Years later, writing for the television show *Life*, I did research for an episode set at the Los Angeles County Coroner's Office. After a tour and autopsy, I saw the main crypt, 130 naked bodies stacked like cordwood, four high, each wrapped in dirty plastic, tied with rope, emanating the smell of meat gone bad, the flickering fluorescent lights throwing shadows across the husks of humans that were no longer humans.

Next to the crypt, hanging on long racks lining an endless corridor, were racks of old, unwashed clothes and shoes. The wardrobe of the dead; what they were wearing when they died.

Pathos was in the corridor, in the sight of those clothes, not in the crypt, among the husks of bodies. Pathos is usually subtle and often found and felt in the unexpected detail.

* * * * *

I have written a number of scripts on a variety of topics, including the death penalty. The most recent was in 2014 for the NBC series *The Blacklist*.

They have all been anti–capital punishment. Along with the episode based on *Kennedy v. Louisiana*, I also wrote a *Boston Legal* episode with Kelley about the execution of a mentally disabled man in Texas.

The episode received an award from Death Penalty Watch, presented during a star-studded dinner. Jackson Browne performed. Our fellow awardees included former Democratic presidential candidate George McGovern and future California attorney general Kamala Harris. James Spader gave an acceptance speech on behalf of the show, which was just as well. Because if anyone asked, I would have to admit an uncomfortable fact:

I am not opposed to the death penalty.

My religious faith supports it. My heart accepts it. I won't be a hypocrite. If the armed robbers who confronted my mother at the bank where she worked shot and killed her, I would have wanted them to die.

But that doesn't mean I cannot tell a compelling story for the other side.

That is what writers, lawyers, and other storytellers do.

To ensure my heart was in the right place, I gave the condemned man my youngest son's first two names.

My wife was not happy.

* * * * *

In *Angels with Dirty Faces*, James Cagney is a hard-case killer, sentenced to die and not afraid of the electric chair. His childhood pal, played by Pat O'Brien, is—as you might expect—a priest.

Fearing that Cagney's gangster has become a hero to America's youth, O'Brien convinces his friend to act "yellow." To convince the Dead End Kids (for they were his costars in the film) not to admire him or follow in his footsteps, Cagney pretends to be scared as he goes to his death.

I borrowed the idea (an homage, not a theft) but dropped the pretense. The condemned man would be afraid and would fight for his life.

In the episode "Death Be Not Proud," the Texas Supreme Court refuses to stay the execution of Ezekiel Borns.

Having failed to save their client from lethal injection, the lawyer played by Kerry Washington (later of *Scandal*) and Spader's character convince their client to fight his executioners. The goal is to show people what it looks and feels like to kill a man who does not want to die.

The final scene of the episode aired as written in the script:

"As the Guards begin to assist his getting on the gurney . . . Zeke suddenly begins to resist. And it's a fight. Kicking, wrestling. The guards have to force him on the table; oddly, Zeke doesn't scream. He simply physically resists. [Kerry Washington's character] has to look away. Shore stares straight ahead, both horrified and admiring. Zeke's going to go out fighting. The guards wrestle Zeke onto the gurney and hold him down as the nurse struggles to strap the injection needle into his arm. The lone Reporter now looks away.

It's ugly. Shore physically turns the Reporter's head to face the action. . . . Guards are pinning Zeke down as the nurse is finding a vein. There's nothing peaceful about this . . . THE CAMERA CLOSES SLOWLY on Shore as we HEAR the physical struggle continue. We eventually FADE TO BLACK as we STILL HEAR the SOUNDS OF THE STRUGGLE. Eventually . . . the sound FADES AWAY. THE END."[3]

Directed by Matt Shakman, with a brilliant performance by the actor playing the condemned man, Sterling K. Brown, it is devastating to watch, and I am proud of having been a part of creating it. But it didn't persuade me that Timothy McVeigh deserved to live.

* * * * *

Powerful as pathos can be in a particular argument, it cannot, by itself, sustain a lawyer's career. The triangle demands all three legs—credibil-

---

3. "Death Be Not Proud," *Boston Legal*, ABC, March 20, 2005.

ity, logic, and emotion. Without the first two, the third is worse than meaningless. It can be fatal.

One of the saddest examples of overreliance on pathos was attorney Stephen Yagman.

* * * * *

Yagman lived on pathos. Anger was his go-to emotion—generating it in jurors so they would go his way at trial, goading opponents into it until they lost their poise.

He once hired a psychiatrist to sit in the back of the courtroom and observe a judge who Yagman felt had been unfair to him.

The next time Yagman drew the judge, he filed a motion asking the judge to recuse himself on the grounds that he was mentally unfit, attaching a declaration from the psychiatrist stating his opinion that the judge was crazy.

The judge was not happy.

* * * * *

If enemies were clients, Yagman would have been flush. And almost all of them were in positions of authority. They were the people he sued—law enforcement, government officials—and they loathed him with a vengeance. Just hearing his name made them flinch. One FBI agent refused to speak Yagman's name, as if saying it would somehow make him appear.

In the mid-1990s, Yagman showed up against me in a drug conspiracy case. The DEA agent in charge was a tightly wound young man who could be charming or threatening, depending on his moods. As I recall, he pulled a gun on another agent during a dispute over paperwork. He only threatened to beat me up once. The idea of exposing him to Yagman's cross-examination seemed like a bad idea.

* * * * *

During jury selection, Yagman asked the judge if he could ask one of the jurors whether or not he was gay.

I can imagine cases where the question of a potential juror's sexuality *might* be relevant. Strike that, actually; I can't imagine one. But if such a case ever did exist, this was not it.

The defendants were charged with conspiring to manufacture PCP. The van they were driving was loaded with the precursor chemicals to make the drug. One of the barrels began to leak. The California Highway Patrol officer noticed the van slowly decelerate from 70 miles per hour to zero—a dead stop. The officer had to pound on the windows to wake the defendants up to let them know they were not moving.

It was a Cheech and Chong movie. But sex, truly, had nothing to do with it.

Still, Yagman had a theory, a story he wanted to tell, and it went something like this: there was a conspiracy, but his client wasn't part of it. The government was conspiring to convict innocent men.

Closeted gay jurors, Yagman reasoned, would be more likely to go along with the government's case, no matter what it was, in order to appear more conventional to their fellow jurors.

The judge was a gentle soul. Cherubic, pink-cheeked, with kind eyes framed by round, rimless glasses, he looked like Ben Franklin and spoke like Mr. Rogers.

A former entertainment attorney, he was a big fan of *Star Trek: The Next Generation*, punctuating his rulings with: "Make it so."

There were no defendants in his courtroom, just friends he hadn't gotten to know yet. They named a Los Angeles County juvenile justice center for him, that's how nice he was.

But he was no pushover. No, sir. He made Yagman explain his closeted gay juror theory twice. Then he granted his request.

The male juror was summoned to the sidebar to ensure his privacy.

Sir, the judge, Mr. Yagman would like to know if you are gay.

I cannot remember the man's reaction, but I do recall wondering if the juror still thought this was still the case about the two guys making drugs.

* * * * *

Yagman's behavior toward me during the six-week trial was polite in the hallway, insufferable in court. The highlight was his closing argument, when he compared me to Germany's good soldiers, the ones who were just following orders—not a Nazi, necessarily, but part of the machine.

* * * * *

Once during the trial, the judge called the three of us into chambers—Yagman, the codefendant's attorney, and myself—and told us to sit down. Peering over his glasses like a disappointed principal, he said that one of us had been heard by the clerk calling another one of us a bad name. And we were going to sit there until the guilty party apologized.

"What was the name?" I asked.

The judge whispered: "Asshole."

I immediately apologized to Yagman.

Yagman immediately apologized to me.

The judge sighed again. We had not been the ones to say it. It was the codefendant's lawyer. And he was not referring to Yagman. He was referring to me.

* * * * *

Yagman's client and his coconspirator were convicted. Yagman's client was sentenced to a staggering 30 years in prison.

Again, if my children ask what I did in the drug war, I will have to tell them this was considered a victory.

* * * * *

But this was not the end of the story.

* * * * *

Years after I left the office, the DEA called to give me a heads up. The DEA agent in charge of the case had just murdered his girlfriend and child. He was now on the run.

"We just thought you should know, in case you saw him," the DEA agent told me. "Since he hated you so much."

Thank you.

They ended up running the agent down, cornering him in New Orleans. Before they could arrest him, he blew his own head off.

* * * * *

The years were only slightly kinder to Yagman.

He was indicted on federal charges, tax evasion among them, convicted at trial and sent to prison.

* * * * *

The only happy ending was unexpected. Among the many pardons President Clinton issued in the waning days of his administration was the one extended to Yagman's client.

Crazy agent dead, Yagman in prison, drug criminal pardoned. The mills of the gods grind slowly and strangely.

* * * * *

Pathos must be used with care, not just because it is unstable, but because it does not always appeal to the better angels of our nature. What moves us is not always pretty.

* * * * *

It was early Sunday afternoon. Services at the Pentecostal church in Anacostia, DC, were over, but the street outside still had a number of families milling outside with their children running around.

The minister and his daughter, a woman in her 20s, began to argue. She was dating a man her father did not approve of, a prison inmate, and he wanted her to stop seeing him. She refused. He hit her across the face with his fist and kept hitting her until she fell to the ground. Children screamed, women wept, men stared in stunned silence. Finally, a group of older women forced him to stop.

The minister, his congregation, the victim, and the witnesses were black. So was the defense lawyer, who wore an African kente scarf in court and struck every white person from the panel.

The minister took the stand. He refused to swear an oath. He didn't recognize the court, he said, and had no intention of stooping to affirm his honesty before it.

The defense lawyer led him through direct examination. The minister was a respected member of the community who refused to spare the rod and spoil the child. He admitted the beating, was proud of it; swore he would do it again in order to save his child from throwing her life away by being with a drug-dealing gangster.

There was no reason for me to cross-examine him. He had admitted every element of the crime. The court had already ruled against his arguing some kind of a necessity defense.

But I was young and stupid and asked him to describe the beating again. Which he did, proudly, confessing a second time.

The jury stared at me, waiting. Instead of sitting down, I decided it would be a good idea to have the minister demonstrate what had happened.

He stood up and walked to the well of the courtroom.

"You be my daughter," he said. "Stand here."

The minister put his giant hands on my shoulder and positioned me directly in front of him.

He looked much bigger from this angle.

A good lawyer takes control of the courtroom; he doesn't give up the role to another character, certainly not to the villain of his story.

But I had.

The minister began screaming at me the way he screamed at his daughter, angrily shaking his finger in my face, his voice rising in anger.

At some point, the minister either slapped me or got his index finger caught between the bottom of my eyeglasses and my cheek.

Either way, my glasses went flying across the courtroom. With as much dignity as I could, I walked over to my glasses and put them on. Now bent, they sat crooked on my face.

"No further questions," I said and sat down. My knees were shaking.

Several jurors covered their mouths to hide the fact that they were laughing at me. Other jurors did not bother to cover their mouths.

Don't worry about it, my supervisor told me later. Try not to get hit again.

During his closing argument, the defense counsel played the pathos card, preached the story of the minister's life's work and motives. The minister was protecting his church's congregation, saving them from drugs and crime; he was a great man and a great father, not a criminal.

"What does Mr. Shapiro know about our community?" the defense lawyer thundered. "What does he know about raising a young girl in today's world?"

Two of the elderly women jurors raised their hands over their head, palms out, their eyes closed, as if they were in church. One yelled, "Amen."

My closing argument was short; my rebuttal was shorter. None of the jurors looked at me. I was going to be the first prosecutor in history to get assaulted while losing an assault case.

The jury deliberated for less than an hour. When they filed in, again, none of them looked at me. The older woman who had yelled "amen" was the foreperson.

"Do you find the defendant guilty or not guilty?" the clerk asked.

"Guilty," she said, turning to the minister.

Race had nothing to with it. The only racists in the courtroom were the lawyers who thought it would.

PART THREE

The Process

SEVEN

The Script

Mel Brooks showed up for a Writers Guild of America dinner several years ago to receive a lifetime achievement award.

Had it been for acting, directing, or producing, he confessed he would not have come. Writing was different. For a writing award he would leave the house.

He started his acceptance speech with a quote from the old movie *Tugboat Annie*. A man asks the captain: "Don't this boat move?"

The script, Brooks said, is the boat. Without it, nothing moves. Not the boat, not the people on the boat, nothing.

* * * * *

There are rules to writing scripts, which should come as a relief to lawyers.

We like rules and love exceptions. It's how we make our living. It's another advantage lawyers have as storytellers. Rather than finding rules confining, we find them comforting. Within rules we can tell an infinite number of stories and create an endless variety of narratives.

* * * * *

Script writing expert McKee refuses to use the word "rules." When he talks about writing movie scripts he prefers to use the word "principles" instead.

McKee also makes use of his own handy triangle, the "Story Triangle," whose three legs consist of "Classical Design," "Anti-Structure," and "Minimalism."

I have stared at McKee's triangle like the ape-people in the beginning of *2001: A Space Odyssey*, but I can make neither heads nor tails of it, except to note it has nothing to do with Aristotle's triangle. McKee's triangle is a tool for identifying types of previously produced movie scripts, not for building stories.

If you prefer the word "principle" to "rule," be my guest. The only mistake is to ignore that there are rules (or principles) and they must be followed. Ignorance is no defense.

* * * * *

The first rule of storytelling is the simplest.

Never tell any story *without* a script.

Are there exceptions to that rule?

No. There are no exceptions to the rule.

I sense you don't agree.

You imagine situations where you might tell a story, off the cuff, on the fly, extemporaneously. In court, dealing with opposing counsel, advising a client, you believe that you have had moments of inspiration when you have suddenly come up with the perfect narrative out of thin air, a story perfectly suited and applicable to the situation, persuasive, a sparkling jewel of rhetoric.

Check your driver's license. You don't see a photo of Oscar Wilde on it?

Everything is better with preparation. Even Oscar Wilde thought so.

* * * * *

Judge McLaughlin used to enjoy holding pretrial hearings at 7:00 a.m. You were expected to be on time, awake, and prepared.

Being prepared meant you were ready to accept without question or comment whatever was contained in Judge McLaughlin's written tentative ruling, already waiting for you when you arrived. That would become her final ruling. No matter what anyone said or did.

I once saw a lawyer, unaware of this. He began to argue a motion, despite the judge's tentative ruling that was squarely against him. "Your Honor," he began, "as I was driving down here, something occurred to me—"

Down went the gavel. Pow.

"The court has no intention of hearing what occurred to you," the judge said. "If you haven't taken the time to write it down first, I am not going to take the time to hear it."

Not that it would have made any difference.

* * * * *

The story begins with a client. By the time they call, many of the story elements have already been created. You must listen to what the client has to say about them. Listen actively, ask probing questions, and do not stop until you have heard what they want, what they fear, what they know.

Listen so hard that you hear not only what they are saying, but also what they are not saying. The client will be your story's central character, or at least one of them. If you do not understand them, you cannot write a script about them.

* * * * *

Once, the general counsel of a corporation called me for advice. The corporation was contemplating a new business opportunity. In explaining the new business, however, it became clear that she hated it and hated her colleagues who wanted to get involved with it. Hated it the way some people hate injustice or the Yankees: loudly and with passion.

Client wants are usually obvious. They want permission to do something, affirmation that what they have already done is legal, or a way around the law if it is not.

The client who calls without a preexisting want exists, I suppose, but they are rare.

This client *said* she wanted my interpretation of the law. But she knew the facts and law better than I did. What she really wanted was not my legal view. She wanted a friend, an ally, someone to help write a counternarrative against the story being told by her colleagues who wanted to go into the new business.

Lawyers and writers are not allowed to be neutral. Conflict is our business. Both jobs demand having a point of view; we base it on the information we have, the law, the nature of the characters, and all the possible implications of what has happened, will happen, or could happen.

I made the general counsel tell me both sides of the issue, making her play the role of the people who wanted to go into the new business. Then I helped her write the script to persuade others that the new business was a terrible idea.

The hard part was getting her to tone down the pathos and bring up the logic. It was a mistake to refer to those who wanted to go into the new business as greedy and immoral. Calling them assholes was also not helpful.

* * * * *

Unlike writers, lawyers are more limited by the story elements they are given. We cannot make things up out of thin air; we must win with what we have.

Think of it like Ron Howard's *Apollo 13*. When mechanical failure threatens the lives of the astronauts, Mission Control back in Houston dump a box of equipment on a conference table, representing the exact things that are in the space capsule.

Out of these things alone and nothing more, the geniuses on the ground must figure out a way to save the day.

Your clients are the astronauts in trouble. You are the engineer. The question is whether you can get them back alive. The materials in the box are the case facts and the law, along with anything else fate has provided.

If you can use the materials to build a persuasive story, you can save them. It depends on your intelligence and creativity. Whether the resolution is happy or sad depends on how well you do your job.

Begin by knowing what is in the box.

You can add to it later. But no rocket scientist—and no plumber—would begin to fix or even diagnose a problem until he or she knew what the problem was and what there was to work with to fix it.

No lawyer should, either.

After you have listened to the client and learned what is in the box, it is time to begin to write the script.

* * * * *

In television, the script begins with a pitch.

What will the episode be about? Rather than imposing the theme on the facts and witnesses, we come up with the most interesting elements that we can.

I once pitched an episode of *The Practice* that would begin with the following opening scene (also called a teaser):

A deranged man runs into the law firm holding a big, bloody knife.

A collection of lawyers who work together is called a law firm. A collection of writers is called a staff. On television shows, they are also referred to as "the writers' room."

After I pitched my knife story, the writers' room debated its merits and potential.

A writers' room can be a hostile workplace—not legally, maybe, but tonally.

It is a combustible environment. There is the free flow of story ideas, the open exchange of strongly held opinions on emotional issues. Add to that enormous time pressure, various personal crises, the egos and ambitions of those involved, the subjective nature of the work, and the hours involved, and it is remarkable that there isn't more violence.

The hope, of course, is that from this clash and conflict, great stories will emerge. Sometimes it works. Sometimes it doesn't.

* * * * *

Once the knife story pitch got some traction in the room, it was on to the next step of the process. It was "boarded," bullet-point style, on white boards and computer screens, with each person in the room contributing opinions and ideas.

Who was the man with the bloody knife? Where did he come from? How would our characters react to him? What were the legal issues?

Someone suggested the police were chasing the man. They would enter the law firm moments after he does. Do they have a warrant? Was this an exigent circumstance? Could they look for the knife? What would the legal implications be? What could the defense lawyers do? What had the guy with the knife done? How did the blood get on the blade?

An episode of a law show is often an expensive hypothetical, built by committee, to be made as emotionally compelling as possible.

The knife idea seemed most interesting if the story centered on Alan Shore, played by Spader, a character with a strong but subjective moral sense, a skeptic, a cynic, not a sociopath exactly, but one happy to straddle the ethical line.

When the police arrive, Shore would declare himself the man's lawyer—though he had never met him—and refuse to let them search the office. In fact, he would hide the knife before they got there.

Each series regular character would have a different point of view on what to do next. It was based on each of their own convoluted backstories, established over the long course of the series.

The ethical lawyer, Eugene Young, played by Steve Harris, was tightly wound, a control freak; he never liked Shore. Young would want to turn the knife over to the police.

Ellenor Frutt—played by Camryn Manheim—was Shore's oldest friend. She brought Shore into the firm and bore some responsibility for his being there. She was more willing to give Shore leeway and the benefit of the doubt.

* * * * *

It is usually obvious when a story idea will turn into a script. It arrives, if not fully formed, at least rich with strong story elements.

Once a pitch has been roughly outlined, it is then turned into a kind of litigation strategy letter, a short memorandum a few pages long. This is sent to the client paying for the services—the studio and network through their many executives. They then weigh in with their ideas and thoughts.

For every idea that grows into an episode, there are many, many more that don't. There are also quite a few that seem promising but die on the vine. Some that should die but don't sometimes become episodes, though in retrospect, the writers wish they hadn't.

After the story area document is approved, a more detailed outline is written in the room. If that outline is then approved, then the script is given to the writer who pitched the idea or farmed out to another writer.

If this process seems unnecessarily complex or tedious, there is a reason. Once a script is assigned to a writer, under the terms of the Writers Guild of America's minimum basic agreement and common practice, the writer must be paid for writing the first draft. No matter how bad it is or how many times it has to be rewritten.

The unfortunate term "gang-bang" refers to the practice of everyone on the staff writing a script together, and then randomly choosing someone to be the official author (names in the hat, with the winner collecting both the script fee and residuals). Emmys have been awarded to such lottery winners.

But all scripts—like many legal briefs and motions—are collaborations, involving the labor of more people than appear on the title page or signature block. Which is one reason why everyone in Hollywood looks at writing awards with some suspicion. Except for those who win them, of course.

A few are credited. Some are not. If they gave Academy or Emmy Awards for appellate briefs to the first name on a signature block, the lawyers below, those who did most of the work, wouldn't be happy.

* * * * *

Once the bloody knife story was assigned to me, I fleshed out the outlined story, building each of the acts with additional scenes, adding action and dialogue.

Following the teaser, each act picks up where the previous one ended, subtly taking pains to reestablish characters, settings, and information from the previous act because the audience may have joined the episode late or missed something along the way.

Whatever happens in the act must be the logical extension of what happened before. Even the most unexpected plot twist must be grounded in the story and character rules already established. Otherwise, the story loses credibility and the triangle collapses.

Except for the final act, each act must end in a way that insures that the audience comes back. Make them laugh, make them cry, but most of all, make them wait. It can be a cliffhanger— someone we care about (love or hate) is in danger, a mystery is about to be revealed; an unexpected complication arises.

The difference in the final act is that there is a resolution of the conflict that has driven the episode. Shows with ongoing storylines like *Homeland* or *Game of Thrones* don't resolve everything. But if the show is going to be satisfying, they must resolve enough conflict to make the experience of watching each episode enjoyable enough to bring the audience back for the next one.

* * * * *

A lawyer structuring the script of his or her story would do well to keep his listener invested. Whether the script is for advising a client, trying to convince a fact finder, or dealing with opposing counsel, the structure of the script ought to have a plot, pace, and momentum that keeps the audience interested in what is coming next.

I wish I could tell you how, exactly, to structure your script to do that. I cannot. It depends on what is in the box. Being aware that pace and momentum matter is a good place to start. A good beginning, an interesting middle, and a clear, cogent ending never fails. It is always a wonder to me how many writers—and lawyers—fail to structure their narratives along even these basic lines.

* * * * *

One trick to writing a script for television or a legal matter is to try to tell the story visually, without a word of dialogue, through action and description. It forces the writer to describe facts, events, and characters in a way that shows what happened rather than just asserting it.

* * * * *

A good example of visual storytelling in a law context came at the end of each episode of the FOX show *Justice*. After a contentious trial, the show ended with the revelation of what actually happened. Not the version of what happened as told by the lawyers, but the truth, the whole truth and nothing but the truth. The way God might have seen it.

Sometimes our heroes were proven right about what happened. Sometimes they were proven wrong. The studio and network preferred our characters to be far more right than wrong, which somewhat undercut the mystery. The idea was sound, even if the execution was not.

The best single version of this type of storytelling managed to convey a complex fact pattern while simultaneously delivering a story about the power of the jury system. And it was done without a single word of dialogue.

The episode involved the death of a woman named Maria and the trial of her husband, Frankie, on murder charges.[1] It looked bad for him. He was in the next room when she died of a shotgun blast. He denied it, but admitted moving the gun after finding the body. Based on where the shotgun had originally been and his wife's depressed mental state, he was sure she killed herself. And he didn't want their children to find out.

Over the course of the episode, our heroes discovered evidence suggesting that the woman's neighbor may have killed her. It was enough to create reasonable doubt in the minds of the jury. Frank was acquitted.

After the trial was over, one of our lawyers wonders if their client might have gotten away with murder. His colleague shrugs.

"Hey, don't ask me what happened. I don't know. I'm just a trial lawyer."[2]

The screen went black.

Then the audience saw how Maria actually died. As they did, the audience also saw what happened in the jury room, as the jury deliberated over whether or not the husband was guilty of her murder—a nifty twin narrative.

Over music, the wordless sequence started in the jury room. The 12 jurors are engaged in early and obviously animated debate and disagreement, pointing and yelling at one another, talking at the same time.

Our focus is drawn to Juror #9, the youngest person there, is a woman in her early 20s. She is trying to get anyone to listen to her. They ignore her.

We then cut to Maria, alive, sitting on her bed, weeping. Frankie is in the next room, on the couch, asleep. We then cut to outside the living room, where the suspected neighbor lurks in the shadows nearby.

---

1. "Shotgun," *Justice*, Fox, December 1, 2006.
2. Ibid.

Back in the jury room, the deliberations have become focused, ordered; the 12 people now sit around the table. An older woman has taken charge as foreperson. She sits at the head of the table. The group is poring over autopsy photographs. Only Juror #9, the young woman, isn't looking at the photos. She is staring at the shotgun, its trigger tied back with a red plastic safety loop. Something about the gun has given her an idea.

We return to Maria as she pulls the shotgun out from under the bed. As she does, we follow her hands on the gun. They seem to pass the weapon into the hands of Juror #9, who is now holding the gun in the jury room, making a point about it to the other jurors as she slips her shoes off.

Now we see Maria on the bed, the shotgun propped on the floor, the barrel aimed at her chest, her barefoot toe reaching for the trigger.

In the jury room, young Juror #9 sits on the table, the shotgun propped in the same position, the rest of the jury watching her conduct an experiment.

We cut back to Frankie asleep on the couch. We see a flash from under the door of the bedroom, hear the sound of the shotgun blast. Frankie jerks awake and rushes into Maria's room to find Maria on the floor, smoke rising from the barrel of the gun and the wound in her chest.

The last scene of the episode read as follows:

"INT. JURY ROOM—DAY

"Juror #9 presses on the trigger with her toe, showing her fellow jurors how it could've happened. Older jurors are impressed and nod. Juror #9 smiles, proud to be part of doing justice. The defense lawyers didn't win the case. Juror #9 did."

The whole sequence took up a page and a half of script. It consisted of approximately 14 separate scenes shot in three separate locations. It took up a little more than a minute of screentime. David McNally, executive producer and cocreator of the series, directed the episode brilliantly. I never wrote anything that more clearly or effectively told the story of what jurors do, why it matters, or why they deserve credit for doing it. And I didn't need a word to do it.

An ear for dialogue is important. But an eye for detail, the ability to think of stories visually, is more useful. It requires that we step away from the spoken or written word and imagine the issues, conflicts, settings, characters, and action in three dimensions. When we do that, we can then describe it to others, in writing or in person, with the details that give a story life and breath and movement.

It is the opposite of being didactic.

We are leading the audience to see the truth for themselves.

* * * * *

Along with solid structure, a sense of pace, and eye for visual detail, a good script also needs a hero and a villain. But it isn't always clear who is who.

I once walked into my office at the US Attorney's Office to find evidence tape covering my neighbor's door. A prank, I figured, until the chief of the section explained: the FBI had searched the office looking for evidence against my colleague.

Ultimately, this colleague would enter a guilty plea to accepting bribes in return for recommending shorter sentences for convicted defendants. The shock was not that he had done it. The shock was that he had been doing anything at all.

"I never saw him doing work the whole time he was here," the chief marveled later. "At least he was doing *something*."

* * * * *

Lawyers are always heroes to me. But I have known a few who were frauds and even prosecuted one who was an outright imposter.

Using a script he carefully wrote out beforehand, the fake lawyer called people at random and said he worked for the Ninth Circuit Court of Appeals. He had identified them as the winners of a class action suit. For a nominal court-filing fee of $50 to $100, mailed to the court's P.O.

Box, they would receive their portion of the settlement, inevitably a figure like $1,567.21, believable because it was so specific.

He didn't get much; had he left it there, he would have gotten away with it. Instead, a month or so later, he called the exact same victims that he had stolen from already.

This time he said he was an FBI agent, informing them that they had been victims of a scam. Fortunately, the FBI had caught the culprit and recovered the money. For the price of the registered mail and handling fees, sent to an FBI P.O. Box, they would get their money returned to them.

The victims told me the first time he called, the defendant sounded harried, bookish, exactly the way the victims imagined that a lawyer would sound. When he called the second time, he had the breezy, confident sound of an FBI agent bearing good news.

Just one victim realized it was the same man. He was 80 years old, but he hadn't lost his hearing or smarts. Thinking fast, he told the defendant he had recently broken his hip and couldn't get to the post office to mail the money. Was there any chance that the FBI agent could come by the house and get the money in person? The defendant agreed.

When he got to the house, he found an old man hobbling on a cane. The defendant strode in. The old man told him to wait a moment while he got his wallet and went into his bedroom; the defendant told him to take his time, there was no hurry.

When the old man returned, he was leaning on a cane, pointing a loaded .45 at the defendant's chest.

"Move and I'll shoot."

The defendant was relieved when the police arrived. The old man's hearing and senses were good, but his hand was shaking just a little bit. Why didn't the old man call the police sooner?

"I didn't want to bother them until I was sure I'd gotten the right guy."

The defendant rejected the plea offer. He resented having a gun pulled on him.

* * * * *

Prior to trial, the real FBI agent in charge of the case said we had to see the old man. We went to the house. He asked to speak to me in private.

"I got something I need to get off my chest," he said.

On December 7, 1941, he was blown off his ship in Pearl Harbor while the Japanese were busy sinking it. He spent the next few years getting even, fighting his way through the Pacific. When the war ended, to his amazement, he was still alive. Along with the other souvenirs he brought home was his sidearm, the very .45 he pointed at the defendant.

"I guess I stole it," he said, voice quivering a little.

He kept it in good working order and was prepared to return it, along with the clip and ammunition. His hands were shaking when he told me. Because he was afraid he'd be facing charges himself.

I told him that he wouldn't be charged, and not just because the statute of limitations had passed around the time of the Eisenhower presidency. But I would have to tell the defense about it. By law, it was impeachment evidence. After all, he did steal government property.

* * * * *

The case went to trial. I gave the defense lawyer a file for cross-examination, containing the man's admission regarding his theft of the gun. Then, like any good lawyer, I drew the poison myself and asked the man to explain himself.

In a quiet, shame-filled voice, the old man "confessed"—in essence—to being a Pearl Harbor survivor, a war hero (he did not use that term) ,and a gun thief.

The jurors were at the edge of their seats, enthralled, in love. One man wiped tears from his eyes, and a woman started to applaud when he was finished; they would have carried him out on their shoulders if the judge hadn't admonished them to be quiet.

The defense thanked him for his service and didn't ask any questions. Not even I could lose that case. The jury found the defendant guilty *before* lunch. Jurors came up to me afterward, yelling at me for bringing up the gun theft and urging me not to prosecute the old man. I didn't.

* * * * *

The hero or villain does not have to be a person. Often, in civil cases or administrative matters, it isn't. But that doesn't mean a hero or villain can't be found.

* * * * *

One of the most persuasive storytellers I ever heard testified before the obscure California State Commission on Government Organization and Economy, which sounds like a joke but isn't.

The topic was climate change. The commission was curious if the state's regulatory agencies or bureaucracies were planning on doing anything to protect the coastline, forests, or jobs put at risk by hotter temperatures and higher ocean levels.

A number of experts and bureaucrats testified. They represented the state's major industries, energy providers, and labor and trade groups and came from across the entire political spectrum. They all had valuable information to impart. But only one managed to deliver it in a memorable, compelling, and persuasive way. He represented the citrus industry.

Barrel-chested as Teddy Roosevelt but twice as animated, he pounced to the witness chair, pulled up the mic, adjusted his rimless glasses, and launched into the greatest story ever told . . . about citrus. California *is* the orange, he proclaimed. The state and the fruit are intertwined, indivisible, now and forever. Orange groves made the state famous. The industry remains of vital importance to the state's ongoing identity and economy.

His presentation had such vim—there was no other word for it—it made you forget that gold was ever found in Sutter's Creek, that

Hollywood ever existed, or that Silicon Valley mattered. No one ever knew or cared more about oranges. His feeling for the Mandarin variety was almost embarrassing. The man had spent his life fighting for the industry. As long as there is a California, he said, there will always be the California orange. Come hell or high water, orange growers will never leave the state.

What if it gets too hot or the sea rises too high to grow oranges?

"We'll move to Iowa."

* * * * *

Not because of the weather or nature, but because of what he called the "obscene regulations" that California continued to heap upon their backs. Citrus was the hero. The government was the villain.

Wasn't there *anything* the government could do to help?

Yes, he thundered, stay out of the citrus industry's way. The situation was well in hand; he and his fellow citrus-growers had everything under control. They were not like their brethren in Florida, he said with a sneer. In Florida, thanks to climate change, the citrus industry was dying off due to what *they* called "citrus greening."

Wasn't he afraid the same could happen here?

"No," he said. "You will never hear that term in California," the citrus man said.

The disease might come here, but not the term. He explained that California growers had done focus group testing on possible disease names relevant to the scourge. "Citrus greening," they realized, sounded too tame. So they settled on "huanglongbing" because it sounded the scariest.

How would that solve anything?

The citrus growers knew that to stop huanglongbing, they needed to spray vast areas of the state with pesticides. In order to do so, they needed the support of urban populations, particularly in Southern

California, where people generally don't like helicopters dumping chemicals from the air. In order to overcome their resistance, the citrus folks wanted to scare as many people as they could into getting with the program.

The man was a wonder. Forthcoming, credible, and passionate, he knew what he was talking about, had an unshakeable understanding of the subject, and cared deeply about it. Yes, he sounded like a lobbyist, why shouldn't he? That's exactly what he was; he wasn't hiding anything.

* * * * *

Inevitably, the hero of your story is the villain of the other side's story. It doesn't matter how heroic your hero is. Indeed, in this tawdry age, the more heroic he is, the more vulnerable he is to being turned into a villain.

* * * * *

Southern California is the bank robbery capital of the world. What we lack in quality, we make up for in volume. Our office only took cases where a gun was used, the robber was involved in multiple robberies, and we had a rock-crushing amount of proof. The rest we left to the district attorneys.

Even with that kind of cherry picking, I still ended up with a few case dogs. There was the robber who wrote his demand for cash on the back of his utility bill, listing his home address; the guy who robbed the bank where he had recently applied for a loan; the guy who had a dye pack of bait bills explode in his pants but went to trial anyway, arguing he found the money on the street—the fact he looked so much like the man in the surveillance photo was just bad luck.

And not all the cases had a ton of proof.

* * * * *

Three armed and masked men walked into the East West Bank branch in Alhambra, California, and robbed it. They were smarter than most robbers and more polite. Having jumped over the teller counter, one of the robbers asked a victim teller if she would, please, hold his gun so he could use two hands to scoop the money into a pillowcase. The teller testified that when the robber was finished gathering up the cash, he took the gun back and said, "Thank you."

The three masked men were also better prepared than most robbers. They fled in a two-door white sports car, which they abandoned a mile from the bank, and switched to a second car, a four-door black Cadillac they had stolen earlier in the day.

An unusually ambitious Alhambra Police Department officer was patrolling a few miles away when the robbery took place. He heard the radio run reporting it, describing three suspects with guns driving a two-door white sports car. There was no other description. Thanks to their disguises, nobody could say what race they were. Quick as a flash, the officer drove to the biggest street linking Alhambra and East Los Angeles and waited.

He did not see a two-door white sports car with three men in it. He did see a black Cadillac with *two* men. The officer decided to follow it. The Cadillac changed lanes, turned down a quiet residential side street, and pulled to the curb in front of a small house.

The officer pulled behind the Cadillac and got out of his patrol car. That's when the Cadillac floored it, tearing down the street. The police officer rushed back to his squad car and radioed for backup. Lights flashing, siren blaring, the squad cop chased the Cadillac. That's when the officer saw the third man pop out of the backseat of the Cadillac.

Up and around the hilly streets of Alhambra, the cars zoomed past streets and schools filled with kids, banging into trash cans, jumping curbs at the corners, smashing into several parked cars. They roared down alleys, sometimes passing terrified drivers, sometimes going the wrong way down streets.

They hit a dead end. The three men tumbled out of the Cadillac, the driver putting the car in neutral, no brake, letting it crash into a fire hydrant, sending a geyser of water 30 feet into the air. The officer grabbed his department-issued MP-5 machine gun and jumped out to chase the men, but forgot to put his own car in park. It crashed into several cars before coming to a stop.

The chase continued on foot, over fences, through backyards, past snarling pit bulls and Rottweilers, until, finally, the cop lost sight of all three men. A more cautious man would have given up, waited for backup, taken a breath. This cop retraced his steps, machine gun in one hand, flashlight in the other, going on his hands and knees, peering into darkened garages and crawl spaces between houses.

Beneath the outdoor deck of an abandoned home, he saw one of the men and ordered him to come out, hands up. The man wouldn't budge. The cop put down his machine gun and flashlight and yanked the man out from his hiding place by his ankles.

The police searched the Cadillac. They found ski masks, clothes, gloves, a gun, and cash traced to the robbery through the recorded serial numbers.

A second man was arrested days later with more of the stolen cash. He pled guilty on the eve of trial. The third man was never found.

My opening statement sounded like a pitch for an action movie. The cop was the star, a superhero, brave, tough, and resourceful. The robbers were the villains. It couldn't be clearer. Jurors smiled at me. This wouldn't take long.

Then the defense lawyer stood up:

"Why did the cop start following them to begin with?"

He just let it linger there like a bad smell.

The men's faces were masked. Nobody in the bank could identify them, not even the victim teller who held the gun and spoke to one of them.

The Cadillac the officer started to follow did not match the description he had of the getaway car. Three men robbed the bank, but the officer only saw two in the Cadillac when he started the chase. Did I mention the officer was white and the men in the Cadillac were not?

* * * * *

The defense lawyer didn't hit the jury over the head with it. He let them fill in the blanks, eliciting their outrage rather than mimicking it. The cop was not a hero. He was a racist.

Other lawyers might have spoken longer and destroyed the moment. They would have used the usual boilerplate—the unnecessary introductions, the perfunctory thanks for their jury service—most of which would have already been covered before they spoke by the court. All these lawyers would have conveyed to the jury was that their client had no story at all.

This defense lawyer knew how to tell a story. And it never changed. His cross-examination of the officer consisted of two or three questions, the best one being:

"Why did you assume the robbers were going to drive to East LA?"

The one juror who lived in East LA stared daggers at me. From thin soil the defense lawyer was teasing out a fair crop of reasonable doubt.

There were no fingerprints or eyewitnesses linking his client to the actual bank robbery. Wasn't it possible his client was just a passenger in the car, along for the ride, uninvolved with the robbery at all?

There was the guilty action of fleeing, but the defense lawyer noted in his closing that the Cadillac did pull over, at least at first. If the men panicked and fled, fearful of the police officer, they had reason to. Look at how the officer endangered the lives of countless innocent people, many of them children, on a hare-brained, dangerous, ego-fuelled joyride. Is this the kind of police work we want to condone?

Everything the man said fit into his story. He had the same facts and law as I had. But he built a clever, consistent, thought-provoking defense with it. He kept the jury out for days.

Eventually, the jury convicted the defendant. But the defense lawyer wrote a better script and told a better story. His guy just happened to be guilty. Justice was done, in that sense. But from a storytelling standpoint, the defense lawyer should have been the winner.

"The race is not always to the swift, nor the battle to the strong," Damon Runyon said, "but that's the way to bet."

* * * * *

The best way to learn to write your script is the same way you learned to write briefs. Read other people's work and mimic it until you get your own style.

For a number of years I have taught law, mostly at USC's Gould School of Law. Usually, the subject was federal criminal law or procedure. One semester, I taught a course on law and film. It was considered such a novelty that the new dean of the law school, in an email inadvertently sent to me, wondered why they were offering it at all.

I tried not to be offended. The relevance of the class was self-evident.

There are deposition scenes in the movie *The Social Network* (2010) that could provide a semester's worth of material for teaching civil procedure and practice. Its story of how Facebook was created is ready-made text for teaching corporate law.

Tony Gilroy's *Michael Clayton* (2007) makes the perfect casebook for teaching professional ethics and responsibility. The antihero lawyer played by George Clooney is a degenerate gambler and fixer who uses his law degree as a license to skirt the law. The only problem is that Clooney looks so good being bad and everything turns out so well for him. These lessons are not necessarily the ones we want to teach young lawyers.

* * * * *

Some films have lost their value as teaching tools. They have become sacred texts that are beyond analysis or questioning. *To Kill a Mockingbird* is the best example. Extraordinary when you think about it. Gregory Peck plays a lawyer who defends an innocent man and loses. Atticus Finch talks about the importance of a fair and impartial legal system, the "great leveler" that guarantees equal and objective justice under the law. But when he is handed the chance to put his principles into practice, when his son is saved by Boo Radley, Atticus Finch goes along with the sheriff's decision to cover up a homicide and obstruct justice.

* * * * *

I spoke with Gregory Peck toward the end of his life. He was sitting outside a grocery store in Beverly Hills, taking in the sun, with a little white dog in his lap. I told him that whenever I addressed a jury, a little bit of me was trying to channel Atticus Finch.

"Yes," he said, with a sigh, more to the dog than to me. "I hear that a lot."

* * * * *

William Faulkner's *Intruder in the Dust* (1948) covers the same time period and territory as Harper Lee's book. It is also the story of a white lawyer and his reluctant defense of a wrongly accused black man.

A disappointing movie version was made of *Intruder*. Will Geer, grandpa from *The Waltons*, and several other left-leaning, blacklisted actors are in it. It came nowhere near achieving *Mockingbird*'s success. But in many ways, Faulkner's novel is the truer, more nuanced story about the law, justice, and race. Perhaps the reason the book isn't more popular is because the white lawyer in it is a racist. And the black man is strong, proud, and angry.

* * * * *

The actress Kim Hamilton came in one day to audition for a small part on *The Practice*. She had played the wife of doomed Tom Robinson (Brock Peters) in *Mockingbird*. She didn't have much screen time, but what is there is powerful. A fascinating woman, she was married to the classically trained violinist, opera singer, conductor, and star of stage and screen, Werner Klemperer. Yes, that's right, the man who played Col. Klink in *Hogan's Heroes*. We cast her as the chief justice of the Massachusetts Supreme Court. It seemed only right. The law had let her down so badly before.

*   *   *   *   *

As storytellers we tend to be cultural imperialists. But America is not the only place that makes law movies. USC boasts an international student body and several of my students pointed this out to me. They also suggested we look at movies from their home country, particularly those that inspired them to become lawyers.

A few were terrific. Britain's Ken Loach's *Bread and Roses* (2000) starring Adrien Brody, an unappreciated film set in Los Angeles about Justice for Janitors, offers a terrific case study of employment law and labor issues.

The best of the foreign films I think, was the 1997 adaptation of author Ferdinand Bordewijk's classic lawyer's tale, *Karactor*, written 60 years earlier. It is the story of a young lawyer who uses his degree to seek revenge against his evil father. It won the Academy Award for Best Foreign Film. There was no need for an American adaptation.

*   *   *   *   *

To Kill a Mockingbird was not on my syllabus. I assumed all the students had seen it. After all, these were the ones who had signed up for the class; they must have some interest in the topic. I was wrong.

Many had seen it but not all of them. Almost none of the students had seen *Philadelphia*, which starred Denzel Washington and Tom Hanks.

Two had seen *The Verdict* or *Anatomy of a Murder*, but neither one saw both.

My students had broad knowledge of current popular culture—the movies out now, the television series on the air. But they had almost no knowledge of films from the past.

I know television is a disposable medium, but most of the law students in my class, situated a stone's throw from LA's big law firms, had never *heard* of, let alone seen, the iconic series *L.A. Law* or a number of other Kelley shows.

Do not fear relying on old stories or foreign ones. They won't be old or familiar to most lawyers or jurors. Nothing is deader than the recent cultural past. Everything is new to the uninformed.

* * * * *

My law and film class assigned students to write a variety of short papers in which they were asked to analyze movies and television series in terms of relevant laws, procedures, and rules of professional responsibility. The final paper allowed the students to focus more deeply on one or more director, genre, film, or television series of their choosing, using the work as texts to analyze and discuss a broader area of the law. More adventurous students could do the same thing by writing their own original movie or television script.

It was interesting to compare the short assignments of the students who opted to submit original scripts. Many of the scripts displayed greater creativity and deeper, more sophisticated thought and understanding of legal concepts than the conventional shorter assignments.

A number of my students had real talent as storytellers. But they had been straitjacketed by the conventions of legal writing, unable to show what they knew or thought about the law itself. They told more cogent and moving stories when allowed to operate in the less restrictive but still structured world of the script. But then again, many of the students were also screenwriters. It is Los Angeles, after all.

* * * * *

When I first met my wife, she was in her third season writing for the comedy series *Roseanne*. By the time we got engaged, she was writing on the show *Friends*. Shortly after we got married, I received a letter from the chambers of a federal district court judge asking that I help his actress girlfriend get a job.

"I am taking the liberty of enclosing a short video which contains excerpts of some of her movies and a copy of her resume. She is very attractive," the judge's letter reads, "although you would not know it from the roles she played . . ."

This particular judge could not have been more unpleasant to me whenever I had the misfortune to appear before him. During one trial, he cut me off in the middle of my opening statement, later barked at me to show him more respect, and, generally speaking, behaved with the judicial temperament of a gassy baby. I named a serial killer after him on one of my shows and told him so. That didn't stop him from trying to use the contact to help his girlfriend. Everybody wants to be in show business.

* * * * *

If you grow up in Las Vegas, you know from birth never to gamble against the casinos. It's a losing proposition. Growing up in Los Angeles, I knew enough to steer clear of Hollywood.

While I was at the US Attorney's Office, a friend of mine left Latham & Watkins to become a television writer on *Law & Order*. Looking for a credible story, he took me to dinner, then wrote an episode based loosely on one of my cases. He even named the evil defense lawyer after me. The role was played by the late, great Alan King. This led to my favorite line of dialogue, spoken by the dyspeptic senior district attorney played by Steven Hill:

"Jonathan Shapiro is so slippery, he could pass you in a revolving door."

Hill's character was named Adam Schiff, the same name as a colleague of mine at the US Attorney's Office. There was a story, perhaps apocryphal, that Schiff received money for the use of his name, or for the producer's failure to have received his permission to do so. The real Schiff tried to write for Hollywood but gave up and moved onto the more logical world of politics. He has served in Congress for many years, though I bet he's still got an idea for a spec script.

* * * * *

Despite my brush with fame, I still had no interest in writing for television.

Then we had twins.

My wife informed me that if I could sell a script and get into the Writers Guild, we could double our health insurance benefits. Fine, I said, but I would do it on my own terms. I would find my own agent, not use her agent. And I wouldn't quit my day job.

I contacted the only agent I knew—a man I had met when he cut in front of me in line at the deli counter of Western Bagel.

One week later, he called back with a job.

"It's a new show," he said, "very hot, and perfect for you—it's about the law, with strong characters, and a really interesting premise."

"Wonderful," I said. "What's the name of the show?"

"You're complaining now?" he snapped.

"No, no," I said, "sorry."

Forget the name of the show, he said. It doesn't matter; show titles change all the time before they get on the air. The important thing was that it had a time slot, so it was definitely going to be broadcast.

"Wonderful," I said. "On what network?"

"You like truck racing?" he asked. "It's the home of truck racing. TNN. The Nashville Network."

"Wonderful," I said.

The name of the show did not change.

Eighteen Wheels of Justice stared Lucky Vanous, a former male model best known for taking his shirt off in a Diet Coke commercial.

He played a renegade cop, traveling through the Southwest in his 18-wheeler, solving crimes and helping others.

His costars included Billy Dee Williams and attorney turned Watergate coconspirator G. Gordon Liddy.

I met with one of the show's executive producers in what appeared to be a converted underground missile launch site deep in the East Valley. He went over the show's bible with me.

* * * * *

Every television series maintains a bible. When you create a show, you get paid to write a pilot, and often, get paid separately to write a bible.

It is more like a last will than a testament. It is a way to get the writer to download everything he or she has created, intends to create, or might create for the show, so that the network or studio that produces the show can fire the creator at some point and still keep the show running.

Like other holy books, the show bible is a founding document. It lays out back stories for all the regular characters, their motivations and goals, the show's overall premise, and storylines that may last over many seasons.

It's also an ongoing record of casts, episode summaries, and location shoots; it often contains wisdom about which stories worked and which did not.

Usually the show bible is written and maintained in the writer's offices and kept on a shelf to be consulted, ritually, at the beginning of every season. It is also referred to in times of confusion or perplexity ("Have we ever done a story about dwarfs?"). Sometimes it is not so much a written document as an oral tradition, passed on from one writer to another.

On shows that run for many seasons the bible can reach several volumes and include commentary, interpretation, and exegesis worthy of a Talmudic scholar. Should the world be destroyed and only the *Battlestar*

Galactica show bible remain, future scholars will have a complete and fascinating understanding of the human race and its history; fictional, yes, but fantastic.

I've always thought that lawyers and law firms ought to make up their own version of the series bible—a formal, constantly updated collection of personal stories, professional rules to live by, memorable or helpful characters, useful resources, and other handy information. Not a diary or journal, but an ongoing record.

It would be a handy resource, a tool for continuity. The act of creating it would make lawyers think seriously about who they are and what they do. It would be an act of mindfulness, an exercise in reflection; a valuable statement of principles.

* * * * *

I don't recall all the commandants in the bible for *Eighteen Wheels of Justice*. There were too many. I do recall that most involved the truck itself. Thanks to some product placement deal with the Kenworth Truck Company, Lucky was the hero of the show, but the truck was the real star.

One rule I remember: The truck never *skids*. It *jackknives*, possibly, but not often, and never because of mechanical or design flaws.

The truck also had to be on-screen as much as possible. How this was to be accomplished in interior scenes, or love scenes, was the writer's problem.

It didn't become my problem because I didn't take the job.

My agent from Western Bagel was furious.

"Do you know how many people would kill for this chance?" he asked me. I did know. The Starbucks of Southern California are full of them, hunched over their laptops, defending their tables like pit bulls.

It wasn't because I was ungrateful. I didn't think I could tell stories about the truck. I was better then about admitting there were stories I was miscast to tell.

Over time, *Eighteen Wheels of Justice* became one of my father's favorite shows.

* * * * *

There has never been a great movie made from a bad script. Not many cases are won with bad scripts, either.

But it is hard work.

"Anyone moderately familiar with the rigors of composition will not need to be told the story in detail; how he wrote and it seemed good; read and it seemed vile; corrected and tore up; cut out; put in; was in ecstasy; in despair; had his good nights and bad mornings; snatched at ideas and lost them; saw his book plain before him and it vanished; acted his people's parts as he ate; mouthed them as he walked; now cried; now laughed; vacillated between this style and that; now preferred the heroic and pompous; next the plain and simple . . . and could not decide whether he was the divinest genius or the greatest fool in the world."[3]

Virginia Woolf jumped in a river and drowned. But it wasn't out of frustration over writing. I don't believe.

* * * * *

During my years working for David E. Kelley, he had several shows on the air simultaneously—*Ally McBeal*, *The Practice*, and *Boston Public*. He wrote most of the scripts for all three shows. Think about that.

An average television show script contains three separate storylines. It goes through numerous rewrites, never fewer than five; it has to be vetted, defended, and noted by studio executives and network lawyers. The sheer labor involved in writing the better part of 66 hours of television (three shows, 22 episode seasons each) in less than a year boggles the mind.

No writer of law fiction has reached so many with such a singular

---

3. Virginia Woolf, *Orlando: A Biography* (San Diego: Harcourt Brace Jovanovich Publishers, 1956), 82.

voice. There are more episodes of other legal-themed franchises—*CSI, Law & Order*—but no one writer wrote more of them himself.

Yes, he made use of the writer's room, taking their ideas and outlines, and allowing some of us to write or cowrite four or five scripts each season. But the rest was all him.

He was the first—and still only—person to win Emmys for creating and producing television's Best Comedy and Best Drama (in the same year).

So why don't people study him more?

* * * * *

There are an infinite number of excellent books about storytelling for lawyers. Among my favorites is *Trial Stories*, a collection of essays edited by Michael E. Tigar and Angela Davis, which addresses the subject in a historical context, considering nine famous trials as stories that reflected and influenced the time and place in which they were tried. Similarly, there is Professor Meyer, who takes a similar approach in *Storytelling for Lawyers*, but expands the scope of material to include classic Hollywood movies to explain story concepts of plot, character, and setting.

Neither he, nor any other writer, to my knowledge, has taken full-advantage of the huge body of television-themed law shows to consider how law stories are told. Nor have they seriously considered the extraordinary impact these shows have both on the public's perception of the legal profession, and on how lawyers tell their stories.

Only a few scholars have lightly mined Kelley's body of work for insights into the changing nature of the legal profession and the role of television in influencing it.

* * * * *

Working with a genius is a blessing and a curse. Kelley's ability to structure a story, to recognize its dramatic points, to know when to reveal information, all seemed innate and effortless.

It wasn't.

Kelley worked harder than any lawyer or writer I ever knew. He just didn't seem to want anyone to know it.

Starting at around 8:30 a.m., after he dropped off his kids at school, he would sit in his office and write by hand on long legal pads. He might eat at his desk or take a lunch break, but he would continue through the afternoon until 5:00 or so before he went home for dinner.

The banking hours were misleading, a New Englander's self-effacing tendency to underplay hardships. In truth, he never *stopped* writing stories.

He would write on scraps of paper during meetings with studio executives, on menus while interviewing directors. He must have written late at night, in the morning before getting to work, and on the weekends. He would often leave work with half a script done and come back the next day with a full draft. Or he would mumble good-bye on Friday with no script then show up on Monday with two.

And this wasn't the only writing he was doing. While feeding hundreds of stories into the television machine, Kelley also wrote new pilots, as well as drafts of movie scripts. They didn't all get made, but they were better than most scripts that did.

He was so prolific that he became his own competition. Executives passed on Kelley material that was better than any other writer could produce because it wasn't as good as material that Kelley himself had already written.

You could see the toll it took on him.

A television production year for a one-hour drama begins in June and runs through April. As one episode is being shot, another is being prepped for production, several are in various stages of being edited, and several more are in the process of being written. It is a war of attrition, a never-ending grind. The machine that makes television shows employs close to 200 people but it shuts down if it isn't fed stories.

Like a veteran ballplayer, Kelley would start the season fit, tanned, and relaxed. Four months into it, he was barely hanging on. Pale and gaunt, eyes red-rimmed with exhaustion, losing weight he didn't really have to lose, he looked like the stories were being bled out of him.

People on the lot would get worried. At lunch at the nearby Johnny Rockets, he would sit, staring at his burger, like he was too tired to lift it.

It wasn't like he didn't have anything else to do. With more money than anyone could ever need, more awards than anyone could ever hope for, more success that can be imagined, he was an otherwise happy, healthy human being with a wife and two kids. She probably doesn't walk around the house in the catsuit from Batman all day, but still, Kelley's wife is the actress Michelle Pfeiffer.

Which led to this inevitable debate on the set:

Why, in God's name, is the man killing himself like this?

The reason was because storytelling mattered that much to him.

He brought a focus and seriousness to storytelling that was the foundation for everything he did. It deserved all he had. That's why he was the best that ever was.

* * * * *

Lawyers shouldn't have to be reminded of the importance of the script. Nothing is more scripted than the law. Among the nations, America's founding document remains the oldest script still being performed.

The Constitution is still what moves the boat.

* * * * *

In 2012, Peter Sagal, best known as the host of NPR's *Wait, Wait, Don't Tell Me*, was asked to produce and star in a multi-episode documentary for PBS on the United States Constitution.

Unhampered by the constraints of a formal legal education, Sagal and his producers used Supreme Court cases as stories to explain what the Constitution is and how it works. It was a wonderful, irreverent, thought-provoking show.

"Most discourse about the Constitution is rooted in ideology and history, like religious texts," Sagal told me. "One side or the other in a debate will say, 'Our Founding Fathers believed this, therefore X must be true.' Which seems pointless. Because, you know . . . they're dead."[4]

They did, however, leave instructions, a manual for resolving conflicts and battling desires.

"I'm a storyteller," Sagal explained. "I see everything from a theatrical point of view."

So does the law. And that includes the takings clause.

"It's one thing to talk about the 5th Amendment and the 14th Amendment and explain the theories and precedents," Sagal said. "It's a different thing to stand in an empty field in Connecticut with weeds growing in it, where a guy's house used to be but now isn't, because the government took it."

Or, "a same-sex couple goes off script and wants to get married; the Constitution doesn't fly out of the National Archives and answer whether they can."

The genius of the constitutional script is that it produces resolution, no matter what the conflicting desires are.

"Our society is deeply divided over the meaning of good and evil. We tell clashing stories about things that matter a great deal."[5] Sagal would agree. And it is all scripted. Not a reality show. A drama with comedic elements, a narrative dictated and defined by the rules of storytelling.

* * * * *

The last rule on writing a script is also simple:

The worst one you write is better than the best one you don't write.

Because the worst one can be rewritten, but no one can rewrite what hasn't been written first.

They don't pay writers in Hollywood to write. They pay us to rewrite.

---

4. Email correspondence, February 7, 2014.
5. Richard F. Duncan, "Wigstock and the Kulturkampf: Supreme Court Storytelling, the Culture War, and Romer v. Evans," *Notre Dame Law Review* 72 (1997): 345.

EIGHT

The Edit

If I could have a superpower, it would not be invisibility or the ability to fly.

It would be the power to edit.

Cut out the bad parts, dub in new lines, move things along more quickly—the power to edit makes one a god, capable of changing fate, removing characters and dialogue, creating a new, better story.

Writing is the most important aspect of storytelling. Editing is the most unappreciated. Before you can write, you have to learn to read. But before you can write *well*, you have to learn how to edit.

What's true in law is true in show business. The writer writes his or her script. The director shoots the script, or his or her version of it. The actors play it. But it is the editor who puts it all together.

The script moves the boat. But the whole thing sinks without an editor.

* * * * *

Here, again, lawyers have an advantage over other storytellers. In the first year of law school, we are trained to edit, to parse, and to rewrite. Usually, it is of other people's work. It would be more helpful if it were our own work.

* * * * *

Great as the Constitution is, it was a rewrite job. The Articles of Confederation was a bomb. The Constitutional Convention convened as a writers' room, with Thomas Jefferson as the head writer. Benjamin Franklin's greatest service to his country was getting Jefferson to take edits.

Chances are good you need editing too, probably more than Jefferson did. You have two choices.

You can try to do it yourself. Or you can ask for help.

My grandfather was a steelworker and a plumber. He used to say he made his money off people who tried to do things themselves. The damage do-it-yourselfers did with their work required that my grandfather do much more extensive—and expensive—work than the original problem would have required.

Choosing to edit your own material makes as much as sense as cutting your own hair or removing your own spleen. It may be convenient. But it won't look great, and someone, at some point, is going to have to fix it.

Editing requires intelligence, fresh eyes, and objectivity. Two out of three is not enough. The writer of the first draft will never be able to manage more than one of them.

* * * * *

Nobody wants to be told that their child is fat, dumb, and lazy.

They don't want to hear it about their script either.

I have seen the most peaceable, sophisticated people almost come to blows in the writers' room of a television show. A woman of a certain age, an experienced and talented writer, once opened up a mouth like a stevedore when someone had the audacity to suggest one scene in her script could be cut. She didn't just bristle. She went crazy.

"You want to go?!?"

A small, bird-like woman, she was on her feet, chirping, challenging another writer to a fight. They had to be separated.

Anybody who has worked on a newspaper knows how dangerous the editorial desk is near deadline. Insults and profanity fly. Scott McKee, an editor of *The Recorder* newspaper, was the nicest man in the world.

Driven crazy by my misspellings, he once threw a stapler at me. Later, he threw a dictionary.

When I worked in the US Department of Justice, I served a rotation in the Appellate Section. Working with the Solicitor General's Office and Criminal Appeals was a fascinating experience. Nothing taught me more about the value of well-crafted fact pattern narrative in appellate practice. It was also the first—but not the last—time I saw lawyers almost come to blows over editing.

Friends who have clerked inform me that even justices of the Supreme Court don't particularly enjoy having a colleague weigh in with suggestions.

Better to accuse someone of being a liar or worse than to suggest they don't know how to write. It touches upon some fundamental sense of being rejected, some deep fear of being exposed.

* * * * *

Lawyers have it easier than some editors.

In film and television, editors get an enormous amount of raw material dumped on them—every shot, every take, every scene, audio, music, and none of it is in order. To accommodate a production's logistics and schedules and to maximize cost savings, filming is rarely done in chronological order.

What the editor has to work with is a daily jumble of images, scenes, or parts of scenes from the middle, end, or beginning of the narrative. These images lack context as well a number of elements that will come later—music, additional dialogue, and special effects.

The editor must take these pieces, or bits of pieces, and turn them into a clear, understandable story.

A good editor can make a story better than the writer wrote or imagined.

* * * * *

Having written their script, lawyers should edit their stories with the same amount of thought and planning. That often means rewriting the script to reflect additional information, better material, or new ideas. It means being flexible, taking advice, changing things to make the story better.

In short, editing requires the exact skills and temperament most writers and lawyers don't have.

* * * * *

There are some people who enjoy being edited. They welcome criticism, regardless of the form it takes. So long as it helps make the story better, they are grateful; indeed, they are happy to hear what others have to say.

I am not one of those people.

I have never worked with such people.

I have never even met them.

But I know they must exist. Because whenever anyone edits me, they always bring these people up to me.

"Good writers appreciate editing," an executive told me. "Quit being so defensive."

* * * * *

There is no shame in hating to be edited. Writing is a personal matter. It is unfortunate but true that when I am edited, I feel as if I am being insulted. Editing touches something in my reptilian brain that triggers a flight-or-fight reflex.

A good editor edits without enraging. To edit well requires empathy, subtlety, and the ability to slip a punch.

Ben Franklin was a great editor because he knew how to write, and because he understood that writers have thin skin. Franklin also understood the importance of being charming, witty, and gentle.

They pay good editors a lot but they don't pay them enough.

* * * * *

An executive on one of my shows liked to turn down each page of a script on which he had a note. As every single page would be turned down, the script looked like a paper fan, covered in line cuts, arrows, and new dialogue.

Wouldn't it be easier to just turn down the pages that *don't* have notes? Or maybe just become a writer yourself?

"If you can't take notes, you shouldn't be in the business," the executive told me.

I can take anything. But nothing says I have to like it.

* * * * *

The murder weapon in one particular episode was a golf club, the killer having smashed in someone's head with one. In my first draft, I had selected a six iron. An executive changed it to an eight iron. I said he'd get more distance with the six.

"Don't be a smart-ass," he said.

* * * * *

After we had pulled two all-nighters to finish the seventh draft of a script, an executive for the network wondered if we might not start over from page one with a whole new story. I threatened to kill him.

"We had another writer in here this morning who was happy to hear our thoughts," an executive told me.

Who was it? I wanted a name.

"That's not the point," the executive said. "You shouldn't be so sensitive."

* * * * *

Great law firms and government agencies produce briefs that are tight as a tick; they manage to be engaging, to tell a compelling story, to persuade. Bad law firms file cut-and-paste jobs, with meandering fact patterns and a catalogue of case citations that are only sometimes relevant. No wonder judges get so testy.

I would think one of the hardest challenges facing those in solo practice would be getting access to editorial help.

I have a suggestion.

Bar associations could do a great service to individual lawyers—and the judges who have to read their work—by offering them access to privileged editorial help.

Not through its own staff, but by organizing other solo attorneys into self-help groups. The model might be the thousands of book clubs that have sprung up across the nation over the past decade.

Clients would benefit from it. Courts that have to plow through bad writing would appreciate it, too.

* * * * *

While not many people want to edit the solo attorney's brief, there is an army of folks eager to edit a television or movie script. The reason is simple. Money.

Precise production budget numbers are oxymoronic, the longest-running gag in show business, legendary as the Sorcerer's Stone, and just as likely to exist. If Hillside or Mount Sinai cemeteries had sections for auditors, they would be filled with the bones of those who had spent their lives in search of numbers they would never find.

The approximately $18 million in production costs for the FOX show *Justice* did not include the millions more spent on marketing. What that number was is anybody's guess. Nobody ever shared it with me, and I asked, many times.

By way of comparison, in the movie industry, approximately *half* of a film's budget is spent on advertising, including digital, print, and broadcast commercials.

That means that for every $100 million budget, *only* $50 million is spent to actually make the film. The rest goes to selling it. It is assumed that less money is spent to promote a television series, in part, because the networks advertise their shows on their own network—they pay for it, potentially at reduced rates, but it isn't free for them.

Based on my conversations with studio executives, advertising representatives, and others involved in the production, I feel very safe in asserting that, conservatively, no less than $4 million was spent advertising *Justice*, though the figure was probably much higher.

Meaning that a major studio and network paid $22 million to tell our 13 law stories about a fictional law firm.

They felt an understandable urge to help tell those stories. Just because they don't write the scripts doesn't mean they are not entitled to have opinions. A free press is not free, and neither is free broadcast or cable television. When storytellers sell their stories to a network, they don't just get storytelling partners—they get *senior* partners.

As we have seen, before a script can be written, multiple executives from the studio, the production company, and the network have to approve the idea. With all that help, you would think the scripts would come out better.

* * * * *

As noted, repeatedly, sometimes the storytelling process does not work out. Indeed, sometimes the process ends in blistering failure.

Law is no different. Usually, it just isn't as public. A lawyer I know who lost a major case continues to celebrate the anniversary the same way every year. He gets drunk and dreams of killing the lawyer who beat him. Unfortunately, we learn more from losing than winning. Such is life.

David Copperfield did not know whether he was to be the hero of his own story. I know I am not the hero of this one.

Admitting failures is my gift to you. I consider it an innovation.

Of all the books that have been written about storytelling, including the large number by and for lawyers, none of them embrace failure—particularly the author's own failure—as educational, let alone inspirational.

History is written by the victors; especially legal history written by lawyers like Gerry Spence, Alan Dershowitz, and Nancy Grace. Indeed, the lawyer autobiography is its own interesting genre.[1] Not surprisingly, the heroes of these books are always the authors themselves.

Writing about the failures of *other* lawyers also comprises a separate genre. A good example is Ralph Adam Fine's *The How-to Win Trial Manual* (5th edition), a provocative book devoted almost exclusively to lawyer storytelling failure. A guilty pleasure to some, it is an excellent source of material for stories. It can be entertaining too.

It is not, however, a book about storytelling. Because Fine is not a storyteller. Fine is a judge in Wisconsin. Fine is a critic. Fine is a kibitzer. There are worse things you can say about a man, but not many.

* * * * *

Call it "the art of storytelling" if you like but never forget that for lawyers and writers, storytelling is a business. We are paid for our stories, or should be. Unless you are a poet or saint, telling stories or writing scripts promiscuously, for free, whatever the purpose, is a bad practice.

As Dr. Samuel Johnson said: "No man but a blockhead ever wrote, except for money." By that standard, really, my only failures as a writer were not canceled shows but shows that were never sold at all.

There was, for example, *Dr. Johnson & Friend*, which had the great

---

1. See "I Represent a Walloon," *California Lawyer Magazine* (August 2001), 47, my homage to the self-aggrandizing lawyer biography and autobiography. Among my favorites, see Terry T. Olender, *For the Prosecution: Miss Deputy D.A.* (1961), with a foreword by Jerry Geisler, its cover boasting: "A Woman Lawyer's Amazing and Often Shocking Experiences in Handling Murder, Robbery and Bizarre Sex Cases."

writer and conversationalist rambling through the British Isles, solving crimes with the help of his younger friend and biographer, James Boswell. I would have watched it.

Greenstein & Tubbs was about a straightlaced forensic accountant and his laid-back surfer partner. They solved crimes, naturally, but with a twist. In the pilot, Greenstein is murdered but returns as a ghost, guiding Tubbs through cases, which is not so easy because Tubbs is a kind of idiot man-child, the result of drug use and blows to the head—not entirely disabled, but close.

"I can solve the case," he would say, "but I'm going to need some help!"

David Straiton, a well-regarded director of *House* and other shows, was to executive produce. We still think it would be an enormous hit.

In 2013, I was asked to develop an American version of Ukraine's number-one television drama.

No, seriously, I was.

The original title of the show was *Sky Court*, though I believe it could also have been translated as *Heavenly Chambers, Judge in Heaven,* or *Death Bench.* Its premise was that when you die, you are judged based on the very last act you committed, good or bad, large or small, meaningful or absurd. Good people are sent to a place that looks like Paris but without the French. The bad go to the Ukraine's version of Arizona.

The lawyers are also dead. They form a kind of Eternal Bar Association. Defense lawyers and prosecutors fight over the souls of the newly deceased. But the cases are really just a thin excuse to debate the existential meaning of humankind's fate in a world devoid of God.

I thought it was the greatest idea I ever heard.

But we shall never know if would be a hit. Because even after we cut out the existential debates and replaced the obese, slovenly Crimean defense lawyer with a beautiful young woman, none of the networks we pitched the show to wanted anything to do with it.

"We tried a dead lawyer show with John Stamos last season. It never got on the schedule."

This was a better idea for a show, I said.

"Sure, but you don't have John Stamos."

Another network complained that it sounded too much like *Defending Your Life*, the great Albert Brooks and Meryl Streep movie.

I tried to distinguish our Russian show from Brooks's movie, but the executive held up his hands to stop me.

"Look, I'll be honest with you," he said, which is never a good sign. "I never saw *Defending Your Life*."

He didn't know anything about it except that what we were pitching sounded too much like it.

"Dead lawyer shows don't work. Not even with John Stamos."

As of this writing, the original series remains on the air in Russia.

* * * * *

Dwelling on failure is no fun. But to ignore failure or the lessons it can teach is always a mistake.

Lawyers do it to their detriment.

Show business won't let you do it at all.

* * * * *

The phone rang in my office. The studio executive on the other end of the line didn't bother to say hello.

"What are you going to do next?"

That's how I found out the first television show I created was canceled.[2] In ten minutes, the studio executive said, I would get the official call from the network executive.

"Act surprised," the studio executive said.

Not a problem. I'm still shocked. It was a good show. People liked it. Just not enough of them watched it.

I was getting ready to meet with the production crew, preparing our

---

2. *Just Legal*, WB, 2005–2006.

next episode. Meanwhile, on stage, the crew and actors were filming the current episode. I had spent over a year working on the show, often seven days a week, 12-to-14-hour days, thinking and worrying about it every waking moment, then dreaming about it when I fell asleep.

Writing a book or a movie is like running a marathon. Take as long as you want but at some point it's going to end. Being the showrunner on a television series is like running until you die. Or are killed.[3]

The show that could not fail had done just that. My partner on it was Jerry Bruckheimer, titan of the entertainment industry, behind countless movie and television hits.

Nobody was going to blame him for this.

* * * * *

The show starred Judd Apatow favorite Jay Baruchel. Canada's version of a young Dustin Hoffman, he was funny, quirky, and brilliant as a young attorney just starting his career.

Don Johnson played his drunken, beaten-down attorney and mentor. The former star of iconic television series (*Miami Vice* and *Nash Bridges* remain worldwide hits), he could not fail to attract a sizeable audience. We believed.

The most interesting man in the world, certainly the most charismatic and intelligent ever to come out of Flat Creek, Missouri, Johnson has lived and loved a large life, one that would kill most men. It had only aged him like fine wine.

"Played golf with Bill Clinton the other day," he told me.

"What'd you talk about?" I asked.

"What do you think?" Johnson laughed: a cigarette-smoky, bourbon-soaked rumble. He made you feel giddy and dirty at the same time.

This was the Great Johnson's gift.

---

3. I am not the first person to draw this analogy. The first time I heard it, it was attributed to David Mamet, author, playwright, screenwriter, and, at the time, executive producer and show runner for a television series, *The Unit*. They canceled Mamet too.

* * * * *

Ten minutes later, as promised, the phone rang again. It was the network executive. The bad news was we were canceled. The good news was we could finish the episode we were shooting.

"I didn't say it was *great* news," he chuckled. I'd heard that kind of chuckle before. It was the chuckle you hear at the craps table from the stickman as he racks in your chips and passes the dice to a new shooter.

Having given birth to a show, the creator and showrunner gets to announce its death.

It's part of the job. I gathered the cast and production crew on the set, thanked them for all their hard work, and offered to represent them at reduced rates should they ever face federal criminal charges.

Then I got drunk.

* * * * *

A week later happened to be the Jewish High Holidays. On Yom Kippur, the holiest day of the year, I was standing with my wife and kids as the sacred Torah passed before us.

"Sorry about your show," one of the rabbis whispered. "I thought the numbers were getting better."

Michael Milken, former junk-bond king, happened to be in our row. He nodded sympathetically.

My mother called me later that night, having observed the holidays with my brother's family at his temple.

"Oh, I wish you could have heard the rabbi's sermon," she said. "It was wonderful. It made me think about you. It was all about failure . . ."

* * * * *

Storytelling failure in show business is disappointing.

Storytelling in law, however, is tragic.

Bad facts don't make bad law. The legislature makes bad law. When the law fails to do justice, it is usually because of their bad writing.

Bad editing by others only makes it worse.

* * * * *

Jordan Davis, age 17, was shot to death in a Florida gas station convenience store parking lot. The killer was Michael Dunn. His son had been married earlier in the day.

When the car with Davis and three other teens started playing loud music, Dunn testified that he very politely asked them to turn down their loud music. The music was hurting Dunn's ears.

One thing led to another. Dunn believed he saw a shotgun. Fearing for his life, he fired ten shots into the van, then went home to bed.

At trial, Dunn was convicted of attempting to kill the three unharmed teens. They were the ones he shot at but missed. But the jury could not decide if he murdered the fourth teen, Davis, the one Dunn shot and killed.

When a verdict only makes sense to lawyers, something usually went wrong in the storytelling.

On MSNBC, former US Attorney Kendall Coffey tried to explain Florida's "stand your ground" law, the script as written by the Florida legislature, the one the lawyers had to work from and the jury had to make sense of. The law said that if Dunn felt his life was in danger, he had the right to stay and fight.

Had he prevailed in a pretrial immunity hearing on the matter, proving that he felt his life was in danger, his case would never have even gone to trial.

Dunn never asked for such a hearing. He didn't have to. Florida's jury instructions on self-defense reflect the stand-your-ground law and allow the defendant all its benefits. The law says that a defendant fearing for his or her life does not have a duty to retreat. Under Florida law, the burden was on the prosecution to prove Dunn did not have a reasonable fear for his life.

Don't blame the jury. The fact that the Florida legislature wrote a bad script wasn't their fault.

* * * * *

Given the story elements—the characters, the setting, the action—it was inevitable that the case would be interpreted in terms of race. Dunn was white. The teens were African Americans. Florida had recently put on the George Zimmerman trial—another white-on-African American murder case—and the result had been outright acquittal.

Lest anyone miss the point, two days after the verdict, CNN's Andrew Cuomo interviewed Zimmerman and asked him if he regretted killing the teenage Trayvon Martin.

Zimmerman stammered, said that he had answered that question before. Then he sat in agonizing silence before saying he had nothing new to say.

Don't blame the media for telling the story. That is their job. They did it to attract attention, to educate, to elucidate, and to do the noble work of informing the public, but most of all, to sell advertisements and make money.

* * * * *

My admiration for a free press is matched only by my understanding that the term itself is an oxymoron.

One morning, during an all-too-rare appearance in class, I heard my constitutional law professor Robert Cole give a lecture on the value of a free press as the bedrock of democracy. Stirring stuff. Made me proud to be a journalist.

Later that day at the newspaper, I was gathering information on the annual take of partners at one of San Francisco's oldest, most respected law firms.

Steve Brill, publisher of *The American Lawyer*, owned our paper, too. Getting numbers for his magazine's Am Law 100 was an annual obligation.

The list was still new then, an innovation, a ranking of law firms based on profits, billable hours, and lawyer satisfaction.

Senior lawyers hated it. Brill was publishing numbers the partners had long kept secret. Nowadays, the list and the Internet provide a steady flow of such information, along with the right to rant about it. Back then, the cat was still in the bag and managing partners were desperate to keep it there.

"This is not a business!" the managing partner raged at me that day. "This is a profession!"

A distinguished graduate of Stanford Law School, this éminence grise of the Northern California bar proceeded to call Brill a string of names that ended with "whore."

"That's a profession too," I said.

He hung up on me.

For five minutes I was the wit of the newsroom.

Then the circulation department called.

"What the hell did you do?"

The law firm managing partner had called to cancel the firm's subscriptions, along with those of every member of the firm—a serious hit for such a small paper.

Law school teaches you that a free press is a wonderful thing. Life teaches you it isn't free.

* * * * *

The district attorney said race was not a factor in the case or she would have charged Dunn with a hate crime.

She had her reasons for not doing so. No doubt they involved the tried-and-true desire of any lawyer shouldering the burden of proof—she wanted to keep things simple.

Race, however, is never simple. It is the messiest of issues. It is emotional; it stirs up passions, making it an enemy of reason. It divides people, when what the DA needs is unanimity.

But just because a story element is hard to handle doesn't always mean you can ignore it entirely, especially when that element is staring you and everyone else squarely in the face.

As will be discussed later, the law depends on a number of fictions and outright lies, but when these reach the point of absurdity, the stories they are based on lose credibility.

Bad editing never makes a bad script better. At best, the DA's decision to pretend race was not a story element made the prosecution look naive. At worst, it made them look disingenuous, like politicians trying not to offend someone; like flat-out liars. This was no way to establish ethos. The prosecution team was going in with one leg of the triangle cut off.

And there were other consequences.

By not admitting race was an issue, the prosecution denied itself access to facts that could have built a rational story.

The judge excluded evidence that might have gone to show Dunn's racial animus toward African Americans, thereby preventing the jury from getting a complete narrative of events and hearing the full story of what happened that night.

The defense lawyer was more than happy to agree race had nothing to do with it. Editing out race as a story element helped his case. It allowed him to argue that Dunn would have acted the same way regardless of race.

Of course, the defense lawyer knew it wasn't true. How do we know? Because of Richard Sherman, Seattle Seahawk cornerback.

* * * * *

During the trial, Sherman's postgame outburst after his team won a play-off game became a bigger story than the Super Bowl.

Critics called Sherman a thug. Sherman took exception, identifying thug as a racist term, the modern, more polite version of calling someone a "nigger."

Dunn's legal team felt the exact same way. They had long and adamantly denied reports that Dunn used the term "thug" when referring to Davis, his friends, or their music.

They did so because they agreed with Sherman. "Thug" is a racist term when applied to young African Americans. They denied Dunn ever used the term because if he had, he would have sounded exactly like the racist he very well may have been.

* * * * *

Don't blame the defense lawyer for the verdict. You can't blame a man for shooting fish in a barrel. He did his job. Blessed with a helpfully narrow set of story elements, he told a story that succeeded in persuading at least one of the jurors that Dunn did not commit murder.

* * * * *

US Supreme Court Justice Robert Jackson famously said that the prosecutor wins when justice is done, regardless of the verdict.

Justice was not done in the Davis case. The DA took a bad script, edited it badly, and told a bad story. It confused rather than persuaded.

Talk about a bad winner, Dunn was reportedly disappointed that he was convicted of anything. A greater number of people were disappointed that he wasn't convicted of everything.

In an effort to make up for her failings, the DA immediately said she plans to retry Dunn on the first-degree murder count. She said it was a matter of principle.

Lawyers always say that when no practical reason is available. Dunn was in his late 40s when he was convicted of three counts that carry a range of 20 to 60 years in prison. In practical terms, Dunn's convictions ensure a life sentence.

The DA wasn't doing anything to increase her credibility, though some in the press hinted that it might help her with African American voters at election time.

* * * * *

A final word about editing—it never ends.

"The Supreme Court has been quietly revising its decisions years after they were issued, altering the law of the land without public notice," *New York Times* recently reported.[4]

So much for the finality of judgment; according to Adam Liptak's article, the Justices make a practice of going back and fixing mistakes, changing language, and rewriting themselves after their opinions are handed down.

In fact, "the court's secretive editing process" has led to confusion, if not consternation. Though "widening public access to online versions of the court's decisions . . . has made the longstanding problem more pronounced."[5]

Lawyers in the lower courts know all about judicial editorial shenanigans. A judge I appeared before in trial once referred to my witnesses in an alien smuggling case as "wetbacks." The trial transcript, however, was scrubbed of the offensive term.

Whether such editing is ethical or not is a question for others. As a writer, at least, I can understand the impulse.

I once stood in a checkout line in Century City behind Neil Simon and felt the need to give him the good news:

"I just got a job as a television writer."

"I'm sorry to hear that," he said. "It will never be right."

Then he walked away.

---

4. Adam Liptak, "Final Word on U.S. Law Isn't: Supreme Court Keeps Editing," *New York Times*, May 24, 2014.

5. Ibid.

NINE

The Performance

Scott Turow's *Presumed Innocent* is a great novel.

It would also serve as a terrific criminal procedure or legal ethics exam. A prosecutor has an affair with a colleague; his investigator destroys evidence, then conceals all he knows; his supervisor is unethical. Spot the legal and ethical issues and try to figure out how it can possibly end well for the prosecutor (for those who never read the book, it does and it doesn't).

Turow's book spent 45 weeks on *The New York Times* bestseller list. Later adapted into a film starring Harrison Ford, it "blazed a trail for other writer-lawyers like John Grisham and Richard North Patterson."[1]

In a thoughtful essay on the book, poet and writer Michael Bourne called *Presumed Innocent* "a turning point in the decades-long process that saw highbrow literature and middlebrow entertainment, once sworn enemies, merge into the hybrid literary world we live in today, in which literary writers routinely use murder mysteries to propel their novels and genre authors routinely grant their characters elaborate inner struggles to add literary heft to their plots."

It isn't just a great book, Bourne asserts; it is an important one that should be on college syllabi: a "wildly innovative work of fiction that upends several genres at once while simultaneously creating an entirely new subgenre of its own."[2]

---

1. Michael Bourne, "The Lasting Influence of Scott Turow's 'Presumed Innocent,'" *Los Angeles Review of Books*, December 4, 2013.
2. Ibid.

I love Turow's book. But I will never forgive him for giving me bad advice. It's right there in the beginning of the book, one of the more famous passages of any law story:

Point at the defendant when you talk about him, because if you can't point at him, then how can you expect the jury to convict him?

* * * * *

My first trial was prosecuting a defendant whose last name was Outlaw. Ron Silver would not have approved—too on the nose.

Outlaw threw a chunk of concrete through a police squad car window, then tried to run away. Outlaw was fat, very fat; almost as big around as he was tall; he did not get far before the police caught him. The charge was assault with intent to kill.

He wanted to plead guilty a misdemeanor. I wanted to let him plead guilty to a misdemeanor. My bosses demanded a felony.

Outlaw was also looking at an attempted murder charge in another case. He pointed a gun at a man and pulled the trigger. The gun jammed. Again, Outlaw tried to outrun the police. He may not have been fast, but he was confident.

The gun could not be fired. It was jammed. His defense lawyer, the redoubtable Abe Blitzstein, was set to put Outlaw on the stand to say he *knew* the gun would not fire and therefore lacked the specific intent to kill anyone.

The senior prosecutor in *that* case wanted to have a prior conviction to keep Outlaw off the stand in his attempted murder trial. Thus, I had to go to trial.

During my opening statement, I pointed at Outlaw.

"That's rude," an elderly woman juror barked at me from the box. "Don't you know not to point at people?"

I do now.

It was not a good start to my career.

* * * * *

During voir dire in another trial, when the judge asked if she knew any-one in the case, another elderly woman juror pointed a finger at me:

"I know Mr. Shapiro and he knows *me*."

I had never seen the woman before in my life.

She lived in an apartment building in Anacostia with roaches, broken lights, and poor ventilation.

"Mr. Shapiro won't fix any of it," she said. "But he still raises the rent."

She believed I was her landlord.

"There are lots of slumlords named Shapiro," the judge said. "This prosecutor isn't one of them."

I did not call the Anti-Defamation League.

The woman did not seem wholly convinced, either. But the judge kept her on the panel and then wouldn't let me use a strike to remove her. He felt it would be unfair.

Thick skin and a poker face are essential to the storyteller.

* * * * *

In *The Articulate Advocate, New Techniques of Persuasion for Trial Law-yers*, Brian K. Johnson and Marsha Hunter offer the lawyer performer an in-depth analysis of the other physical attributes they believe you will need to be a successful lawyer storyteller.[3]

There are chapters such as "Controlling Your Lower Body," "The Face," "Tone as a Tactical Choice," "The Questioning Curl," and "What Do You Do With Your Hands When You Are Not Gesturing?" There are checklists for spine alignment and vocal tone, and "Mantras of Self-Instruction."[4]

---

3. Brian K. Johnson and Marsha Hunter, *The Articulate Advocate, New Techniques of Persuasion for Trial Lawyers* (Phoenix: Crown King Books, 2013)..
4. Ibid.

"Your face should look at ease and comfortable with no visible tension, a look best described as neutral alert," they write. "To achieve neutral alert, part your lips slightly—no more than a quarter of an inch—and breathe through both your mouth and nose. When your lips are slightly parted, they cannot tense, scowl or tuck."[5]

I tried. I drooled. I stopped.

There are easier and more enjoyable ways to learn how to become a better storyteller.

Watch good performers do it.

* * * * *

The reason why Michael Badalucco is successful is because he is serious about preparation. Each of his scripts for *The Practice* and other shows I cast him in were as marked up as a first-year law student's casebook.

Badalucco parsed every word, highlighting important ones, jotting notes from a dictionary and thesaurus to understand the various meanings of the words in the script. The capitalizations and characterizations are all his.

In the closing argument Badalucco presented to the ABTL, the defense lawyer is defending a man charged with soliciting an undercover police officer posing as a prostitute in a hotel bar. It was a perfect example of storytelling built with ethos, logos, and pathos. Insofar as the conference was held in a hotel with several bars, it also seemed timely. But it was Badalucco's performance that made it work.

Badalucco's character begins his closing argument by building ethos, conceding that it's appropriate for the police to prosecute men who solicit prostitutes.

In the margin of Badalucco's original script next to these lines of dialogue, the actor wrote a note to himself: "It's ok. It's acceptable."

---

5. Ibid., 48.

The lawyer concedes his client could have been stronger and resisted the solicitation. "But he wasn't," Badalucco's lawyer says. "He was weak."

The closing argument next moves to logos, using the facts to make a reasonable, logical argument. While it is one thing to stop someone from committing the crime they intended, "it's something else to seek a person out who's sitting at a hotel minding his own business." The policewoman pretended to be a secretary and "hinted that sex is in the offing."

This is entrapment, Badalucco's character says: "That's defined as when a person is lured into the commission of a crime that he has no predisposition to commit. And that's this case."

Next to the word "entrapment," Badalucco wrote the words "HE WASN'T LOOKING FOR A HOOKER," along with the words "deceive/trick."

Based on the evidence established at trial, the lawyer argues that the defendant had no criminal record and was not an appropriate target for law enforcement's limited time and resources.

"Big picture . . . is this what we want the police to be doing? Staking out law-abiding people, baiting them into committing crimes then busting them?"

Next to these words, Badalucco wrote: "IT'S DESPICABLE."

Next to the word "baiting," Badalucco wrote: "Teasing them in hotel bars." Next to "big picture," he wrote in the largest hand of all: "ARE THEY *SERVING* US OR ARE THEY *PROTECTING* US?"

At the bottom of the script, Badalucco wrote himself a reminder: "REGARD THEIR ACTIONS WITH CONTEMPT/DISDAIN = REJECT AS *UNWORTHY.*"

Having established ethos and logos, Kelley moved to pathos. Badalucco's character starts with sarcasm, always a dangerous technique, but valuable when earned.

"Thank God we have the police to go out and find the weak and lure them into committing crimes. Come on," the character says. "The police are supposed to protect us. Not trap us."

The closing ends with a rhetorical question: "Is this the government we want?" Badalucco circled the word "we" and underlined the last line. Underneath it he wrote: "TELL *THEM* IT IS WRONG."

The whole thing took less than two minutes of screen time, not even a single page of written dialogue, single-spaced. Yet it managed to do everything a closing argument can and should do.

* * * * *

Badalucco is a classically trained actor. That he became such a great lawyer on television was a testament to his talent, training, and to the material he was given to play.

Real lawyers don't get Kelley to write their closing arguments or get Badalucco to give them. But we can learn to do a better job of it by studying Kelley's writing and Badalucco's performance.

And nothing says we have to limit ourselves.

There are other types of storytellers who have just as much, if not more, to teach lawyers about how to perform stories well.

* * * * *

In a 2012 TED talk about what stories are, former Pixar Animation director Andrew Stanton began his speech with a Lenny Bruce joke.

He modified it slightly, delivering it in a Scottish dialect (presumably because he did a good one). But the punch line stayed the same. As in the original, Stanton's version ended with the narrator complaining that despite all his other achievements, people only think of him as the man who had sex with a goat.

Animators like animals—think of Walt Disney—but Stanton was not suggesting they want to mate with them. He wanted to get people's attention. He got it. His point was that jokes are stories, and thus, a good place to begin to understand how stories work.

Jokes and stories do have much in common, and there is much the lawyer storyteller can learn from jokes and those who deliver them. Each has a beginning, middle, and end. They are not mere factual recitations of events. They are constructs. They are designed. They are not spontaneous. Thus, they are artificial, unnatural, and manipulative. Not that there is anything wrong with that. It just has to be acknowledged. They may be short, self-contained, stand-alone narratives or mini-stories that are part of a larger overall narrative. They can be written, oral, or even silent. But they must have a reason for being.

Lawyers should never tell jokes. Like lies, jokes have no place in the legal profession. William Shatner's attorney Denny Crane *was* a joke. But he almost never discredited the role by telling one.

Furthermore, "lawyer jokes" are never funny, especially when told by a lawyer. Self-hating acknowledgement that others misunderstand or dislike you is revealing, maybe, but never funny. But that doesn't mean we can't all learn something from comics.

* * * * *

The dressing room of the Improv Comedy Club in Brea, California, feels like an appellate court's attorney lounge before oral argument.

Three professionals in a small room, two of them sitting on a sagging couch, their knees almost touching, the third man standing with his back pressed against the opposite wall, all of them lost in thought, thinking about what they are going to say, going over their notes.

The thin dressing room door opens directly into the main room. It does nothing to block out the sound of the sold-out crowd. The comics are too engrossed in preparing for the performance to care. The hideous wrought-iron sunburst clock on the wall is missing some rays. Show time is in six minutes.

* * * * *

Each comic in this dressing room represents a separate phase in a storytelling career. They parallel a lawyer's journey.

The one standing against the wall is the youngest; he's at the associate stage. Tonight he is the emcee, an entry-level position. He is itching to tell stories but doesn't really know how and isn't finding it easy to learn. This evening his main responsibility is to introduce the other comics and close the show with as little damage as possible.

In between, he is allowed to tell the best stories he can, to get the most laughs possible, to learn how to do the job better.

By day he works as a physical therapist. At night he hustles for stage time. He is a rookie with almost too much intensity. He holds a stack of note cards, four or five inches thick, covered front to back with potential material. Some are full stories; others are just pieces of stories. There are hours of material in the stack. Tonight he will get to use less than ten minutes of it.

He flips through the stack of cards with the intensity of a lawyer going through his notes, knowing he won't have time to do more than touch upon his best points.

* * * * *

The younger of the two men on the couch is the opening act. He is in his late 30s, a veteran of the circuit, a thoroughly confident and competent professional.

He is at an interesting place in his career, on the cusp of either becoming a big star or never going any higher. Like a lawyer who has been doing it for some time, the opening act has proven he knows his business and has reached a level of success in it. He is good at what he does. The question is will he get better.

Most lawyers get to this point. To get better requires a lot of work, being ruthless about the quality of your work while coming up with new material and better ways to deliver it.

Having traveled a hard road already, the opening act can see that the road ahead only gets tougher. He also knows it is the only route to greater things. But it comes with risk. New material and deliveries almost always bomb, at least at first. After spending years coming up with a good thing, changing it risks losing the audience, upsetting the paying customers, angering the booking agents, and enraging the club managers. Nobody wants to lose a paycheck.

The siren song of the easy road is seductive for stand-ups and lawyers. Stay on it, keep doing the same thing the same way, using the same material, not getting better but not getting worse, and the reward is stability and safety. It isn't dangerous to anything except ambition.

The emcee, whose greatest ambition at the moment is to *be* the opening act, would give anything for the *chance* to get on the easy road.

* * * * *

The headliner, inevitably, by definition, chose the harder road. And having chosen it, he can never quit it. The star of films and television, a successful author, now in his 50s, he doesn't do stand-up for the money. Anything else he could do would pay him exponentially more.

Nor does he do it for the fame. He has had his fill of that. If that was ever the goal, it isn't the goal now. Like a rich dessert, a little bit of fame goes a long way, and too much is a very bad thing.

He is genuinely shy off stage, quiet, known to walk around the block and down flights of stairs to avoid crowded lobbies and elevators. He is not necessarily fearful of the crowd. He is cautious. He knows how quickly things can turn bad on a Saturday night when people have been drinking. Yet he drives two hours from his home to be in front of these strangers.

Like the managing partner of a firm or the rainmaker, headliners are drawn to center stage and the biggest stages possible. They don't just like to be there. They need to be there.

The emcee cannot really imagine in his wildest dreams ever becoming the headliner. The opening act can imagine it, can almost taste it, in fact. Whether he will take the hard road to get it—knowing the risks—remains an open question.

* * * * *

The clock strikes eight and the energy in the room spikes. There is a knock on the door. It's time. It feels exactly like the dressing room of the Fabulous Forum, back when I used to cover fights as a contributing editor for *The Ring* magazine. These are serious men, specialists, aware that things could go horribly wrong.

* * * * *

Like lawyers, stand-ups make their living by storytelling. It takes commitment to do it well, hours of practice to make it seem natural. It often requires a lot of travel, working with tough characters, and business sense to collect the fee up front whenever you can.

The emcee's stories are observational, based on his life, about working at a fast-food chain. ("The woman asked to see the chef. I said, 'Ma'am, it's a fast-food restaurant, we don't *have* a chef.'")

He gets some laughs, but the material is thin and he doesn't get the most out of it. He swallows the last line of a story, interrupts the laughs too soon, makes bad choices, dropping profanity for its own sake, joking about the older people in the crowd, turning what could be strengths into negatives. He handles the audience but does not move them. In short, he is exactly where he should be, based on his experience. He's learning.

* * * * *

Five minutes after he starts, the emcee passes the stage to the opening act who takes over like a dad taking back the wheel to the family car. The opening act is African American. The vast majority of the crowd is not. He addresses it immediately in his deliberate, Southern accent:

"I am feeling very black at the moment."

The room laughs. For the next 15 minutes it doesn't stop. The only interruptions are for ovations and the opening act's wise choice to take a sip of water, not because he is thirsty, but to give them a chance to catch their breath.

* * * * *

Now it's the headliner's turn.

Spare a moment to appreciate his guts. To go out there *after* another comic has already done it, to be confident enough to know you can meet, match and beat what the other man has done, requires more confidence than most people have.

The set is a model of thoughtful plotting and pace. It starts off slowly. This is not a sprint. It is a 55 minute race; endurance is required from both the performer and the audience. The laughs begin to come in waves, small, then building, steadily.

The stories are each a few minutes long. They involve family, spouses and children. They are tied together but not so obviously that you notice the stitching.

The narrative is about the headliner's life now, the myth of what he thinks *should* be versus what it actually *is*. His delivery is the calmest and most comfortable of the evening. The crowd relaxes into the set, safe in the knowledge that however the story starts, it will go someplace worthwhile. The waves of laughter get bigger and come closer together.

At approximately 50 minutes, the headliner lets them know this will be the last story. He's aware of time and aware that *they* are aware of time.

He ends his set with a story about a goat.

It is neither the old Lenny Bruce joke nor the revised TED talk goat joke, told to shock people in order to get their attention. This goat story is the culmination of the evening's narrative, the payoff of the previous 50 minutes. It brings together all the stories about marriage, kids, hope versus reality; everything that came before it was designed to lead to this ending.

The laughter it elicits is the deepest and richest of the night. It was earned. Built with credibility by a master storyteller, consisting of logical parts that fit together, the story also delivered a surprising emotional wallop.

* * * * *

Minutes after the headliner takes his last bows and the emcee tells everyone to drive home safely, they are back in the dressing room in the same positions as before—two on the couch, the emcee at the wall. They are going over their notes again, getting ready for the second show.

They edit based on the earlier show's reaction. The emcee replaces the fast-food story with another one about getting older. It isn't funnier, necessarily, but it wins more of the audience's affection.

The opening act repeats a story about a supermarket. It got a big laugh during the first show but only triggers a small response in the second show.

Later, it will be dissected, the consensus being that by changing the order of the story elements, the opening act ruined the story's timing and pacing.

The headliner changes out sections, varies the pace, uses slightly different phrasing for a story about his child and school. But the goat story is the closer. And once again, it works like a charm.

To be funny on demand is no easy trick. Lawyers use storytelling to persuade others on matters of life and death, justice and injustice; the stakes could not be higher.

At least they don't have to be funny.

* * * * *

Comic Lives: Inside the World of American Stand-Up Comedy is a great book on the craft of storytelling. Lawyers could learn much from it.[6]

After months watching sets and interviewing working comics—Jerry Seinfeld, George Carlin, Jay Leno, Carol Leifer, and Alan King—the author broke down how they did their job, developed their material and style, and continuously honed their craft. Now a part of the required reading list for anyone interested in performing stand-up, the book is

---

6. Even if the author is my wife, Betsy Borns-Shapiro (the "Shapiro" is silent).

also an interesting historical document, written at the height of the popularity of comedy clubs.

Like the lawyer, the comic lives or dies on the basis of "perfectly sculpted layers of words, chosen, discarded, and re-chosen night after night, according to the whims of the paying jury, until they have been polished to the final sentence, phrase and syllable."[7]

Great lawyers bring the same seriousness of purpose to the task, the same commitment to preparation and detail.

The fundamental relationship between the storyteller and the audience is the same for lawyers and comics. The storyteller is in charge; the one who holds the mic controls the situation. But it isn't a one-sided conversation. For it to work well, it can't be. The stand-up, like the lawyer, has to be attuned to who they are speaking to and must be able to judge the quality and strength of their responses and their understanding of the information being conveyed.

The book quotes George Carlin who said that unlike a "poet, painter, composer, symphony musician, even rock musicians," a comedian presents his story as he makes it, not as a finished product. "The appreciator of the art gets to vote all the way through, about every five seconds, on whether the work of art is going the way they'd like. And if it isn't, the comic gets the message immediately and can change it." The only person who comes close to that, Carlin said, "is a jazz soloist who has the ability to change what he's doing."[8]

* * * * *

To put it another way, listening is about getting information. This information includes noticing whether the person you are talking to is listening and cares about what you are saying.

---

7. Betsy Borns, *Comic Lives: Inside the World of American Stand-Up Comedy* (New York: Simon & Schuster, Inc., 1987), 235.
8. Ibid., 284.

The lawyer who can't tell he or she is boring the audience shouldn't be practicing any type of law that involves engagement with another human being.

I am afraid I have no idea what type of law that would be.

* * * * *

Finally, let us conclude with some technical considerations that may strike you as shallow. Again, if shallowness offends you, you should skip the next few pages.

* * * * *

Out of the 150 or so crew people who work on a one-hour television drama, more than two-thirds work on making sure the actors look good.

The wardrobe department dresses them. Make-up and hair departments groom them. The largest group—the lighting department, including grips, electricians, gaffers, and the director of photography—make sure they are lit to optimum attractiveness.

Lawyers often complain that television law shows are not realistic. Cases happen too fast, we get the law wrong, a judge would never say that or rule a particular way.

Nobody ever complains that the lawyers look too beautiful, dress too well, or that the lighting is too flattering. Lawyers are not that observant. But they should learn to be.

* * * * *

During Monday morning arraignment in DC Superior Court, the courtroom was full of people. You didn't need a program to tell who the players were.

The men under the age of 25 were all charged with low-level drug offenses. The men over 25 were there for a violent crime or property offense. Any man in the drug trade over the age of 25 was either dead, in prison already, or across the street in federal court charged with more serious crimes.

The younger, better-dressed men and women who were charged with prostitution were arrested on 14th Street. The further you moved away from 14th Street, the more likely the accused was older or more obviously addicted to crack.

There was never any problem picking out the drug dealers' lawyers. They dressed the part—earrings, ponytails, shiny suits and dirty shoes; low-cut blouses, too-high heels, and tight skirts. If they were on a show, the producers would fire the wardrobe department for being too obvious.

No lawyer should dress in a way that makes his or her client look like the kind of person who would hire a drug lawyer.

Appearance can be deceiving. Which is all the more reason to make sure one's appearance does not deceive others into assuming the worst about you or your client.

* * * * *

Hair, make-up, and wardrobe are not taught in law school. Nor should they be, no matter useful the lessons would be.

That said, the richest and most expensive lawyers use the same stylists as a number of Hollywood actors and executives. They won't admit it, but they do.

* * * * *

As we have seen, lawyers can be miscast as storytellers, but there are things they can do about it.

The bigger challenge is what to do when other characters—the clients, the witnesses—are miscast in their roles.

And unlike experts, they cannot be recast.

* * * * *

People say there are too many lawyers. In Hollywood, they say there are too many actors. The actual number is hard to know. The Department of Labor does not keep the statistic. The actor unions don't provide specific information. The conservative estimate is 100,000 or so.

The vast majority of these actors are unemployed, chronically underemployed, or dead, meaning that they are not working but, thanks to digitalization, available.

Yet the moment you write a script, none of them are right for the part.

Week after week directors, producers, and writers hold casting sessions, auditioning hundreds of actors.

The sessions are inevitably held in windowless offices with the feel of a jury room. The lighting is poor, the air stale, the carpet drab, the furniture chipped, and the chairs mismatched, often at least one of them broken and dangerous. Hour after hour, actors come in, none of whom are right for the part.

"Let's cast the next guy who comes in who can act."

This usually does not speed the process along.

* * * * *

In law, most of the players cast themselves. You must win with what you have. You cannot write their dialogue. Their truth is your truth. But there is much you can control.

You are scriptwriter, editor, and executive producer as well as director. You decide whether to make them part of the story and how they will be used to tell it.

You must work with them. Not rehearse them; *work* with them so they understand the legal process, what they can expect, and what is expected of them.

It would be incompetence not to work with them. The whole purpose of hiring you was to tell your client's story in the most effective way possible. It means working with the characters to make sure they understand that this is—in Goffman's words—a presentation. And each of them has a role to play in presenting the story.

* * * * *

The first direction to give any of the characters in this story is obvious.

"No matter what happens, always tell the truth." Be precise in your language.

Next, let them know, in your first meeting, that you are not rehearsing with them. Rehearsals are for actors. They are not actors. You are never going to hand them the script you have written and edited. You would be a terrible storyteller if you risked letting your worst critic—the other lawyer—get a copy.

You have to dress them and make them look presentable. Oliver North was no longer on active duty when he testified before Congress in the Contra-gate scandal, but his lawyers made sure he was wearing a Marine uniform.

I'm not suggesting costumes. Clean clothes, as nice as the client can manage, appropriate for court, though that is not always easy to describe in this benighted age of style.

* * * * *

A final word on presentation:

When I was eight, my father talked to me about sex. When he was done, he asked if I had any questions. I asked him what sex felt like. He hadn't mentioned it.

He stared at me, disappointed.

"It doesn't make you nauseous."

Storytelling is one of the universal human activities and it serves many important and useful purposes.

It should not make you or the audience nauseous.

PART FOUR

The Practice

TEN

Lies That Tell the Truth

"I used to think I was getting at the truth in court, but I see now that the truth is greater than the sum of the facts," Arthur Train wrote. "Besides, you can't get the truth from a witness. The rules of evidence don't permit it."[1]

Stories are never the whole, unvarnished, unadulterated truth. They wouldn't be stories if they were. Storytelling is not the complete transcript of events.

"There is an accuracy that defeats itself by the overemphasis of details," Justice Cardozo wrote. "I often say that one must permit oneself, and that quite advisedly and deliberately, a certain margin of misstatement . . . The picture cannot be painted if the significant and insignificant are given equal prominence. One must know how to omit."

Cardozo was talking about writing style, suggesting that lawyers and judges adhere to basic rules of storytelling in their work. To be effective, they should plot and pace their story, focus on what is important, and edit out what is not.

But he was also acknowledging that the law itself "never can represent the truth in the usual conception of the term, but only a special kind of truth, which might be called the 'legal truth.'"[2]

"Legal truth," like "legal ethics," is an oxymoron that often reveals deep truths about the law itself.

---

1. Arthur Train, *Yankee Lawyer: The Autobiography of Ephraim Tutt* (New York: Amereon House, 1943), 374.
2. Ibid.

To study law stories is to discover just how much of the actual law is an agreed-upon legal fiction, if not an outright lie. Some of these lies are repeated so often that the storytellers themselves forget that they are lies at all.

* * * * *

Tom Connolly is a big, broad-shouldered, redheaded Irish American from Nebraska. He has no patience for lies.

That is why he agreed to defend Dr. Steven Hatfill, wrongly accused of murdering people by mailing anthrax-laced letters. He was innocent. It was a lie to suggest otherwise. Repeating the lie over and over again did not make it less of a lie.

"When the two most powerful institutions in the United States—the federal government and the press—decide to tell flat-out lies about your client, it's bad," Connolly told me over the telephone in March of 2014.

When they did it to Hatfill, Connolly decided to make them pay for it.

* * * * *

Dr. Hatfill had experience researching and developing biological weapons for the United States government. He possessed the unusual sets of skills and know-how to turn anthrax into a weapon.

Hatfill wasn't the only one with this background or expertise. But he was an odd duck and a handy candidate to blame. The government couldn't prove he did it. They couldn't even gin up enough evidence to arrest him, let alone indict him. So they called him "a person of interest" instead.

The term makes Connolly want to put his fist through a door.

There is no such thing in law as a person of interest. No legislative body ever created it. No court ever recognized it. It is the figment of a sick imagination, a piece of government double-speak worthy of George Orwell. You might as well call someone a witch. It is not, has never been, and can never be, a legitimate legal distinction.

It's bad business when the federal government denounces a citizen without due process. It's the kind of thing totalitarian governments do.

It is also the worst kind of storytelling, an abomination of the rhetorical triangle. It is a lie built on misuse of government authority, weak logic, and public fear. If labeling someone a person of interest isn't the most egregious example of an unfair and unjust governmental act, then nothing is unfair and unjust.

* * * * *

Tom Connolly's father, Justice William M. Connolly, still serves on the Nebraska State Supreme Court. Both men take acts of injustice personally.

Nebraska police once grabbed Justice Connolly because they thought he looked like Charlie Starkweather, the serial killer, then on the lam. Justice Connolly didn't particularly like getting arrested for something he didn't do.

When Tom was a boy, his father was the county attorney. He would take Tom to crime scenes and pull him out of school to watch closing arguments.

Born and bred to try cases, Tom is now arguably, pound for pound, the best trial lawyer of his generation, which is saying something. Tom is not a small man. A former college football player, he looks a like the Notre Dame mascot on steroids: a very large, scary leprechaun.

* * * * *

To appreciate what Hatfill and Connolly went through, context is important.

The FBI was already under intense criticism for not using the available intelligence to stop the 9/11 attacks. The anthrax murders, coming so quickly after the jet attacks, seemed to be part of a larger, coordinated terrorist plot. The nation was near panic. The Bureau faced unprecedented pressure to solve the case.

When they could not, they did the next best thing. They let the public think that they had solved it. They just hadn't done all the paperwork yet. Through leaks and public statements to a willing, eager press, the nation's most powerful law enforcement agency told the world a big, fat, comforting lie. They knew who the culprit was. All would be revealed in good time. Go back to bed, kids, everything is just fine. The hungry media ate it up.

"The press would call me day and night," Connolly remembers. "They would say, 'The FBI says your guy did this or that. What's your response?'"

It was like a bad joke.

"What's my *response*?" Connolly yelled at them. "You shouldn't even know my guy's *name*. Why do I have to counter the FBI's false narrative? The man is presumed innocent. He owes you nothing."

The press was offended. Connolly was being a bad sport. He wasn't helping tell the story the FBI wanted them to report. It was surreal. Connolly calls it, "a paradigm shift of how I was taught things are supposed to work."

During this whole time, as the national and world media besieged him for comments, Connolly's answer never changed. It was also never reported accurately. Here, published for the first time, in its entirety, was his response:

"If the FBI wants to convey to the American public that my client is a mass murderer, there's one way to do it, the only way to do it—indict him. Otherwise, shut the fuck up."

* * * * *

Connolly was my mentor at the US Attorney's Office in DC.

"God, you're awful," he moaned during a trial recess.

In what sense, I asked.

"In the sense that you're an asshole." Tom can be impatient.

Why had I beaten up the witness so badly?

I said because he was so hostile; the guy was killing my case.

"He's your *own witness*," Connolly yelled.

That was true. But Tom didn't have to yell about it.

* * * * *

According to the applicable Code of Federal Regulations, law enforcement is *never* supposed to identify suspects in criminal cases *except* in the narrowest of exigent circumstances. Like if a child is about to die, or a nuclear bomb is about to blow up—something you would see on a television show.

Even then, the only information that is supposed to be released is the name of the person, his or her age, and the potential charges.

Leaks *about* the investigation, the evidence, speculation about the suspect's character, information about his or her background, personal life, or medical history, or theories of the case are *never* supposed to be released.

No one knows who created the "person of interest" character, but I hope it was not a lawyer. Maybe it was a press office hack. Whoever it was slunk back into anonymity, having never claimed authorship. I like to think they were ashamed of what they had created. They should have been.

* * * * *

The first victim of the "person of interest" nonsense was Richard Jewell, unfairly tagged with the lie after the Atlanta Olympic bombing case.

Jewell later sued various media outlets and won. What he could not do, however, was sue the government officials responsible for using the term in the first place.

When other storytellers commit slander or libel, they get sued.

When government storytellers commit slander or libel, they get immunity.

Connolly could only find one official reference to the term "person of interest." It was contained in a letter from the Department of Justice confirming that the term had no legitimate legal meaning and *shouldn't* be used. Ever. Yet Attorney General John Ashcroft himself was on the record using the term to describe Hatfill.

Why, exactly, would the FBI want to write a sequel to the Jewell case?

Because it worked; it usually does, for a time. The public was mollified. Congress stopped its criticism of the FBI. Indeed, making Hatfill a scapegoat achieved the storyteller's purpose perfectly. The press reported the story eagerly, without proof, without solid evidence, even when it made no sense.

* * * * *

At one point in their investigation, law enforcement leaked the fact that a box had been found at the bottom of a pond near Hatfill's home. Bootstrapping on their own improper release of this information, unnamed government sources then speculated that the box was used as part of a complicated process to weaponize anthrax spores underwater.

Connolly laughed when the press asked him about it. He thought they were joking.

"The spores are 100 times thinner than a human hair. If they get around moisture, they clump up, making them harmless," he said.

"I told the press people to call their 10th-grade biology teachers and ask them if it was possible to keep spores like this dry underwater but they expected me to do their job for them."

"I told them, do a story about how the FBI has no idea how anthrax works. They didn't do that either."

Connolly knocked down as many of the false leads and rumors as he could. But it was an impossible task.

"How do you prove a negative?" Connolly still wonders. "The press accepted what the FBI said without questioning or vetting any of it."

The media, prone to self-congratulation, should have been ashamed of itself for the role it played in helping to destroy Hatfill's reputation and life. Instead, it continues to spin the person of interest lie.

"One of the main reasons I took the case was to stop the term being used," Connolly said. "I did such a good job, they got a show called *Person of Interest* on CBS, and the term is used all the time."

* * * * *

Once, during a lunch break, when we were both in trial, I made Connolly help me prepare my closing argument instead of his own.

As we rushed back to court, I inadvertently took his coat instead of mine.

I looked like a kid wearing his father's suit.

Tom looked like Chris Farley in *Tommy Boy* ("Fat guy in a little coat, fat guy in a little coat . . .").

* * * * *

Connolly managed to save Hatfill from arrest or indictment. Then he came up with a novel theory to get around the government's traditional immunity.

He jerry-rigged a relatively obscure provision of a 1960s federal privacy statute connected to the Freedom of Information Act. Basically, it created a cause of action when the government improperly gathers and unfairly releases private information about a citizen.

"We argued that the government collected records on Dr. Hatfill, not to charge him or try him, but to create a bad narrative about him."

The government, in an unprecedented move, ultimately settled for a reported $5.8 million to make the case go away.

"What shocked me wasn't the government's willingness to create a false narrative," Tom said. "It was their willingness to sacrifice another human being to keep the narrative alive."

People get incensed when someone uses a racially insensitive or sexist term. They should take up arms over the term "person of interest." It's a government-funded rumor campaign, a lie that, in the modern age, can circle the globe a dozen times before the truth can even begin to get out of the starting gate—if it ever even does.

The "person of interest" lie reveals ugly truths about what law enforcement is capable of, but it is not the only one.

* * * * *

"Truth in sentencing" is another oxymoronic, legal lie. It is not limited to the United States.

Drazen Erdemovic was one of the mass murderers of Srebrenica, convicted of killing up to 100 Muslims by the International Criminal Tribunal for the Former Yugoslavia convening in The Hague.

With time served, he was released from prison after four years. The crime was amoral. The sentence was immoral. To call it justice mocked the notion of justice itself.

Erdemovic was treated with due process, given the benefit of the presumption of innocence, allowed to challenge all evidence, given every nicety denied to his victims. Then, having been convicted of multiple acts of genocide, he served much less time than an American defendant convicted of selling cocaine.

The same year that Steven Spielberg's *Schindler's List* won the Academy Award for Best Picture, concentration camps were springing up in Serbia. And Rwanda was just around the corner. Law stories are important. But it's a lie to overstate their power.

* * * * *

I wrote an episode of *The Practice*, "Pro Se," in which a defendant wanted to testify in his own defense in a murder trial and lie about what happened.

The lawyer, knowing her client was about to lie, was legally prohibited from presenting perjury to the court. She informed the judge outside the presence of the jury about what her client intended to do.

The judge promptly let the defendant take the stand, swear the oath, and then tell one lie after another.

This was all proper and legal, of course, according to the relevant rules of professional responsibility and ethics, as well as the Court's holding in *Nix v. Whiteside*.[3]

The script was based on my own experience watching this exact scenario play out in DC. There is something terrible about watching the law allow—if not endorse—such bold-faced lying.

But it is not the only time it happens. Concealment, too, can be a form of lying.

* * * * *

Some of the most persuasive and compelling stories I ever read will never see the light of day. They are true stories. But the law hides them, perhaps out of fear that they reveal too much about the law and the lack of justice in it.

They are the stories contained in presentence reports (PSRs). By federal law, they are never to be released to the public.

PSRs are a creative collaboration between many writers. This includes prosecutors and defense lawyers, law enforcement and medical personnel, crime victims, and the defendants themselves.

The PSR writer herself is responsible for conducting interviews, summarizing reports, and pulling all the information together into a cohesive whole.

The unsung talents of the criminal justice system, PSR writers often produce nonfiction stories of the highest quality. Each PSR a biography of the convicted, the life story of someone considered to be society's worst; but it is also a record of the worst society can do to someone.

The purpose of the PSR is to recommend a sentencing range based on the defendant's crimes, past and present. On another level, the PSR

---

3. 475 U.S. 157 (1986).

provides what is surely the most comprehensive consideration of who the defendant is, how he got to this point in his life, and what is to be done with him now.

If anyone had taken the time to look this closely at defendants before they were convicted, maybe they could have saved them from being convicted at all.

Of the hundreds of PSRs I contributed to and read as a prosecutor, the number of defendants with learning disabilities or correctible but untreated physical problems—such as needing glasses—was heartbreaking. With just a little help at the right time, many of their lives might have been different.

Far greater were the number of defendants—surely the majority—who came from a broken home, were raised by single mothers or grandmothers, were victims of sexual or other types of abuse, were addicted to one substance or another, or simply came from poverty.

The justification for keeping PSRs under seal is to protect privileged information—the mental and physical health records of the defendant, attorney-client materials—and the privacy of victims, witnesses, and others.

But that is a lie. Government officials redact privileged and private information from documents before making them available in discovery or to the public all the time. When the government doesn't or refuses to, the Freedom of Information Act makes officials do it.

The real reason the government doesn't release PSRs is because they tell the stories of men and women who never had a chance—poor people, most of them, who were often victims of crimes themselves before they became perpetrators, products of ungodly childhoods. To understand, to some degree, is to forgive. Forgiving criminality never got anyone elected to anything in this world.

Real truth in sentencing would involve not only telling the judges the stories of these people but telling the public as well.

I say that as a former prosecutor who remains pro-prosecution. I have never handled a criminal defendant's case in my life and never will.

But no one who reads PSRs can have anything but empathy for many of the people who get caught up in the criminal justice system.

More than bad character drove most of them to commit their crimes. It is a lie to deny this but it has been told so many times, we forget the truth.

There would be real value in letting the PSRs out. They would constitute an invaluable body of objective information for scholars and policy makers in fields ranging from early childhood development to health care, criminology, sociology, and government.

And they would show the American taxpayer and voter how the law is applied in their name against their fellow human beings.

* * * * *

"Acceptance of responsibility" is another law lie.

The Constitution's 5th Amendment guarantees the right against self-incrimination.

After being convicted, before an appeal is allowed, a defendant *may* reduce the sentence in both the federal and most state systems by admitting guilt and accepting responsibility.

But after the appeals are exhausted, the defendant's *only* hope of getting parole is to show remorse, which means accepting responsibility for what happened, even if he or she did not do it.

The result is a classic prisoner's dilemma. Maintain your innocence, remain the wrongly convicted victim of injustice in the eyes of family and friends who have supported you throughout your ordeal.

Or, go along with the lie of those who wrongly convicted you, at the cost of your reputation and soul, and go free.

* * * * *

That was at the heart of "Killing Time," the episode of *The Practice* for which Charles Dutton won the Emmy. He played Leonard, wrongly convicted of murder, a man who had always maintained his innocence.

After 15 years in prison, he appears before the Massachusetts Parole Board. In order to obtain his freedom, he must take responsibility for a crime he did not commit.

His lawyer, Eugene Young, confronts his own conflict. He defended Leonard at his murder trial and lost. Now a better, more experienced attorney, he feels enormous guilt for having failed to save an innocent man.

The lawyer's duty of loyalty is to the client who is desperate to go home. But the rules of professional responsibility and ethics demand that the lawyer not counsel his client to lie, even to obtain his long-denied freedom.

* * * * *

Dutton knew all about the law. He was a graduate of the Yale School of Drama, a Broadway star in the plays of August Wilson, and one of the nation's greatest actors.

He also served almost ten years in prison for manslaughter and weapons charges.

His understanding of and commitment to the part was extraordinary. He understood why his character won't—*can't*—confess to a crime he did not commit. To do so would make him a collaborator in an injustice in which he was the victim.

* * * * *

This was a law story *about* law stories themselves—specifically, the stories the justice system forces participants to tell in order to affirm the system's own credibility, its own ethos.

The original intent behind making a defendant admit his or her guilt reflected a belief in the perfectibility of man, the possibility of reform, the importance of taking personal responsibility, not only for one's actions, but also for one's character.

While the theory may be enlightened, the actual practice isn't. It's a straight, hard-nosed bargain. In return for joining the government's theory of the case and affirming that the trial was fair and the result just, the wrongly convicted defendant gets out of prison.

And the system gets to pretend it doesn't make mistakes.

* * * * *

There are other lies the system tells to affirm its credibility. The one with the biggest impact is the lie that plea agreements are entered into voluntarily and free from compulsion.

Anyone with even a passing experience in the justice system knows they are not. I often stood in court, halfway through the entering of such a deal, watching as the judge went off the record to give the defense lawyer time to quietly take a client aside to bully them into going through with it.

Once, it took the court close to two hours (of which perhaps 15 minutes were on the record), to finally accept a one-count guilty plea in a loan fraud case where the parties had stipulated to the sentence.

Sometimes screaming in anger, sometimes weeping in frustration, the defendant vacillated between following her lawyer's advice and demanding a trial. She wasn't guilty, she said. Someone had forged her signature, but she wouldn't identify who it was. Exhausted, she finally gave in and entered the plea.

It wasn't incompetence on the lawyer's part. The risk of losing at trial and getting a higher sentence was too great. But to say the plea was entered voluntarily and free from compulsion was an outright lie everyone agreed to tell. Because if they didn't, the system would not only lose credibility, it would collapse under the weight of giving everyone the due process they are entitled to. Health care and education are not the only things rationed in this country.

* * * * *

Law lies are not limited to issues of guilt and sentencing.

Prior to one narcotics trafficking case, the defendant filed a motion arguing that he was mentally incompetent to stand trial. The indictment identified him by his legal name, as well as by his alias—"Bugsy." People who knew him swore he was certifiable.

He was sent to a federal facility for evaluation and, as required by law, examined by a prosecution expert. The man I used often worked for the office. He always seemed to find the defendants competent to go to trial and sane when they got there.

Bugsy returned to court for a hearing covered in his own feces, which he had gotten into the habit of applying to his hands and face. The psychiatric experts conceded he had mental problems but could not agree he was legally incompetent to stand trial. Everyone agree he was crazy but not "legally crazy."

After a short trial, Bugsy was convicted, and given a 20-year mandatory prison sentence.

* * * * *

There are many lies in the civil law, of course, the greatest being that it is a fair and just system, despite the fact that "80 percent of the legal needs of the poor go unmet," and the majority of Americans cannot find, afford, or receive legal representation when they sue, are sued, get divorced, or otherwise have to appear as a party in a civil case.[4]

* * * * *

I confess that sometimes television writers also tell lies.

I once wrote an episode of *The Practice* about a man charged with murder. At trial, a psychiatrist testified that the man's inability to recall exactly what happened may have been affected by a previous shock he

---

4. Ethan Bronner, "Right to Lawyer Can Be Empty Promise for Poor," *New York Times*, March 15, 2013.

had experienced just prior to the shooting. These two shocks, taken together, in close time proximity, affected the man's cognitive ability, just as they would for anyone suffering from post-traumatic stress disorder. Referring to established conditions from the DSM, as well as peer review studies of the issue, the doctor identified the condition known as "twin positional traumas" (TPTs) as the likely cause for the man's lapses in memories.

There is, of course, no such thing as TPT. It sounded like something the OB/GYN talked about when my wife was carrying twins. But time was short, the script was late, and it sounded true, television true. At any rate, it was only to be a temporary placeholder until we came up with something better.

Unfortunately, everybody seemed to like it, and I got busy with another script, and the episode was shot with it in, having been cleared by an army of studio and network clearance departments and their lawyers.

It was the only time I made anything up like that. I felt bad about it. Especially when the executive producer called and suggested we do a whole script about twin positional traumas and I had to admit that the condition didn't exist.

Had I done it in a real case, I would have been disbarred. There is a difference between television truth and legal truth. But they have one thing in common.

Neither is the actual truth.

ELEVEN

PowerPoint Versus Pixar

My nominee for the greatest law story of the year was a commercial that ran on cable television. In 30 seconds, it managed to explain complicated legal issues *and* inspire people to pursue justice.

"If you purchased a computer, video game system, or other electronic device between 1998 and 2002, because your nine-year-old had to listen to, watch or email her favorite boy band, chances are you paid too much."[1]

Has any cause of action been described better or faster? Whose nine-year-old daughter *didn't* use the computer to listen to and watch her favorite boy band?

The young male narrator's voice is ironic rather than commanding—a deadpan comic's delivery. The commercial's soundtrack is a subtle low electronic score that gives the static images life, a sense of movement. It builds as the narrator explains *why* you may have paid too much.

"That's because the makers of DRAM, one small piece in those devices, are accused of fixing the price for the part, ending up costing you more money at the register."

No CGI, nothing expensive; the graphics are straightforward, deceptively childlike. The makers of the computer part are represented by four stick figures, faceless, genderless.

They sit around a table and share a single thought bubble, like in a cartoon; there are no words in the bubble, only dollar and cent signs.

---

1. DRAM Claims, "DRAM: $310 Million Settlement," https://www.youtube.com/watch?v=4RFo_GnWFYg/.

Next is a drawing of a stylized cash register with more money signs: "Don't say bye-bye-bye to your hard-earned money," the narrator says. The graphic also shows a wallet with three bills sticking out, under the words "BYE BYE BYE."

"Join the millions nation-wide entitled to a refund." There is a graphic of the earth circled by stick figures of men, women, and children. "It only takes five minutes to file a claim," the narrator promises. The next graphic shows a clock and a toll-free phone number and web address under the words, "IT'S EASY!" all in caps.

"It's your money," the narrator says, "get it back!"

It was all done with ten simple slides. If a lawyer had the guts to use it as an opening statement, it would be the greatest presentation ever.

* * * * *

Nobody can say when human beings first began to rely on graphics to tell stories. Prehistoric cave paintings suggest the art is as old as our most ancient ancestors. But over the last 30 years, technology has changed how we create and share stories in remarkable ways.

When I began trying cases, butcher paper and marking pens were the standard way prosecutors summarized information. Defense lawyers and law firm attorneys used fancy preprinted boards.

Now, failure to use PowerPoint, CGI reenactments, and three-dimensional imaging is considered lazy if not outright malpractice.

Go online and you will find a number of companies and consultants eager to help you use the new technology to tell your story, for a fee, of course.

* * * * *

Eric P. Mirabel is an intellectual property attorney in Houston, Texas. He is the author of articles in the *Journal of the Patent and Trademark Office Society*. He is also a rapper, possibly the first one to put out a footnoted video.[2] It tells an identity story, explaining the kind of law Mirabel practices, his talent for it, using the exaggerated braggadocio appropriate to the genre.[3]

"My 'song' is effectively a 3.5 minute ad/brag about my abilities and services—in the rap tradition." In keeping with that tradition, Mirabel just wanted to be heard.

In an email, Mirabel explained that the rap video was part of his campaign to reach a specific, underserved segment of the market—injured veterans who want to start a business; people "who want their piece of the American dream instead of help filling out benefits forms (other lawyers can do that)."[4]

Before turning to music, he contacted several charitable and bar organizations "for vets and injured vets," offering his legal services, "and got NO RESPONSE (not even a 'thanks' please consider donating)."

Rap was his way to get noticed. If the song gets him enough attention/hits to move his name to the top of Internet search engine lists for "IP lawyer," it could be worth a lot.

* * * * *

That a lawyer would communicate through rap matters more than the quality of the rap itself.

Mirabel's rap song is no more outlandish or ridiculous than many rap videos. And he doesn't see it as any more or less "demeaning to the profession" than the "Hit by a semi-trailer?" attorney ads he already sees on television and billboards.

---

2. Joe Patrice, "Lawyer Touts Practice Through Rap Video. Yes, This Is Real," *Above the Bar*, March 19, 2014, http://abovethelaw.com/2014/03/lawyer-touts-practice-through-rap-video-yes-this-is-real/; Thomas Connolly, "This IP Lawyer's Footnoted Rap Video Could Be the Best Thing on the Internet," *Legal Cheek*, March 14, 2014, http://www.legalcheek.com/2014/03/this-ip-lawyers-footnoted-rap-video-could-be-the-best-thing-on-the-internet/.

3. Ibid. "Other lawyers wish they had this kind of career. / 'Cause I patent your mama, / Make you pay to see her."

4. Email correspondence, March 23, 2014.

As to whether a rap music video works as a lawyer marketing tool remains an open question. "I guess if mine's some kind of runaway success, some might say 'yes,'" Mirabel said. "But they'd be smart to wait and see."

One suspects that Mirabel is not doing this for monetary reasons. He has not posted the video on his firm's website. Yet *he* has clearly gotten something out of it.

Whether it is any good is beside the point. It is good to him. It is an expression of who he is and what he does. It is good story; it has added joy to his practice. It has given personal meaning to what he does.

Can Larry Parker say that?

* * * * *

In February 2014, during a speech before the New York State Bar Association broadcast on C-SPAN, Justice Ginsburg said she was surprised that younger women were not, as she said, "more fired up" about issues of women's rights. She was asked how women attorneys, in particular, can help make sure that equality gains are not lost in the future.

Tell the story of the struggles women went through to be treated as equals. "Find an audience," Ginsburg said, "and educate them."

Easier said than done. It is getting harder to find an audience all the time.

Movies used to begin with the low rumbling "ohm" of the Big Bang and the words "The Audience is Listening" on the screen.

They are not listening now.

The marketplace of ideas that lawyers and writers operate in is not a 19th-century emporium. It does not cater to a small, select clientele of knowledgeable consumers.

It is a 24-hour-a-day convenience store. The goods are not always the best quality, but the variety is endless.

Each of us is one small voice in a loud and crowded field of storytellers. To be heard requires more than knowing that storytelling is important. To be effective, good storytellers must also acknowledge and respond to how the audience and its expectations have changed.

* * * * *

When I started writing for television in 2000, a one-hour television script for broadcast television ran about 50 pages, which meant 52 minutes of screen time, the other eight minutes or so going to commercials.

Now on broadcast television, a one-hour television shooting script is often 46 pages, and the screen time is 42 minutes or so—shorter even than a one-hour therapy session (which, as almost every member of the Writers Guild knows, is just 50 minutes).

I don't believe this reflects a shorter national attention span. Indeed, based on overall screen time—television, film, and the combined content of the Internet, delivered through an ever-expanding universe of devices—people are actually spending more time watching and listening to stories than ever before.

The problem is getting them to watch *your* show.

There is nothing more painful than sitting with someone as they watch an episode you wrote. The distractions—phone calls, bathroom breaks, texting—are endless.

Increasingly, even the screen on which they are watching your episode contains advertisements *during* your show. At an especially dramatic or comedic moment, the name, date, and time of one of the network's other shows will appear like a ghost, in an eye-catching silent promo.

Their sole purpose is to take the attention of the viewer away from the story being told; like a lawyer making objections at trial to throw his opponent off stride.

I am no Shakespeare. But Shakespeare never had to deal with signs thrust from the wings advertising the new Christopher Marlowe play.

* * * * *

Cable networks (HBO, Showtime) and on-demand sites (Hulu, Netflix) don't air commercials during their shows. An hour on those networks is closer to an actual hour. These networks and platforms continue to grow in popularity, peeling audiences away from the broadcast networks.

When offered the chance to watch something with fewer commercials and longer periods of content, the audience takes it.

It isn't that the American attention span is getting shorter. It is American's tolerance for advertising that is getting shorter.

* * * * *

Technology requires that all storytellers, including lawyers, rethink how to communicate with the audience.

Once during a first-year contracts course, Professor Jack Coons called on me to discuss the holding of a case. I offered to interpretively dance my answer.

Choreographers use the language of dance to tell complex stories all the time, I said. In structure, what is a pas de deux but the wordless representation of offer, acceptance, and consideration, its coda the final performance?

"You didn't do the reading, did you?" Professor Coons asked.

No, I hadn't.

Coons moved on to another student, disappointed, and not just in my lack of preparation. Coons had a terrific baritone voice. He used to sing the national anthem at the Oakland Coliseum before A's baseball games. He would have loved to see somebody dance the law.

In fact, lawyers interpretively dance the law all the time. They do it through expensive choreographed video, CGI, and computer reenactments. Based on the facts, characters, and law of a case, it is all storytelling. It is in this interpretive dance of the law that technology has had its greatest impact.

* * * * *

Much has been written about the "*CSI* effect." Having been exposed by the technological wizardry of crime detection on television shows, jurors expect that they will be applied to real cases. And they hold the lawyers responsible when they are not.

Unacknowledged is the "Vine Effect." In 2013, the Vine mobile app began to enable users to make and post six-second video clips that can then be posted on social media. It is among the most downloaded and popular apps of all time, allowing tens of millions of Vine users to produce and publish over one million stories.

Watch them. Most are crude slapstick, but a few convey a surprising amount of information and emotion in an absurdly short amount of time.

I am not advocating that you present a legal story through Vine. I am suggesting that the Vine Effect means that millions of people know how to tell stories in video form, reaching millions of other people with their stories through cheap and easy-to-use technology. They should expect lawyer storytellers to do the same.

In a world where anyone can tell a story to everyone else visually and quickly, the demands on lawyers and storytellers to be compelling and quick have never been greater.[5]

* * * * *

The story of how the three American broadcast networks once had a monopoly but don't have it anymore is an old story. Less appreciated, however, is how little it matters. Hundreds of new channels, the advent of cable networks, and thousands of digital channels have given screen viewers lots of choices. But the networks are still making billions of dollars. Their power and reach remain enormous; indeed, in relative terms, they have increased.

Like all predators, they have adapted, buying a number of the newer channels as well as starting their own. Through the studios they own,

---

5. See Hanson R. Hosein, *Storytelling Uprising: Trust and Persuasion in the Digital Age*, 3rd ed. (Seattle: HRH Media Group, 2012).

operate, and contract with, the major networks remain main content producers as well as providers. Independent channels (of which there are almost none) and digital outlets are to the big-three networks what mom-and-pop shops are to Wal-Mart. In theory, they are competitors; in reality, they are not yet costing network executives a tremendous amount of sleep.

* * * * *

More consumer choice has meant more shows. But it has not necessarily meant a greater diversity of shows.

Two years ago, another David E. Kelley show, *Harry's Law*, attracted 11 million viewers, making it, at the time, NBC's highest-rated scripted television show.

It was canceled.

Drawing 11 million people to watch a show is no longer enough. The problem was they were the wrong kind of people—too old, not part of the 18-to-49-year-old demographic, the golden target for advertisers eager to reach those with the largest amount of disposable income.

As the audience has splintered, broadcasters have become increasingly more interested in attracting the audience that advertisers want to reach most.

If you are over the age of 49, the major broadcasters don't want you and don't make shows for you.

Not because they don't like you. They *are* you. CBS, run by Sumner Redstone long after he turned 90, attracts the largest group of people over 49, making it the number-one network in the country. But they are not happy about it. Every development season, its executives tell agents, writers, and producers that it is looking for shows to "young down" their audience.

* * * * *

What does this mean to the lawyer storyteller?

Only that we live in a world where the audience—including our clients, witnesses, judges, and jurors—are increasingly being catered to in segments, divided by age, race, and gender. Billions of dollars in advertising and entertainment dollars are spent producing tailor-made content for each of these groups; the vast majority of it spent on the 18-to-49-year-old demographic.

What moves each of these groups is known—or thought to be known—by the networks and advertising companies. It drives their marketing campaigns, determines where they spend their money and how they tell their stories.

A lawyer storyteller who is not aware of audience fragmentation, how stories are being told to various demographics, is not listening.

* * * * *

Easier, quicker access to the Internet increasingly allows the audience to be less passive all the time, to shout their opinions, digitally, or to fact-check what they are hearing in real time.

The implications for lawyers are obvious. In her ABA article "Can the Jury Trial Survive Google," Professor Caren Myers Morrison cites numerous cases in which deliberating jurors in criminal cases violated the court's instructions and did their own legal and factual research.[6]

Morrison notes that jurors don't like being told they can't blog their friends or look up sentencing information on their smartphones. Information is power, technology has empowered all of us, and nobody likes to give up power. Jurors should but don't follow the court's instructions. Other than sequestration and seizure of their phones, iPads, and laptops, there is no way to ensure a complete information blackout.

---

6. Caren Myers Morrison, "Can the Jury Trial Survive Google," *Criminal Justice* 25 (Winter 2011): 4.

A practical answer would be to shorten trials. If exposure to outside influence is the issue, than the only practical solution is to limit the quarantine time during which jurors must refrain from outside contact with the world.

Morrison suggests another answer is to "reform the jury system so that jurors can be more engaged in the proceedings."[7]

This means letting them take notes, ask questions, and begin deliberations before the closing arguments.

The idea of jury participation has the corny appeal of a Norman Rockwell painting or a Frank Capra movie: the average American Joe or Jane has more sense than a roomful of lawyers and judges. Giving jurors the chance to ask questions reaffirms democratic principles and encourages civic participation. Since they have no personal interest in the outcome, giving them the chance to ask questions seems logical. They are the fact finders, the truth seekers, the only real noncombatants in the adversarial system.

It sounds like a good idea.

It isn't.

* * * * *

Judge Linda H. McLaughlin's bench sported an old-fashioned pencil sharpener and containers of precisely sharpened pencils and pens, the exact same number in each container, grouped by color—yellow for highlighting, black for orders, blue for drafts, and green for internal communications. She was a tidy person, precise, prissy.

She once threatened to hold me in contempt for "sass."

She used to let jurors take notes and encouraged them to write out questions.

"Just raise your hand, the clerk will bring the question to me, and we will go from there," Judge McLaughlin promised.

---

7. Ibid.

Trial began; opening statements, first witness, and a hand would pop up in the jury box. The juror would hand the note to the clerk, nodding proudly to the others as it was handed up to the bench for Judge McLaughlin's review.

"Oh, dear," the judge would say with a frown, "I can't read this. The handwriting is . . ."

Her voice would trail off. Sometimes she would hand the note to her clerk. "Can you make any sense of . . . ?"

The clerk would stare at it, then shake her head and shrug, handing it back to the judge.

Sometimes Judge McLaughlin would make the juror walk out of the box and up to the bench to read the question quietly to her. Then she would thank the juror and wait as he or she slunk back to sit down.

"The juror has asked a question," the judge would say. "It is improper, so I won't be asking it."

She gave the shamed juror the icy, condescending smile of a particularly cruel head nurse at a mental hospital.

On the rare occasions when she did find the question relevant, she would read it exactly as written, emphasizing grammatical errors.

"The juror asks: 'Who [sic] car defendant driving when arrested?'"

Pursing her lips, the judge would quietly take a red pencil from the red pencil container and correct the note, before reading it again:

"*Whose* car was the defendant driving when *he was* arrested?" she would read, before turning to the juror. "That's better, isn't it?"

There were not many joys in Judge McLaughlin's courtroom. One of the few pleasures was the chance to see how nonlawyers liked trying to do the job. Again, the Germans *must* have a word for it.

One question was usually enough. The jurors stopped raising their hands, stopped taking notes, and sat there in silence, glad not to be called on.

Lawyers have a hard time asking proper questions. And they are trained to do it. It's what keeps Judge Fine up at night. Asking jurors to do it is like asking them to help out with their own surgery. Wanting them to help isn't enough.

* * * * *

Morrison thinks the jury trial will survive. It has shown itself to be a remarkably hardy institution. But nothing that lasts such a long time stays the same. Over the last, say, 100 years, the institution has adapted to gender equality, desegregation, and changes in the rights of the defendant. Morrison is right to suggest that it will adapt to new technology as well. The question is whether lawyers, like bad comics, will make the mistake of confusing props with good material.

Handing technology to most lawyers is like handing the keys to a Porsche to someone who never learned to drive stick. It is a great car but it won't take them where they need to go.

Pixar, the greatest animation company operating today, does not rely on technology to tell stories. Instead, it relies on an expanded version of the rhetorical triangle to create universal stories of depth and meaning.

Technology is no substitute for good storytelling. If anything, it makes bad storytelling look worse.

* * * * *

My FOX show *Justice* was all about technology's role in law storytelling. It centered on a boutique LA law firm specializing in high-end trials, using every conceivable means of technological wizardry to gather information and present its case.

Victor Garber starred, among others, and was wonderful. Law stories based solely on technology, however, proved not to be a recipe for success. It was a good show, credible and smart. All it lacked was heart and a reason to watch it.

* * * * *

In storytelling, the delivery system matters much less than the content. More important than technology is the sophistication we bring to analyzing the substance of stories.

Professor Daube understood this. His genius was to apply classic rhetorical techniques to new delivery systems. He did it when analyzing law stories in the Bible, in modern literature and film, or in contemporary laws and cases. He created new understanding out of an endless variety of material by applying classical principles to their construction and meaning.

Technology and cultural mores change. The basics of storytelling do not.

* * * * *

Several years ago, an executive at Dick Wolf's production company had an idea for a new show. He wanted a writer.

I met with two producers. The hero of the new show, they explained, was a talented lawyer in a large law firm who had a secret. He was a closeted gay man.

It sounded like a groundbreaking idea for the 1972 television season. As this was 30 or so years later, I bowed out. I don't say yes to every bad idea.

For the storyteller, it is more important to understand cultural change than technological change.[8]

* * * * *

Make friends with change. Understand it. Knowing your audience means knowing that their attitudes and sensibilities are in a constant state of flux. And change is happening faster than ever before.

During my background check for getting hired as a federal prosecutor, I was warned that my marijuana use could prevent my being hired.

Why? I answered my personnel forms truthfully, admitting to having *never* tried pot, not once.

"Yeah, see, that's a problem," the young FBI agent said to me. "It isn't the initial crime that brings people down. It's always the cover-up."

---

8. Dick Wolf's genius has always been to do the same show—*Law & Order*—over and over again, with only the slightest variation. Innovation is not his brand. It doesn't have to be.

Had I not noticed the forms were signed under penalty of perjury?

I *had* noticed. But it was true, I swore, despite growing up in LA during the 1970s, attending public school, and leading an otherwise normal, healthy social life, I somehow never got around to trying pot.

She shot me a stare that could toast bread.

"I drink a lot," I said, trying to be helpful. The silence was beginning to hurt my ears. I gave a nervous chuckle. It came out like a seal bark.

"We know about the *drinking*," she said, flipping through my file.

They had talked to college roommates, old bosses. They had even visited my childhood home and talked to the neighbors.

I knew this because my parents, who still lived in the same house, heard the scream. Across the street, sweet old Mrs. Carlucchi, born in Sicily, lay in her doorway, holding her head as two FBI agents tried to calm her down.

"He's a good boy," she cried. "He's a good boy!"

Somehow, I passed my background check, despite my lack of marijuana use.

Later, when I prosecuted an espionage case that required the highest security clearance available, the FBI didn't seem bothered by my increased drinking, various moral lapses, or the fact that I kept breaking office equipment in various states of rage and frustration.

All they cared about was whether I was still sticking with the marijuana denial. I had to. It was still true.

Now that marijuana is legal in many states, the federal government is considering loosening restrictions, and there is no longer much stigma attached to prior use. There is also no reason for anyone to lie about it.

I suspect the FBI agent still wouldn't believe I have never tried it.

* * * * *

One of the most ethical lawyers I ever worked with—a man who lectured on legal ethics at the Department of Justice and in US Attorney's

Offices—was one of the finest prosecutors the nation ever had. He was also gay.

In the mid-1980s, that was still a red flag on background checks, something that was thought to compromise national security—blackmail material.

So this ethical man—and a host of ethical Justice Department officials and US Attorneys—hid the truth. Don't ask, don't tell was not an innovation. It was how people protected themselves and their coworkers. They lied.

Change is influenced by, and reflected in, the stories we tell. How much is impossible to say.

Whether television and film portrayals of gays and lesbians helped change attitudes, or whether they merely documented the changes as they occurred, is a chicken-or-the-egg riddle. It's impossible to say which came first. All we know for sure is that they are related. It wasn't a straightforward process. And we no longer make liars out of good people.

* * * * *

In *The Verdict*, Paul Newman's character belts Charlotte Rampling and bloodies her lip. The crowd in the theater where I saw it actually *cheered*.

A Hollywood movie now would never have its hero hit a woman, no matter how much she betrayed him. Murder her in some spectacularly graphic or violent way, maybe, but not hit her.

* * * * *

To be clear, *Dirty Dancing* is not a law movie. But it turns on what was a crime in the context of the story. Set in 1963, the hero played by Jennifer Grey learns to dance the merengue so that another girl can go get an illegal abortion—which Grey's character tries to pay for. Abortion has been legal a long time. But no Hollywood movie today would put its hero anywhere near the issue.

I have sat in writers' rooms and watched men and women writers make numerous attempts to write such a story. No studio or network would allow it. The idea of portraying abortion as a legal right, let alone a possibly heroic or moral act, is impossible. Were the movie remade, Jennifer Grey's character would be more likely to sleep with the other woman or murder her in some spectacularly graphic or violent way rather than try to help her get an abortion.

For all the talk of liberal bias, it is remarkable how conservative American storytelling has become. The only gun story you cannot tell on network television involves regulation. I have written countless episodes with spectacularly graphic and violent murders committed with guns. Each time I have suggested writing a story about lawyers suing gun manufacturers, the idea has died in the room.

* * * * *

I once wrote a script that insulted a highly protected and sensitive class: American billionaires. "All great fortunes in America are built on one great crime," I wrote. "If they catch you, they send you to a country club prison; if you get away with it, they build a university for you."

Balzac said it first, but what was true in 19th-century France is also true in modern America.

The producers and executives thought it was the stupidest thing they had ever read. Especially since a number of people I named bought billions of dollars' worth of advertising.

Technology and society change. Some things do not change. The business of storytelling is business: the profit margin matters.

TWELVE

Heroes, Villains, and Exposition

The system of apprenticeship lasted for thousands of years, went away, and is now staging a modest comeback. And for good reason: it works.

We have mostly considered storytelling by analyzing stories themselves; breaking them down to their component parts and figuring out how and why they succeeded or failed. Another way to learn storytelling is to consider the lives and experiences of great storytellers in order to understand their motives and methods.

* * * * *

The Salesman

To say Leonard S. Shapiro sold furniture fails to convey the passion he brought to the task. Furniture *mattered* to him. Other than life, death, and the welfare of the nation, furniture was *all* that mattered.

He fought for furniture like it was a moral issue. He pushed wall units like they were war bonds. He advocated for credenzas like they were family. Death row inmates got less committed representation than my dad's least expensive line of lamps.

He started as a salesman on the floor at Sears and worked his way up to become a manufacturer's representative, selling to stores.

"Nobody can afford cheap furniture," he'd say. The idea struck him as immoral.

* * * * *

My dad's sales territory was vast, bigger than many states. It started in the south in Yucaipa, near Palm Springs, and snaked up through the Central Valley, to the mountains of Yosemite; from the state's eastern border all the way to the Pacific. "From the deserts, to the sea, to all of Southern California," as the late local broadcasting legend Jerry Dunphy used to say.

Over a 40-year career, my father covered more than a million miles and never missed a yearly sales quota. His reward was getting a higher quota the next year.

This was despite the fact that the furniture he sold was laminated, heavy, traditional, and old-fashioned. To paraphrase Dodger announcer Vin Scully and the old Farmer John hot dog commercial, it was the easternmost in quality but *not* the westernmost in flavor.

Most customers told my dad no, thank you. He might go days without a sale. Three sales for every ten attempts was a good percentage. A sensitive man, he took each rejection hard. But what upset him more were buyers who didn't understand the business.

One complained he was selling desks that contained "particleboard."

"Not particle board," my father corrected him firmly. "Chip core."

This was denser and lasted longer than particleboard. In fact, it was better than solid wood because, with lamination, it never warped or cracked. If you didn't believe him, my father could give you the name and address of a store that specialized in solid oak furniture.

"Go on a hot day," he would say. "If you're quiet, you can hear it cracking,"

* * * * *

I made a number of trips with him over the summers, staying in motels, eating in diners, waiting in the car, or coming into the store with him. Most buyers were happy to see him. He was not only liked, as Arthur Miller would have said it—my father was well liked.

Some buyers just happened to hate all salesmen. Once, weighed down with armfuls of fabric swatches, my father and I walked from the car toward the entrance of one store on an unbearably hot Bakersfield or Fresno day, I can't recall which, only to be confronted by the hostile owner:

"Lenny, get him the hell out, I don't want or need anything."

I died a little.

My father put down his fabrics in order to shrug and say "no problem." He then launched into the story of the last man who threw him out, and the business the store lost because they didn't get to see the new line.

But it hurt him. It hurt me. He put up with it to make his living. And he sold the rat bastard a bunch of desks.

* * * * *

Lawyers are the butt of much humor. Some of it is mean-spirited but it is nothing compared to the shabby disdain shown to salesmen. Even the roughest lawyer bashing carries a tinge of respect, an understanding that however loathsome and dishonest its members, the profession is powerful.

A salesman has to earn respect.

* * * * *

Dad always wore a suit and tie. Not because he wanted to. It wasn't more fun or comfortable to wear suits and ties back then. He wasn't exactly a fashion plate, either. Not tall, not thin—his clothing size was "squat"— my father understood the value and purpose of a uniform.

"I was selling my credibility," he said. "Dressing nicely was part of it." But just *part* of it. Clothing did not make the man; being honest, reliable, prepared, and knowledgeable did. Clothes did not *create* his image. They reflected and reinforced what was already there.

This was a man who knew the territory and understood his line.

* * * * *

Part of his job involved teaching store salesmen how to sell the products his company made.

"Product knowledge meetings" took place in the morning, in conference rooms or showrooms, before the store opened. Dad brought donuts and the story of King Tut.

When King Tut died, his body was placed in a tomb. Thousands of years passed. Imagine all that happened next.

Jesus and Muhammad were born and died, great empires rose and fell, the Dark Ages came, the Renaissance—he could go on for as long as they were interested.

Then, in 1922, adventurers discovered King Tut's tomb. When they opened it and went in, among all the treasures, what do you think was in the best shape?

The laminated furniture, he would say, in awe.

* * * * *

His father died at 49, a naval shipyard worker and victim of asbestos.

On his 18th birthday, my father left home and joined the Air Force for a four-year hitch. After a battery of induction aptitude tests, they declared him a whiz at languages, much to his surprise. A diffident high school student, he had been on the "four-four plan," working a junkyard job four hours a day and attending class four hours a day.

The Air Force sent him to Syracuse University to learn Russian. The faculty was comprised of former White Russian army generals and members of Kerensky's government. The rest of the students were college boys. Most of them were officers.

It was forbidden to speak English after the first day of class. After 10 to 12 hours of studying, they were forced to listen to Russian on headphones as they slept—subliminal learning.

Of the 200 or so airmen and officers who started, a handful, perhaps 20, graduated six months later, not merely fluent in Russian, but almost incapable of speaking anything else.

My dad was one of them.

They sent him to a secret listening post, 17 miles off the Siberian coast, monitoring Soviet military air traffic. He was there for two solid years.

Now, close to 60 years later, he can still speak Russian, even though he rarely gets the chance. A recent Russian immigrant was amazed. Not only was Dad's grammar perfect, it was courtly Russian, the type the tsar's family might have spoken:

"Whoever taught him was very educated."

* * * * *

I was surprised that the day he retired was the last time he ever discussed furniture. I am certain he has not thought much about furniture, either. His passion was not furniture. It was advocacy, telling stories to get customers to appreciate and purchase what he was selling. It happened to be furniture, but it could have been anything.

Dad wanted to be a lawyer. His two sons, both lawyers, learned a lot from him about how to be a lawyer.

Tell stories to convey information about what you are selling. Make sure you know what you are talking about. Anticipate the other person's story. Tell your story in a credible way. Show respect for people by dressing well. Never embarrass anyone ever, because they will never forgive you for it.

I always regret not following his advice, particularly the part about not embarrassing people.

* * * * *

The Country Lawyer

A Harvard law student tells his professor he is dropping out of school.

"Abraham Lincoln never had a formal education," the student says.

"Yes," the professor says, "but just think how far he could have gotten with a Harvard degree."

* * * * *

Any lawyer storyteller must come to grips with the greatest storytelling lawyer in American history, if for no other reason than because he remains such a fascinating, confounding figure.

The nation's most beloved president, self-taught and brilliant, irreligious yet martyred, a suicidal depressive who remained extraordinarily engaged in life—Abraham Lincoln was nothing if not complex.

Yet if forced to describe Lincoln in one word, you could do no better than to call him what he often called himself: a storyteller.

* * * * *

"Lincoln not only remembered and told a great storehouse of anecdotes and jokes and stories; he told them with a great storytelling talent."[1]

"In the role of storyteller," his partner Edward Herndon wrote, "I am prone to regard Mr. Lincoln as without equal."[2]

"In fact, Mr. Lincoln's fame as a storyteller spread far and wide. Men quoted his sayings, repeated his jokes, and in remote places he was known as a storyteller before he was heard of either as lawyer or politician."[3]

* * * * *

Nobody grows up wanting to be Stephen Douglas.

If forced to describe Douglas in one word, you might say "short" or "loser" but not "storyteller." To read the Lincoln versus Douglas debates is to appreciate what an unctuous, unpleasant little roly-poly of a man he must have been, someone who saw himself as too good, too smart, and too proper to stoop to storytelling.

Douglas had every advantage. He was far better educated than Lincoln,

---

1. William Lee Miller, *Lincoln's Virtues* (New York: Vintage Books, 2003), 73.
2. Edward Herndon, *Herndon's Life of Lincoln* (New York: De Capo Press, 1983), 249.
3. Ibid., 94.

more sophisticated, with greater access to information, and, according to reports of the time, a stronger, more pleasing voice and style. But Lincoln beat him like a drum.

* * * * *

Spare a moment to think about Lincoln's law partner Edward Herndon as a storyteller.

The president's murder was the last Northern casualty of the Civil War; he was shot on Good Friday and dead by Easter. But Herndon refused to be Lincoln's St. Paul. He was too ornery and honest a lawyer for that.

He had spent years staring at Lincoln's mud-caked boots on the desk; he knew the smell of the man and all his bad habits. Hagiographers were beginning to turn his annoying officemate into a saint.

Herndon thought the truth made a better story. His goal was not to debunk the Lincoln myth. It was to show all Lincoln overcame. What made Lincoln great, Herndon believed, was his humanity, his imperfections, from the mole on his face to his depression. The result is a portrait of a man in full, flawed, contradictory, and human.

Many people, including Mary Todd, never forgave Herndon for it. For a half-century, the nation mostly ignored his Lincoln, preferring the one-dimensional martyr to the more vexing truth.

* * * * *

Herndon's Lincoln is the kind of lawyer law schools *don't* want to produce:

"I may truthfully say, I never knew him to read through a law book of any kind. Practically, he knew nothing of the rules of evidence, of pleading, or practice, as laid down in the text-books and seemed to care nothing about them."[4]

---

4. Ibid., 271–271.

Lincoln is also not the kind of lawyer a law firm would want to hire. He "detested the mechanical work of the office. He wrote few of the papers—less perhaps than any other man at the bar work. Such work was usually left to me."[5] "Lincoln knew no such thing as order or method in his law practice. He made no preparation in advance."[6]

Lincoln was also the last man you would want to hire if you were *really* in trouble. "I think he was of less real aid in trying a thoroughly bad case than any man I ever associated with," Herndon recounted. "If he could not grasp the whole case and believe in it, he was never inclined to touch it."[7]

But the real career killer, and the one that must have rankled most of all, was the fact that Lincoln "never believed in suing for a fee. If a client would not pay on request he never sought to enforce collection."[8]

No one can document the faults of a lawyer better than his partner.

* * * * *

Maybe it is Herndon's fault that while we claim to admire Lincoln, we don't try to teach lawyers to be *like* Lincoln. Not even Abraham Lincoln University School of Law does it.

Its motto is "The World Is Our Campus," but its address is Mid-Wilshire in Los Angeles. Established in 1996 by attorney-CPA Hyung J. Park, and offering its entire curriculum online, the school's website states:

"The institutional mission of Abraham Lincoln University is to be a respected international provider of quality certificate, undergraduate and graduate degree programs primarily in law, business, technology and arts and sciences."

No courses on Lincoln or the art of storytelling were offered.

They aren't at Harvard, either.

---

5. Ibid., 251–252.
6. Ibid., 252.
7. Ibid., 431 (quoting attorney and Lincoln associate Leonard Swett).
8. Ibid., 261.

We do Lincoln a disservice not to recognize his mastery of the rhetorical triangle, or why he deserves to be part of the law school curriculum. "The first impression he generally conveyed was that he had stated the case of his adversary better and more forcibly than his opponent could state it himself."[9] Making all the best arguments he could for the other side, Lincoln established his own credibility for fairness and reason.

"When this was done he presented his own case" with the "force of his logic."[10] A master of establishing ethos and using logos, Lincoln was equally adept with pathos.

Lincoln famously used an 1857 farmer's almanac to prove that his client, William "Duff" Armstrong, could not have been seen committing murder in the moonlight because the moon wasn't out that night.[11]

But what won the case, according to Herndon and others, was less Lincoln's use of reason (the almanac) than the emotional appeal of his pathos-filled closing argument. It was "his tender and pathetic pleading for the life of the son of his old benefactor" (Armstrong's father, an early Lincoln mentor), and his personal, long-time friendship with the entire Armstrong family, that earned the acquittal.[12]

In John Ford's *Young Mr. Lincoln*, Lincoln's trial victory is much more the product of this pathos than his ethos or logos.

* * * * *

For the next 70 or so years after Lincoln's death, books and popular portrayals of St. Lincoln ignored Herndon's more nuanced version.

During this same period of time, Lincoln—the storyteller—was all but silent. Biographies and reminiscences downplayed his storytelling

---

9. Ibid., 431.
10. Ibid.
11. Ibid., 288.
12. "Defense of Duff Armstrong, as recounted by Juror John T. Brady," Illinois State Historical Society, Lincoln's Defense of Duff Armstrong, April 2010.

abilities or ignored them entirely. Only minor gods tell stories. Lincoln was too good and godly for storytelling.

The best example of this is John Drinkwater's West End play *Abraham Lincoln* (1919). The play was an enormous success, though it is almost unreadable today. It portrays Lincoln as devoid of humor, incapable of telling a story. The play was later made into the first of many silent films about Lincoln. He was played by an attorney, University of California, Hastings College of Law graduate Frank McGlynn Sr.

Walt Disney, that great leveler of American history, finished the silencing of Lincoln the storyteller. In the theme park exhibit "Great Moments with Mr. Lincoln," the robotic Lincoln lip syncs from speeches. He does not tell stories.

* * * * *

John Ford was the first storyteller since Herndon to present Lincoln as the storyteller that he was. Indeed, it is at the heart of *Young Mr. Lincoln*.

Yet even here, Lincoln's stories lost much of their bite and meaning. Divorced from their context, separated from their settings, they were homogenized, sentimentalized, made safe for public high school orators and Rotary Club luncheon speakers.

* * * * *

In Steven Spielberg's *Lincoln* (2012), written by Tony Kushner, the president is portrayed as a political strategist, calculating how to get the 13th Amendment passed. As noted by others, this is not a Lincoln who belongs to the Ages so much as a Lincoln who belongs on MSNBC.

But storytelling is central to Spielberg's *Lincoln*. At one point in the film, Lincoln himself apologizes before announcing that he must tell a story right now, even though it drives one of his cabinet members out of the room.

The story Kushner chose to have Lincoln tell reveals an entirely new version of Lincoln the storyteller, one that differs from Herndon's or Ford's or Disney's.

* * * * *

In the movie, during a stressful moment of war planning, Lincoln spots a portrait of George Washington. It prompts him to tell a story. It involves the American ambassador to Great Britain going to the bathroom at the residence of a British official and finding a portrait of Washington over the toilet.

When the smart-alecky British official asks the American what he thinks of the portrait's placement, the American says that it makes perfect sense. After all, nothing makes an Englishman shit faster than seeing George Washington.

* * * * *

For lawyers and writers, *why* and *when* someone chooses to say something are as important as *what* they actually say. Story choice, timing, and presentation matter as much as content. Why did Kushner choose to have Lincoln tell this *particular* story at this *particular* moment?

* * * * *

One obvious reason is to offer a light moment in a dark movie. It also showed Lincoln's documented need for levity, particularly during times of stress. These are all understandable, defensible artistic choices. Yet the story hit the wrong note. It gets laughs but only at the expense of the historical record and Lincoln's character itself. The evidence suggests that while it might have been a story Lincoln told, he would not have told it at that particular moment, in that particular setting.

"It has been as often as charged that Lincoln narrated vulgar stories; but the truth is he loved a story however extravagant or vulgar, if it had a good point."[13] No matter how funny or dirty the story, "if it exposed no weakness or pointed no moral, he had no use for it either in conversation or public speech."[14]

Throughout the movie Kushner shows Lincoln thinking and speaking like a lawyer, such as when he lectures his cabinet on the legal necessity of the 13th Amendment. These are the realist moments in the film, when the real Lincoln seems before us. These moments are what make the Washington story so jarring.

* * * * *

Notice that Spielberg shot the storytelling scene as a theatrical set piece, as if emphasize that Lincoln's storytelling was done for its own sake. Daniel Day-Lewis sits on a desk before a large group of men, an actor performing on a stage before an audience. He holds a cup in his hand like a prop. He takes sips from it as a timing device, self-consciously, not because he is thirsty, but to give the story pace, to let the narrative build.

This Lincoln is neither Herndon's imperfect sinner nor the saint in the Drinkwater play nor John's Ford's cracker-barrel philosopher. This is Lincoln as an actor, performing a role, putting on a show.

* * * * *

Were he alive today, Lincoln would find that the rules of storytelling have gotten more complex. He would be criticized as insensitive for telling jokes that stereotyped people on the basis of race, national origin, and their accents; for using profanity, for lacking decorum and taste.

He would also be attacked as a plagiarist. He called himself a retail dealer in story, taking a Balzac story, for example, relocating it in Indiana,

---

13. Edward Herndon, *Herndon's Life of Lincoln* (New York: De Capo Press, 1983), 94.
14. Ibid.

and then passing it off "for a purely original conception."[15] Great storytellers all steal from Balzac.

Just think of what CNN or FOX could do with such a transgression.

* * * * *

Like all great stories, the story of Lincoln changes with the times. As others have said, each age has its own version of the man, one that reflects its own particular standards, ethics, and obsessions. This is what makes him relevant. This is why he is an evergreen for historians, authors, filmmakers, lawyers, and every other type of storyteller.

* * * * *

The Wise Man

The homeless guy at Café Roma greeted David Daube as "The Crypt Keeper." Daube always waved and smiled back. After getting his coffee, Daube would shuffle to a booth and sit down next to a person who was already there.

"May I?" he'd say. "Or would you prefer privacy?" He was always cold. He sat at tables with strangers for their body heat.

His accent was unique; high Oxbridge via Freiburg, Germany. Fluent in many languages—living and dead—his speech pattern had strange, ancient tones.

From his raincoat he would pull out crossword puzzles clipped from various newspapers and magazines. In pen, he would fill in the boxes as if he were copying DMV forms, answering one clue per puzzle, then another one from the other, completing two or three in a few minutes. Each puzzle was in a different language—English, French, German, and Hebrew.

---

15. Ibid.

* * * * *

Daube was born in Germany in 1909. He was the first male on his father's side not to become a rabbi since the 14th century. Who knows why he never became a rabbi himself? I only know what others have said; that he was too independent a thinker, too eager to question authority, too much of an iconoclast.

Yet his knowledge of Talmudic law was profound; his ability to read ancient texts in their original language was unparalleled.

Daube earned his doctorate in law but had to flee Nazi Germany before he could receive it.

Grateful though he was for sanctuary in Britain, it did not change his nature. Despite being a loyal British subject, he ended up in a jail during World War II because he refused to take a loyalty oath to the King. Many of his fellow prisoners were Nazis and their sympathizers.

"People are more struck by the asininity of the law when they are trapped by it than when they are left off," he wrote.[16]

* * * * *

Daube ultimately became the Regius Professor of Civil Law at Oxford and a fellow of All Souls College. His groundbreaking work, *The Rabbinical Jesus*, was the first of the modern era to interpret the Gospels, not in terms of Pauline Christianity, but through consideration of the *ipsissima verba*, the original words of Christ, as understood through the rabbinical codes of the time. There are currently four fat volumes of his work, filled with such storytelling.[17]

At one point, every professor of civil and Roman law at Oxford and Cambridge had been his doctoral student. His wide-ranging abilities as

---

16. David Daube, *The Jottings of David Daube*, ed. Calum Carmichael (New York: YBK Publishers, 2008), 88.

17. David Daube, "Messianic Tests: Appeasing or Resisting the Oppressor," in *New Testament Judaism: Collected Works of David Daube*, ed. Calum Carmichael ed., section 2, vol. 2 (Berkeley: University of California, 2000), 93–95.

a writer and intellect meant "he could have held any one of five Chairs, the other four being in non-legal subjects."[18]

Many Jewish scholars seemed to feel he was too Christian in his interests and perspective. Some Christians who still seemed ambivalent about the fact that Jesus was a Jew—and a rabbi, yet—seemed troubled that a Jewish scholar was advocating a secular, historical understanding of the Holy Word.

Daube did not care. To Daube, the story of Jesus, and everything else, was based on factual and legal realities of time and place. By relying on original text and laws, he interpreted the Christ story and New Testament theology on their own terms in a manner so persuasive that his analysis was impossible to ignore or deny.

* * * * *

He lost family, friends, colleagues, and career to the Holocaust. Yet he returned to Germany after the war to help accused war criminals seeking leniency. He felt some of them were also victims of the Nazis. Like Martin Buber, he opposed the execution of Adolf Eichmann.

Yet he also pointed out there was a biblical basis it. The Bible does not really say "Thou shalt not kill." The ancient, priestly Aramaic word used was "murder." The term "to kill" is used throughout the Bible to describe and celebrate the slaughter of defeated tribes, right down to their animals.

Daube's writings often supported the story of his opponents. He was too honest a scholar to alter the truth merely to suit his purposes.

* * * * *

How he ended up in Berkeley remained something of a mystery. There was a woman involved; at least, that's the rumor. A true romantic, in the 19th-century Germanic mode, he was nothing if not passionate.

---

18. David Daube, *The Jottings of David Daube* (New York: YBK Publishers, 2008), 88.

His classes on Roman and biblical law drew two types of students: the religiously inclined and those looking for an easy two units.

Daube's lectures were fascinating. "He could take any branch of the law at any time and bring to bear on it the most wide-ranging insights drawn from historical, literary, theological, and popular sources."[19]

A lecture on ancient laws relating to abortion began with the story of life, how it has been defined over the ages and by whom. He cited Talmudic definitions and rabbinical law relating to compensation to be paid to the mother if a fetus was destroyed; followed the story through Roman law, the late Empire, the Dark Ages, and the Enlightenment; and ended with the current state of the law and the situation in an East Bay women's clinic.

A playful intellect, Daube wrote serious interpretations of nursery rhymes, once writing an article that famously and convincingly argued that Humpty Dumpty referred to a siege weapon used during the English Civil War during the 1643 battle for the city of Gloucester.[20]

He was also fond of limericks, acrostics, and bawdy—never dirty—stories.

* * * * *

Daube loved stories. He would tell them and draw them out of his students, fellow professors, and street people. They were essential to him, the method by which he expressed himself.

Once, when the fire alarms went off in the law library, a librarian found Daube in his office, refusing to leave. He was reading a story, enjoying it, and wouldn't dream of getting up.

"Time was I took a sweetie to bed
When I felt in the mood for a caper.
By now I fear I make do in instead.
With the local evening paper."[21]

---

19. Ibid., xi.
20. Ibid., 45–48.
21. Ibid., 182.

Two people carried Daube, still sitting in his office chair, out of the library.

* * * * *

Toward the end of his life, Daube described himself as a Zen Jew. He always seemed tolerant of most people. Exceptions included those who failed to appreciate the value of a good story or lacked the ability to tell one. Of a particular detective novel, he wrote:

"It is of redeemed dullness. The man murdered is uninteresting, the murder is uninteresting, the people involved on whatever side are uninteresting, the process is uninteresting, the language is uninteresting, and if I go on, this note will become equally unbearably uninteresting."[22]

* * * * *

In 1948 or 1949, Daube was having a drink with friends in Strasbourg when an older man came into the bar. Everyone stood in respect.

Early in the war, the man had been the mayor of an occupied town. Partisans killed a German soldier. In retaliation, the Germans rounded up a group of the town's young men, among them, the mayor's only two sons. They were all to be executed.

Rushing to the German headquarters, the mayor "gained access to the Commandant, the window of whose office in fact gave out to the yard with the twelve or so victims already lined up for the firing," The mayor begged for his sons' lives.

"The Commandant, nonchalantly waving toward the window, said: 'All right, you can have one.'"[23]

---

22. Ibid., 76.,
23. David Daube, "Messianic Tests: Appeasing or Resisting the Oppressor," in *New Testament Judaism: Collected Works of David Daube* (Berkeley: University of California, 2000), 93.

In William Styron's fictionalized version of a similar horror, the fictional Sophie chooses to send her girl to death in order to save her son, never to know if she succeeded, never capable of overcoming her guilt.

Daube's story was real and had a more complex ending. The mayor must have been an extraordinarily principled man. Unlike Sophie, he took the only ethical choice available. He refused to choose at all. To pick one son over the other was to become a collaborator in their murder. He left. And both boys were murdered.

Another scholar might have ended the story there, using it to explore the complex nature of resistance, the morality of refusing to participate in evil, the power and meaning of one man's example.

Daube ended the story by explaining what happened when he told his wife what the mayor had done.

She was unimpressed.

"A mother would have taken one home with her," Daube's wife said. The mayor lacked the courage to deal with the guilt of his choice. If Daube had been in that situation, he had better have come home with one of the boys.[24]

Daube told this story in a class lecture about the wisdom of women in the Old Testament. He also wrote about it in an essay on the nature and moral complexities of resistance to tyranny.

* * * * *

Daube noted that snobs have always looked down at rhetoric. In ancient times—Daube joked that he was there—rhetoric was fiercely attacked by Greek and then Roman philosophers as "an unworthy second best, being satisfied with the likely approximation of truth, rather than the absolute."

Aristotle helped establish rhetoric's value as a legitimate new discipline so that "in the course of time, there was room for both old-fashioned philosophy, new-fashioned rhetoric and various combinations."[25]

---

24. Ibid., 94.
25. David Daube, *The Jottings of David Daube* (New York: YBK Publishers, 2008), 25.

Daube thought people looked down on him too. At Berkeley, he wrote, "they love to have a European doing these strange things—Roman law, Jewish law, law and literature."

But they do not respect it.

"They love it, but a true American jurist ought to do tax or corporation or anti-trust law, and ought not to devote himself seriously to the luxuries I am concerned with. In a sense I am the call-girl of Boalt Hall."[26]

It didn't seem to bother him that much.

* * * * *

His tenth honorary degree came from Harvard University, but he was too ill to attend the ceremony.[27]

"I sowed and hoped but nothing grew.

Don't reap.

I found a friend but she withdrew.

Don't keep.

Now death is near, thank God I'm through.

Don't weep.[28]

I dream about him now and then.

Storytellers never die."

* * * * *

The Cynic

The law profession is a confidence game. The job is to instill confidence that you know what the law is and what you can and cannot do with it.

Clarence Darrow was a confidence man.

26. Ibid.
27. Ibid., xi–xii.
28. Ibid., 181.

America's first mass media celebrity lawyer, forefather of today's cable channel talking heads, Darrow's career is a case study in the power of self-serving storytelling.

"There is no justice in or out of court," Darrow said. Since the system was rigged for the rich and powerful, the only thing Darrow promised his clients was a good show.

His "sense of law as theater had been at the heart of [his] legal technique for nearly half a century."[29]

Like all confidence men, Darrow was first and foremost a showman.

"The audience that storms the box-office of the theater to gain entrance to a sensational show is small and sleepy compared with the throng that crashes the courtroom door when something concerning real life and death is to be laid bare to the public," Darrow wrote. "Everyone knows that the best portrayals of life are tame and sickly when matched with the realities."[30]

Darrow claimed his brand of storytelling relied on logos, on reason, that he was a clear-eyed realist, a facer of ugly facts and undefeatable truths, a debunker of myths, willing to speak truth to power. He saved the lives of Leopold and Loeb through equal use of reason and emotion. He technically lost the Scopes Monkey Trial battle but won the war for the teaching of evolution.

An atheist, Darrow didn't believe in God or religion, nor did he believe in conventional marriage, though how much his wife knew about that is an open question.

What Darrow did believe in was Darrow.

Like Lincoln, another Illinoisan, Darrow remains iconic, the ideal of a principled lawyer. The question is: does he deserve to be?

* * * * *

29. David E. Stannard, *Honor Killing: How the Infamous 'Massie Affair' Transformed Hawai'i* (New York: Viking Press, 2005), 366.
30. Ibid.

No lawyer took greater pains to tell the story of his life. His purpose was to make money by promoting his reputation and credibility as a defender of the poor and downtrodden.

Darrow's autobiography was a bestseller and remains in print, as does a number of his other books. With one notable exception, they were written not so much to further the cause of Darrow's clients as to burnish Darrow's reputation and feather the Darrow nest.

* * * * *

In 1912, Darrow was indicted in Los Angeles County on criminal charges of jury tampering and bribery arising out of his defense of the McNamara brothers. They were charged with blowing up the *LA Times* newspaper building, killing a number of the kind of low-paid, disenfranchised, hardworking men Darrow always claimed to care about.

Darrow was tried twice but avoided being convicted of the charges against him. Geoffrey Cowan's excellent *The People vs. Clarence Darrow* provides plenty of evidence to suggest he got lucky.

When it was over, Darrow self-published a copy of his defense closing argument. It was the only story he ever wrote that didn't sell. It was also the only one written to save his reputation rather than promote it.

* * * * *

Less known—because Darrow spoke and wrote as little about it as possible—was Darrow's last trial. Brilliantly described in David E. Stannard's *Honor Killing: How the Infamous 'Massie Affair' Transformed Hawai'i*, it was the shameful final act of a morally complex career.

In 1931, the wife of a naval officer stationed in Pearl Harbor accused five nonwhites of gang rape. When a jury failed to convict the men, the woman's husband and his mother arranged for the kidnapping and murder of one of the suspects, Joseph Kahahawai.[31]

---

31. Ibid.

"The national press described it as a justifiable lynching and an 'honor killing,' while the American public rose up almost as one—to support the killers. In the spectacularly publicized trial that followed, the country's greatest criminal trial lawyer, Clarence Darrow—for his largest fee ever—sailed to the islands to defend the lynchers, a sad ending to a noble career."[32]

Stannard laid out Darrow's methods with meticulous, harrowing detail. For all his talk of the power of reason, his defense was pure pathos, mercy based on the notion that the white lynchers had been driven to kill Kahahawai in retaliation for what they believed had been done to the husband's wife.

"Justice is not laws, he told the jury, it is about 'feelings,' is about 'instinct,' and since the earliest man it has existed independent of laws, independent of rules that can destroy it."[33]

There wasn't a whiff of logic or reason to any of it. It was an appeal to the gut from the gutter.

It didn't work. Darrow lost the case. Apparently, there *can* be justice inside a courtroom.

After the jury convicted his clients for the lynching, Darrow said: "I couldn't believe it. I couldn't think or understand how anybody could be that cruel."[34]

The ending of Darrow's career wasn't so much sad as predictable. He was always a bit of the flimflam artist. The stories he told as a lawyer worked, mostly because they were solidly built and presented well. He was a master. But that didn't make him a saint.

* * * * *

In 1974, Darrow's autobiography was adapted for the stage by David W. Rintels. A hit on Broadway, it was later broadcast on NBC, with IBM as

---

32. Ibid. From the book flap and promotional materials.
33. Ibid., 370.
34. Ibid., 380.

its sponsor. Darrow hated big business but might have enjoyed the irony. He certainly would have welcomed the notoriety.

The play was produced and performed by Henry Fonda, star of *Young Mr. Lincoln*. With all due respect to Gregory Peck, no actor in the history of American film created more influential or iconic law characters than Fonda. Consider his turn in another classic about storytelling and the law, as the initial lone vote for acquittal in the original *12 Angry Men*.

Fonda's character in that movie provides a fine example of Aristotle's rhetorical triangle; he persuades the others to join him by using just the right amount of ethos, logos, and pathos. One could do worse than studying Fonda's performance in that movie to understand how the rhetorical triangle works.

* * * * *

Like Lincoln, we perceive Darrow through the prism of our times. Fonda's Darrow is a liberal, a Democrat, a progressive, a pacifist, a foe of the corrupt rich and powerful—in short, the antithesis of Richard Nixon, Watergate, the war in Vietnam, and so on.

In 2014, a revival of Rintels's play opened in London at the Old Vic theater. Kevin Spacey, star of Netflix's *House of Cards*, played Darrow. Spacey is a great actor, famous for portraying the deliciously corrupt and perverse. In its review, the *Telegraph* said: "This remains a masterclass in how to woo an audience." This was in reference to Spacey's performance, but the same could also have been said of Darrow himself.

* * * * *

The Justice

I sometimes name murderers in scripts after judges I appeared before. It is not because I hate judges. Some of my best friends are judges. But I would not want to appear before them. They are fine people. They do important work, like dentists. But I avoid deathbeds and judicial investitures for the same reason: I hate to see good people go to the other side.

Judges don't have to convince clients to hire them or to follow their advice. They don't have to get juries to agree with them. They don't have to convince opposing counsel to give up or compromise.

An exception that proved the rule was Thurgood Marshall, one of the bench's greatest storytellers. The leading lawyer of the civil rights movement and US solicitor general, he became an associate justice of the US Supreme Court.

On March 3, 2014, in an appearance in Los Angeles, Sandra Day O'Connor recalled Marshall's constant use of storytelling to advocate among his fellow justices.

No one else told better, more relevant law stories, O'Connor remembered, or had more life experience to draw from.

When Marshall retired, O'Connor said she missed the stories, and so did the other Justices.[35]

Since she retired from the Court, Justice O'Connor, in books and lectures, has been trying to pick up the slack.

* * * * *

In 2014, Justice O'Connor starred in a short movie I wrote and produced for the National Association of Women Judges (NAWJ).

The goal was to tell voters the story of what judges do and why it is important that we have a free and fair judiciary that isn't controlled by special interests or a particular group.

Of course, if judges did a better job educating the public themselves, the NAWJ wouldn't have had to make the film to begin with.

Justice O'Connor arrived on the day of filming prepared, didn't change a word of the script, and asked for additional takes, just like the best actors. Our film was later nominated for three Emmy Awards, including one for writing.

---

35. Sandra Day O'Connor, speech, Town Hall Los Angeles & the Jonathan Club, Los Angeles, CA, March 3, 2014.

Judges are not the only ones who need to do a better job telling the story of what they do and why it matters.

Lawyer bashing is an American tradition. But so is appreciating that we are a nation of laws, and more than anyone else, lawyers are the ones who guarantee that we stay that way.

Alexis de Tocqueville knew this. He admired American democracy but recognized that it was always a fragile thing, vulnerable to the whims of majority rule.[36]

"I cannot believe that a republic could hope to exist at the present time if the influence of lawyers in public business did not increase in proportion to the power of the people."[37]

Say what you will about the French, American lawyers never had a better friend than Tocqueville.

He saw lawyers as instruments of good. He believed they are protectors of individual rights who make the Constitution's ideals a reality. He saw them as fighters of government overreaching and the power of the rich and connected. He admired them as keepers of the "civic wisdom" of laws and procedures that make America a free, open, and successful society.[38]

If today's public doesn't quite look at lawyers the same way, we have no one to blame but ourselves.

Bar fees paid to publicize disbarments and suspensions would be better spent telling the stories of how lawyers police the politicians and the police, protect due process, and try to make equal justice under the law a reality.

---

36. Phil C. Neal, "De Tocqueville and the Role of the Lawyer in Society," *Marquette Law Review* 50 (1966): 607–608.

37. See Alexis de Tocqueville, *Democracy in America*, trans. Gerald E. Bevan (London: Penguin Books, 2003). To be sure, some of what de Tocqueville liked about lawyers may not be what all of us like about ourselves. "Men who have made a special study of the laws," he said, "derive from occupation certain habits of order, a taste for formalities, and a kind of instinctive regard for the regular connection of ideas, which naturally render them very hostile to the revolutionary spirit and the unreflecting passions of the multitude." Ibid., 615.

38. Ibid.

The national narratives of other nations are built on creation myths of divine right, military might, and various dogmas. Our national narrative is process-based, law-based, written by lawyers and protected by lawyers.

Now, more than ever, lawyers owe it themselves to tell that story. If we don't, one day we may find ourselves in the same leaky boat as the judges.

* * * * *

Enormous amounts of money are being poured into what had previously been sleepy, nonpartisan judicial races. Attack ads aimed at sitting judges are being financed by a variety of special interests.[39] They take the good work judges do and make it seem horrid.

To uphold the law, judges sometimes have to do unpleasant things like suppress evidence because of police misconduct or set bail for someone presumed to be innocent. In the hands of paid political consultants, acts of proper judicial conduct are easily turned into Willie Horton stories.

Lawyers are not immune. In the 2014 South Carolina gubernatorial campaign, the Republican Governors Association (RGA) ran ads against Democratic state senator Vincent Sheehan, accusing him of being a "trial lawyer" who "made money off criminals."[40]

Four of the nine members of the governing body of the RGA—Chris Christie (NJ), Mike Pence (IN), Tom Corbett (PA), and Susana Martinez (NM)—*are* lawyers.[41] They have taken political contributions from lawyers. So have *all* the other members of the RGA. But that didn't stop them from attacking the profession.

---

39. See Matthew J. Streb, *Running for Judge: The Rising Political, Financial, and Legal Stakes of Judicial Elections* (New York: New York University Press, 2007); Billy Corriher, "Big Business Taking over State Supreme Courts," Center for American Progress, August 13, 2012; Alicia Bannon and Lianna Reagan, "New Politics of Judicial Elections 2011–2012," Brennan Center for Justice, October 23, 2013.

40. David Nir, "Republicans Continue Their Assault on Criminal Defense Lawyers With Revolting New Campaign Ad," *The Daily Kos*, April 22, 2014, http://www.dailykos.com/story/2014/04/22/1293760/-Republicans-continue-their-assault-on-criminal-defense-attorneys-with-revolting-new-campaign-ad/.

41. See the Republican Governor's Association website at http://www.rga.org/homepage/.

If any of them are still capable of feeling shame, they should be ashamed of themselves for this.

* * * * *

For the record, I don't really blame judges for not being good storytellers. I blame them for seeming to go out of their way to prevent *me* from telling *my* story.

I recognize it is their job. I appreciate that they are doing their best; they are only human. They make mistakes. If they didn't make them—let alone so many of them—there wouldn't be the need for all the appellate courts in the world.

Storytelling is neither required nor encouraged on the bench. But if judges want their influence to extend beyond one case—to have their opinions read and relied on by others—they need to learn to tell stories well. Most do not.

Lawyers have no excuse.

* * * * *

The General

I had dinner one night with the late Jack Valenti, former LBJ aide, later president of the Motion Picture Association of America, creator of the ratings system, a great lobbyist for the entertainment industry, and a great storyteller in his own right.

I asked him about an old friend of mine who wrote a memoir of his experience working for President Clinton.

"I don't want to say anything bad about him," Valenti said in his refined Texas drawl, a cross between Foghorn Leghorn and James Baker.

"He's your friend," Valenti said. "But he's a whore, son. He's a whore."

* * * * *

Anyone fortunate enough to work for a great figure has a duty to keep their confidence. Lawyers especially. They could pull his fingernails off, Valenti said, but no historian would get him to reveal all he knew about President Johnson. A few years later, Valenti did write a memoir. It was not a tell-all by any means.

If what I am about to say is a violation of Valenti's advice, I apologize.

* * * * *

There was a rumor that Janet Reno's Secret Service code name was "Big Country." She enjoyed playing basketball with local women's college teams. She had a dry sense of humor and a reserve that masked real sensitivity.

I don't believe she was born tough. I believe she became tough out of necessity. Her mother was apparently a hard-living, independent character, often unkind. As a young woman in the then still male-dominated world of law enforcement, Reno got even tougher.

She was not a great storyteller. She made up for it with attention to detail, smarts, and hard work. You don't get keep getting elected DA of Broward County, Florida, and then reelected, without being persuasive.

For several weeks, I worked on the team that prepared DOJ's presentation to the joint committee of Congress that was investigating the handling of the siege of the Branch Davidian cult in Waco, Texas.

* * * * *

The executive branch plays the role written for it by the House and Senate. The nation's most influential critic, the Supreme Court, passes judgment on the script and the performance. But Congress is the writers' room, the collective creator of countless law stories.

Not a *real* writers' room. If it were a real writers' room, the writers would have been fired and the series canceled long ago. Anyone who ever drafted indictments based on federal laws, or tried to advise a client on how to stay on the right side of them, knows that a lot of the laws Congress writes don't make a lot of sense.

But nothing is worse than when Congress stops trying to write the laws and starts trying to enforce them. The stories are never good.

* * * * *

The Clinton impeachment was the perfect example.

In the interest of full-disclosure, I note that the day the president's videotaped grand jury testimony was released happened to fall on the High Holidays. They were so desperate for a talking head to defend Clinton on MSNBC that I did it. God forgive me. I think He will, too.

It is not always remembered, but days before the Senate was converted into a court of law, the Republican leader of the House, Bob Livingston, resigned after his own marital infidelities were uncovered. A standard had been set. The Republican argued that it should apply equally to everyone, including the president.

The congressmen appointed to prosecute the case were experienced attorneys, credible professionals who still managed to seem less like fair-handed prosecutors and more like what they were—politicians.

They never managed to put together a good story as to why Clinton's actions, particularly his lies, justified his removal from office. *They* believed it. But feeling pathos is not the same as eliciting it in others.

* * * * *

No Republicans ever came up with a persuasive story for impeachment until 2014, when Senator Rand Paul stumbled on one. The White House, Paul suddenly realized, is America's most important workplace. President Clinton was the First Boss. Lewinsky was an underling, powerless. If what Clinton did with her was not a form of sexual harassment—or a hostile workplace for the other interns—then there are no such things.

In her 2014 memoir, Lewinsky writes that her relationship with Clinton was consensual, as if that matters. There was never any claim that Clinton forced himself on her.

The point was that the White House is a federal workplace. The relationship between boss and underling is highly regulated. Had a supervisor at DOJ done what Clinton did with an intern—and then lied about—he would lose his job.

Had he done it with *my* daughter, I would have wanted to punch him out.

Had the prosecutors told *that* story in a cogent, consistent way, to the exclusion of all others, the Senate's verdict might not have been different. But it would have been a better story. And it might have done the country and the nation's workplaces a service.

Or was that not the point?

* * * * *

Some in Congress decided the Waco story was going to be Reno's undoing. Some in the Clinton administration, which did not love her independence, were thought to be rooting against her. Names of her possible replacement were being floated loudly enough for them to end up in the media.

Our team held mock hearings in the Attorney General's office. I played the role of a specific, aggressive and abrasive congressman, using his past comments on Waco as my guide.

"Go after her hard," one of Reno's advisors told us. "Be as rough as you like. She can take it."

I accused the Attorney General of killing men, women, and children whose only crime was their religious faith.

Their blood is on your hands. How can you justify that? How can you live with yourself?

Her answers never changed, not from the first day to the last. When she spoke to Congress. Sometimes her voice cracked. Sometimes her eyes filled with tears. I don't know for sure, but I think she prepared to testify because she wanted to make sure she didn't lose composure.

She went over the material, not to shape it, but to master it. Nobody ever had a more honest, consistent, or ethical witness.

* * * * *

An avid viewer of Watergate, Irangate, and various confirmation hearings, I always wondered what the serious-looking people sitting behind the congressional witnesses were doing there. Were they all family, friends; were they all lawyers? What was their role exactly?

During the Waco hearings, I was one of those people. You can see me in the news coverage and in one of the documentaries about the tragedy, a tired-looking Zelig with a bad haircut from the congressional barbershop.

The late Republican congressman Sonny Bono was a surprisingly aggressive questioner. During one of Congressman Bono's passionate harangues, as we sat behind the witness, a senior attorney with the FBI, grim-faced and serious, hastily wrote a note and handed it to me:

"I can't believe this guy fucked Cher."

Apparently that's what the people sitting behind congressional witnesses do.

* * * * *

Several weeks after the hearing, I received an autographed photo from Reno. The accompanying note read:

"I just wanted you to know how much I appreciate all you did to insure that our presentation at the Waco Hearings was accurate, objective, and thorough."

It was also true and fair.

* * * * *

Denny Crane
What was that, exactly?

A walking example of ethos, a man who dropped his *own* name and became his own catchphrase; the epitome of lawyerly megalomania and self-regard; a silverback, a rainmaker and named partner; a legend, and not entirely in his own mind, which, as the seasons progressed, he began to lose.[42]

I write of William Shatner's *character*, you understand, not Mr. Shatner.

Denny Crane is a lecherous, monomaniacal showboater who has lost much of his mind, apparently to mad cow disease. He is Shore's soul mate and conservative sparring partner, channeling Vice President Dick Cheney to defend, not very persuasively, the war in Iraq or polluters.

Environmentalists, he declares on a salmon fishing trip, are "evildoers."

"Yesterday it's a tree, today it's a salmon, tomorrow it's 'Let's not dig Alaska for oil 'cause it's too pretty.' Let me tell you something," he says. "I came out here to enjoy nature. Don't talk to me about the environment."[43]

Shatner offscreen was delightful, witty, odd, capable of discussing everything from Morgan horse breeding to the mystical properties and powers of tap water. He's known to relax in his dressing room in a shorty robe, napping to the music of techno-lesbian pop; he's possibly the last man on earth to still own or use Hai Karate cologne.

On-screen, Shatner played a gun-toting, right-wing, sexually promiscuous, and predatory attorney; he was, nevertheless, capable of lawyerly brilliance. A great storyteller, though the stories were about him rather than the client.

He only *seemed* to be a cartoon. Anyone who had ever worked with a successful CEO, politician, or managing partner or had to appear before a federal judge knew there was more to Denny Crane than a joke.

---

42. If you missed the odd cultural phenomenon that was Shatner's character, he is currently doing a one-man show, "Shatner's World: We Just Live in It," in which he discusses the part. There are also endless references to Shatner's character in a variety of mainstream and law-based media, including Donald J. Labriola, "'But I'm Denny Crane!' Age Discrimination in the Legal Profession after Sidley," *Albany Law Review* 72 (2009): 367; "Cultural Commentary: The Morays of Diminished Capacity in Boston Legal," *Disability Studies Quarterly* No. 1–2 (Winter/Spring 2007): 27.

43. "Beneath the Quirks, There's Always a Message for the Masses," *New York Times*, February 13, 2006, a not terribly positive review from critic Alessandra Stanley, who was not terribly fond of the show.

"I am the lie that tells the truth," Jean Cocteau said, quoted in Philip Core's *Camp: The Lie That Tells the Truth*. A sensibility and style, camp is exaggerated emotion, purposeful ridiculousness, an obvious pose, utterly affected and self-conscious, always theatrical.

Film director John Waters is a master of camp. He has written about his obsession with the law. He has taught in prisons, befriended a number of inmates, and has lobbied for the release of Manson Family member Leslie Van Houten.[44] A regular court observer, he hosted a show on infamous domestic murders with the campy title *'Til Death Do We Part*, for the now-defunct Court TV.[45]

Like John Waters, Denny Crane was camp. Absurd and exaggerated, he was the lie that told the truth about the pomposity and self-delusion of a certain segment of the legal profession.

That was why people responded to it.

* * * * *

Years after the show went off the air, Shatner became a spokesman for the Milwaukee-based Hupy & Abraham law firm.

"We thought he was just an awesome choice as a representative for the law firm," Jason Abraham said. "You just get a big credibility factor when you use someone like him as your representative. That's something we take very seriously."[46]

Denny Crane would be proud.

44. John Waters, *Role-Models* (New York: Farrar, Straus and Giroux, 2010).

45. Scott Martelle, "Court TV to Try Scripts, Irony and John Waters," *Los Angeles Times*, October 20, 2010.

46. David Burke, "Shatner's TV Pitch Gets Law Firm with G-C Office Noticed," *Quad City Times*, April 27, 2013.

Conclusion

I have seen worlds where lawyers don't tell stories.

They are bad places.

If you doubt the power of lawyer storytelling, go visit one of them.

* * * * *

The Federal Immigration Office in Anaheim, California, shares a parking lot with Disneyland.

Signs with Mickey and Donald look down on the people waiting silently in line to go through the security metal detector. The monorail whooshes over their heads.

Inside there is a large waiting room, a real-life version of "It's a Small World." Every nation on earth seems to be represented. Instead of wearing native clothes, they are dressed in the universal wardrobe of the poor.

And nobody is smiling and singing.

Many seek political asylum.

On this day, a woman from Darfur, the victim of genital mutilation, waits for her case to be called. Her eight-year-old son sits next to her. His case is up for consideration today as well.

Both the woman and the boy watched as members of a fundamentalist rebel group murdered members of their village, including the woman's parents.

She has never learned to read or write. As they wait, her son reads *Highlights* magazine to her. It isn't clear she understands what he is saying. The boy soon falls asleep, sucking his thumb, his head against her shoulder. He cannot sleep at night. He has nightmares about seeing his grandparents shot to death.

They cannot afford an attorney. They are not appointed an attorney. They are not legally entitled to an attorney.

Yet they are expected, this illiterate woman and this little boy, to tell their stories themselves, within the spaces and constraints of the political asylum petition, signed under penalty of perjury, showing that they meet the legal standard to stay in America.

If they do it wrong, if they misstate the facts, intentionally or not, if they fail to state their case in a compelling way, they will be sent back to the Sudan. Their village is gone, their people are dead; if they go back, they face arrest for leaving the country illegally or life in a refugee camp.

Don't tell this woman or her son that storytelling isn't important.

They have almost nothing in the world but the clothes on their back and one another. But they would give whatever else they had for a lawyer to help them tell their story.

They were lucky that they didn't have to. They had lawyers who volunteered to help them. Other asylum seekers that day did not.

* * * * *

Less dramatic, though no less absurd, is a world where the issues are not life and death. But don't bother trying to tell the parties that.

For several years, I served in Los Angeles Superior Court Small Claims and Traffic Divisions as a judge pro tem.

Not so much to do justice. But to solve this nature versus nurture question: Does being a judge make people crazy or are judges crazy before they get on the bench?

During training, we were told there are two approaches to the job. Apply the law to the best of your ability and understanding. Or do whatever you think is best, so long as it is not illegal or in obvious conflict with the facts, as you are able to decipher them.

What they don't mention is that it is impossible to do either one. If my job was to come up with the right answer, nobody seemed that interested in helping me.

* * * * *

For several hours at a time, sometimes in Van Nuys, sometimes in Beverly Hills or downtown LA, I would observe the rich tapestry and beautiful mosaic that is Southern California. Except half of the people there wanted to kill the other half. It would have looked like the cantina scene in *Star Wars*, except those monsters were having a good time.

To paraphrase Kingsley Amis, the fights were so vicious because the stakes were so small.

Unencumbered by legal technicalities, they presented their stories, and you know what?

They were *horrible*.

Nonsensical, meandering, but always told with great emotion—like bad poets, small claims court litigants are always sincere. Hell is paved with good intentions, but it is decorated with sincerity.

* * * * *

A woman sued her ex–business partner and lover. She mentioned the lover part without being asked. She accused the other woman of having stolen equipment from their now-defunct photography studio.

"I want her to give me back the equipment," the woman yelled. "And I want her to admit she's a fucking bitch."

She had asked for the same things in her written complaint too.

* * * * *

There seemed to be a lot of cases involving air compressors. Apparently, air compressors make up a large part of the nation's economy. And all the people buying and selling them are Israelis. Yet none of the compressors ever work, according to the plaintiffs.

The defendants, in contrast, swore they had never sold or even *heard* of an air compressor that did not work and blamed the plaintiff for not knowing how to work it.

"You say I'm lying?" the plaintiff asked.

"No," the defendant yelled, "I'm saying you're stupid!"

"Gentlemen," I said, "please, do not talk to one another."

"That bastard," the plaintiff said, pointing a finger at the defendant. "Him, I don't want to talk at all!"

The plaintiff threw his hands back and thrust his chest at me:

"If I am lying, kill me!"

Keep in mind that we were talking about a $150 air compressor.

* * * * *

Small claims court offers an insight into our natural desire for justice, and how ugly that desire can be.

The man who was tired of the neighbor's barking dog really did want the dog put to sleep.

The woman suing because her neighbor used her trash bin really did want permission to dump *her* trash in *his* front yard.

* * * * *

Yet not everyone wanted blood. The man with a large divot in his forehead just wanted his money back.

He and his wife, a pleasant older couple from Tarzana, had paid a handyman to tile their bathroom ceiling, for some reason. The tiles had gotten loose. One fell, crashing onto the man's head as he got out of the shower, knocking him out cold and opening up a giant gash on his head.

"There was an awful lot of blood," the wife said quietly. "I thought I was going to lose him."

The ambulance arrived in time to keep him from bleeding to death. The trip to the ER involved a number of stitches and an enormous bill. But they were not asking for damages to cover any of it. They just wanted the handyman to pay for the broken tiles, a few hundred dollars.

The defendant refused to pay. He had his own story to tell. The tiles should never have been on the ceiling. He told them they would fall off. They insisted. Why should he be held responsible for their bad decisions? He was a handyman, it said so right on the side of his truck; his job was to be handy, not to be a structural engineer. He had done exactly what they asked. How could he be held responsible for their stupidity?

"And if they had asked you to build a bomb in their basement," I thundered, "would you have done that too?"

The man blinked at me. He didn't make bombs. What was I getting at?

* * * * *

There are no small claims to the people involved. Winning or losing a few hundred dollars in a legal case significantly affects their business and personal income. Equally or more important, however, is the people's desire to be heard.

They want to tell their stories, because they think they will get something out of it. They may not all get justice. When they get the chance to have their say, what they end up with is catharsis, the relief of at least having a resolution. The process matters more than the result. When the small claims trial is handled right, both sides leave feeling a little better.

* * * * *

The tragedy is not just that most Americans can't get someone to explain the law to them or represent their interests.

It is that they don't even get anyone to help them construct a basic narrative that allows them to tell their own stories effectively.

It matters. Small claims and traffic court will be the only day most of them will ever get in court. Without anyone helping them tell their story, the whole thing is designed to guarantee that half of them will go home unhappy and unsatisfied losers. And the experience will color their view of the courts and the legal system. Do you think it will make them better, more law-abiding citizens? Do you think it will make them more or less likely to pay their taxes or vote?

Law professors and law firms might not care. There is nothing sexy or impressive about small claims court. But it impacts the lives of millions of Americans. And it ought to work better.

* * * * *

Nonlawyers practicing law is an anathema to the profession. But helping people put their stories together doesn't have to involve giving legal advice. It involves talking with them first, creating a narrative, walking them through their story and helping them tell it.

It seems like the least the system can do. Until society extends the right to representation in all cases, not just criminal cases, a lawyer ought to at least be willing to let other professionals help their fellow citizens have a fighting chance. After all, as we have seen, even the smartest lawyers have trouble telling a good story.

* * * * *

If lawyers won't help nonlawyers tell their stories better, they should at least try to tell their *own* stories better.

This book does not purport to be the last word on the subject. The subject of storytelling is far from an empty field, but it remains an open one. If paid consultants feel there is money to be made in teaching storytelling to lawyers and nonlawyers, there must be something valuable in it. If writers still have new things to say about vampires, for example, and what can or should be done to cats, the topic of storytelling itself should be inexhaustible.

As we have seen, there are many types of stories lawyers tell in their work. The most effective ones are built with the legs of Aristotle's marvelous triangle in mind.

There are stories of identity. These are the narratives lawyers tell to explain who they are, what they do, and what the law is. They are stories told to potential clients to get hired, presented to finders of fact to establish credibility, all shared, in one way or another, in the service of ethos.

There are also puzzle stories; narratives that lawyers present to convince a client, colleague, or fact finder to decide something in the lawyer's favor, or to persuade a client to take the lawyer's advice. Reason—logos—is at the heart of puzzle stories.

There are lawyer stories designed to appeal to the brain and touch the heart. If you don't care truly, deeply, and passionately about the case, the client, or the issue, you cannot elicit those feelings in others. Emotion in storytelling matters as much as the other two legs. It is also the one that is the most problematic.

But regardless of the type of story, the reason *why* lawyers tell stories never changes. Lawyers tell stories to persuade.

* * * * *

Finally, I want to point out one last type of story lawyers tell that is almost never discussed, even though its importance cannot be overstated.

These are the internal narratives—the stories we tell ourselves about ourselves, the overall epic of our lives in the law.

Whether you are the hero or villain or the exposition of your career depends on the narrative you create over the course of your career. No one can be a great lawyer or storyteller without first being aware that this internal narrative exists and that it matters.

What you do with this narrative doesn't matter to anyone but you. Do with it what you like. You may share your personal story with spouses, bartenders, shrinks, and colleagues. Or you can keep it locked away, privileged and confidential.

It is the great internal memo, the ultimate product of your work. This is the story of your professional life, as only you know it. You cannot put a dollar figure on it. It all depends on how valuable you think self-knowledge is.

I have been lucky that over the years, many lawyers have shared their personal stories with me. It has led me to conclude that we are an interesting group.

Imperfect, sometimes intemperate, we are sworn to uphold—whether we like it or not—basic American principles of fairness, equality, and the peaceful resolution of human conflict. That makes what we do noble, something to be proud of.

It is a good story. We ought to tell it.

Index